DO NOT REMOVE
CARDS FROM POCKET

THE SELF-HELP DIRECTORY

THE SELF-HELP DIRECTORY

*A Sourcebook for Self-Help
in the United States and Canada*

JOE DONOVAN

Facts On File

The Self-Help Directory: A Sourcebook for Self-Help in the United States and Canada

Copyright © 1994 Joe Donovan

Facts On File, Inc.
460 Park Avenue South
New York NY 10016
USA

Library of Congress Cataloging-in-Publication Data
Donovan, Joe.
The self-help directory : a sourcebook for self-help in the United
States and Canada / Joe Donovan.
p.   cm.
Includes bibliographical references (p.   ) and index.
ISBN 0-8160-2621-1 (acid-free paper)
1. Self-help groups—United States—Directories.   2. Self-help
groups—Canada—Directories.   I. Title.
HV547.D65   1993
361.7'025'73—dc20   93-12074

A British CIP catalogue record for this book is available from the British Library.

Facts On File books are available at special discounts when purchased in bulk quantities for businesses, associations, institutions or sales promotions. Please call our Special Sales Department in New York at 212/683-2244 or 800/322-8755.

Text design by Catherine Hyman
Jacket design by Fred Pusterla
Composition and manufacturing by the Maple-Vail Book Manufacturing Group
Printed in the United States of America

10 9 8 7 6 5 4 3 2 1

This book is printed on acid-free paper.

Dedicated to
Self-Helpers Everywhere

CONTENTS

ACKNOWLEDGMENTS

I would like to thank Neal J. Maillet, Kathy Ishizuka and Randy Ladenheim-Gil, my editors; Grafton Mouen, my computer programmer; Jim Carden, who helped perform the laborious but crucial clerical process in which we contacted by mail or telephone all groups listed in this *Directory* to confirm the accuracy of the citations; Edward J. Madara at the American Self-Help Clearinghouse; and, most of all, the many self-helpers I had the pleasure to meet by phone and letter during the preparation of this book.

What Is "Self-Help"? An Introduction and a Bibliography

"Self-Help": The Term, the Concept

One way to begin a study of self-help is to hack through the lush undergrowth of terminological and conceptual misunderstandings that have surrounded the phenomenon.

First of all, the term "self-help" has, in the discourse of some social scientists and human services providers, been replaced rather inconsistently by "mutual aid" and a variety of other terms, including such tortuous locutions as "peer-oriented support systems." The argument is that these other terms—but especially "mutual aid"—better describe the phenomenon's salient feature: people helping themselves by helping others, with the emphasis on the latter part of the definition. In this sense, "self-help" is one of those terms, like "original equipment manufacturer" in computer marketing, that mean the exact or near opposite of what they would seem to imply. Nevertheless, "self-help" continues to be preferred—however unconsciously—ironically, sometimes even by writers who argue for "mutual aid." Writing in professional journals, social scientists use "mutual aid" in their first references to the phenomenon, but switch to "self-help" for subsequent ones. One exception is Harvard human services guru Phyllis Silverman, who consistently uses "mutual aid" in her many writings on the subject; see the bibliography for a selection. The reason for the enduring popularity of "self-help"—the term this book will use—seems fairly obvious: It has fewer syllables than any alternative.

Though it may exert hegemony over competing terms in the English language, the term "self-help" remains shrouded in mystery. "Self-help" does not appear at all in, for example, the index to *The Encyclopaedia Brittanica*, 15th edition, in *The Macmillan International Encyclopedia of the Social Sciences* or, interestingly, in *The Oxford Dictionary of New Words: A Popular Guide to Words in the News*. The second edition (1989) of *The Oxford English Dictionary*, citing passages by Carlyle and Shaw, does contain an archaic definition of self-help: "the action or faculty of providing for oneself without assistance from others." But this definition and that in *Webster's Third New International Dictionary of the English Language Unabridged* (1986) are, of course, the exact opposite of what the term means in social scientific parlance.

A definition of the social-scientific term may be found in Robert A. Barker's *Social Work Dictionary* (1991). Unfortunately, this book, published by the National Association of Social Workers, hopelessly muddles the situation by including separate entries for "self-help groups" and "self-help organizations" and "mutual aid groups" and "mutual help." Read as a whole, these various entries imply there is a difference between "self-help" and "mutual aid"; for example, Barker makes the specious assertion that "mutual aid groups are similar to self-help groups except they may have professional leaders." All of this results in a distinction that doesn't appear reflected elsewhere in the literature, certainly not in Phyllis Silverman's definitive short statement on the phenomenon in *The Encyclopedia of Social Work,* 18th edition (1987), from the same publisher as Barker's volume. Unfortunately, as already noted, Silverman—with logic though not usage on her side—prefers the term "mutual aid."

Users of the term "self-help," must recognize the two meanings attached to it, one grounded in social science and human services (which is the one that will concern us), another in contemporary popular culture, or pop psychology, to be exact. It is difficult to imagine a bookstore in the contemporary United States or Canada without a section labeled "Self-Help." Among the classics of this literature are Dale Carnegie's *How to Win Friends and Influence People* (1937) and *How to Stop Worrying and Start Living* (1948), W. Clement Stone's *The Success System That Never Fails* (1962) and a work by Napoleon Hill whose title—quoted here in full—is *Think and Grow Rich; Teaching, For the First Time, The Famous Andrew Carnegie Formula For Money-Making, Based on the Thirteen Proven Steps to Riches, Organized Through 25 Years of Research, in Collaboration With 500 Distinguished Men of Great Wealth, Who Proved By Their Own Achievements That the Philosophy Is Practical* (1972). Well-known recent titles in this genre of "self-help" literature include Robin Norwood's *Women Who Love Too Much* (1985) and John Bradshaw's *Homecoming: Reclaiming & Championing Your Inner Child* (1990) and *Bradshaw on: The Family: A Revolutionary Way of Self-Discovery* (1990). This literature will not concern us, strictly speaking; its books will not appear in the Bibliography that concludes this chapter—enumerating this vast literature would require a separate monograph. True, these self-help books are sometimes used in self-help groups. Norwood's *Women Who Love Too Much*—certainly one of the most influential works in contemporary popular culture—has been the basis for groups concerned with codependency. And devotees of these self-help books share at least one salient feature with participants in self-help groups: a consumerist, do-it-yourself orientation toward taking problems of one's mental and physical health partly or even wholly out of the hands of professionals and solving them on one's own. The domain of "self-help" books, however, is the individual, not groups. And groups are what our "self-help"—as in, self-help *group*—is all about. Leonard Borman has stated (Lieberman and Borman, 1979) that the "self-help" in such "self-help books" is "the antithesis of self-help seen in common interest groups where members become means to the ends of one another."

"SELF-HELP": DEFINITION AND HISTORICAL BACKGROUND

While there is some disagreement about what to call them, there is a good deal of consensus on what self-help groups are. The concept may be defined fairly adequately in a few sentences: A self-help group is a voluntary small-group organization of peers who share a common problem and who meet to discuss their relevant experiences, and provide support and exchange practical information for dealing with the problem. Many individuals, especially the disabled or societal "outcasts," such as gays, feel isolated and belittled; by gathering in a group, they alleviate this isolation and experience empowerment. A self-help group is not for profit, though members usually support its activities through voluntary, nominal contributions; involvement by professionals is minimal or nonexistent. The key dynamic of self-help is what Frank Riessman has called the "helper-helpee principle": When human beings, by sharing experiences and giving advice and support, help other human beings with whom they share a common problem, the helpers typically find themselves helped; they are better able to cope with the problem in question, and derive the additional benefit of a general psychological state of well-being. The helpees, in turn, become helpers, who help others, derive the same benefits and so on down the line.

Today, we are in a golden age of self-help. But according to Petr Kropotkin (1824–1921), the seminal Russian self-help theorist, revolutionary, philosopher, and geographer, self-help is hardly a new phenomenon; it's as old as human society itself. Kropotkin theorized that while Darwinian "survival of the fittest"

obtains in biological contexts, it is superseded—or at least tempered—in human society by the tendency or urge to help others when weakened by need; otherwise, society is impossible, or so the theory goes. In their classic sketch of the prehistory of the modern self-help group, "Self-Help Groups in Western Society: History and Prospects (1976)," Alfred H. Katz and Eugene I. Bender trace a history that dates back over more than a millennium. In medieval Europe, craft guilds extended aid to needy members; later, public assistance laws sought to provide such benefits on a universal basis. Certainly, the increasing social, economic and health problems of urban areas, which grew precipitously after the breakdown of the feudal system and, later, under the pressures of the Industrial Revolution, created a clear need for such sources of help. Among the earliest were occupational groups known as Friendly Societies. These outgrowths of the medieval guild provided, through special funds, for the relief of members fallen prey to sickness, infirmity and old age. Among the services offered were loans to the needy and burial for those who died destitute; social activities—a key feature of modern self-help groups—included outings, feasts and club nights. By 1800 nearly 200 societies, such as the Society of Carters, the Fraternity of Dyers and the Ancient Society of Gardeners, were founded. Interestingly, while society at large blessed the Friendly Societies, employers often denounced them as breeding grounds for political agitation and class struggle; as such, the societies were progenitors of modern self-help groups with a significant consciousness-raising component, such as women's or gay groups.

In colonial America, continental traditions of mutual aid were continued in some settlements but stifled in rural, agricultural settings, where the richness of the land and population dispersal favored the development of individualism and autonomy. By the mid-19th century, however, the deleterious effects of the Industrial Revolution created in the expanding U.S. urban centers an environment of social need that fostered the growth of organizations—above all, trade unions—that provided help to members. Benefits included housing, banks and worker education. Also forming organizations were the different ethnic groups that appeared during the successive waves of immigration during the 19th and early 20th century. Notable organizations of this type included the Greek Pan-Hellenic Union, *Landsmanschaften* organizations of Russian and Polish Jews and the Polish National Alliance.

Around the time of World War II, a variety of organizations were founded that, in the problems they address and the means they employ, begin to outline the contours and often foreshadow the content of today's self-help scene. They include, above all, Alcoholics Anonymous, founded in 1935. AA's "Twelve Steps and Twelve Traditions" are the starting point of today's burgeoning "12-step" program of recovery. AA, in turn, derives from a variety of earlier phenomenons, including 19th- and early 20th-century European and American religious organizations in which public confession of guilt played a key role. AA's founder, Bill Wilson, was himself a member of such an organization, the Oxford Movement (later renamed Moral Rearmament), which encouraged members to share their character defects and failures at group meetings to achieve spiritual progress and self-improvement. Other significant organizations that appeared at this time include societies of parents of children with handicaps—for example, the United Cerebral Palsy Foundation, founded 1949; and Recovery, Inc., one of self-help's distinguished senior citizens, established in 1937 by Dr. Abraham Low so that ex-mental patients could

help each other avoid relapses into chronic illness.

TYPES OF SELF-HELP GROUPS

While it's possible to create a single-sentence definition of self-help groups, it's difficult to offer an equally compact scheme for classifying all such groups. There's an enormous variety within the self-help groups, which number more than 500,000 and involve over 15 million people active today in the United States and Canada.

True, in the popular discourse, "self-help" has become equated with just one narrow—though important and widespread—type of group: those of so-called recovery programs, based on the Twelve Steps and Twelve Traditions of Alcoholics Anonymous. This genre of self-help has been the object of great journalistic scrutiny, much of it bemused if not mocking. One particularly influential and caustic account was *I'm Dysfunctional, You're Dysfunctional; The Recovery Movement and Other Self-Help Fashions* by Wendy Kaminer (1992). Not surprisingly, so-called recovery self-help groups—which have served as a lint trap for contemporary pop psychology (especially John Bradshaw)—have even been the butt of stand-up comedians. Al Franken, a member of TV's popular *Saturday Night Live,* regularly delights audiences with his impersonation of Stuart Smalley, the psychobabbling host of a TV recovery self-help program, *Daily Affirmations.* Those laughing the hardest are probably audience members who had themselves attended such recovery meetings and recognized the eclectic concepts and tortured jargon in Franken's hysterical self-help jabbering.[1]

---

[1] For an excellent account of the highly suc-

But social scientists and human service providers—for whom self-help is a serious topic of inquiry and source of benefits for their clients—know that the vast majority of groups are not recovery groups. In the growing professional literature on self-help—cataloged selectively in the Bibliography that follows—are numerous studies that offer typologies of self-help groups. Some are quite elaborate; in "Mutual Help Organizations (1976)" M. Killilea provides a 20-category taxonomic scheme, which Alan Gartner and Frank Reissman flesh out with numerous examples in *Self-Help in the Human Services* (1977, pp. 8–11). Others are simpler, and at least one bears repetition here. The National Institute of Mental Health (U.S. Department of Health & Human Services, 1988) has suggested the following three classifications of self-help groups:

Groups for People with Mental and Physical Illness

Contrary to popular perception, the largest category of self-help groups contains those organized around specific health problems, ranging from the most common (heart disease, cancer, diabetes) to rare diseases affecting a mere handful of people nationally. (Because of their wide geographic dispersal, these groups may "meet" electronically via telecommunications hookups—see Appendix III.) Since chronic health problems affect 50% of the population and account for over 70% of all patient examinations, it's hardly surprising that this category is so large. There is a self-help group for most major diseases cataloged by the World Health Organization.

Although mutual support and helping members to cope with stress are, to a greater or lesser extent, features of all self-help groups, they are especially important to groups in this category, especially when a member is making a transition into membership status, for example, a cancer patient who has just received an ostomy, or a person who has just tested positive for HIV.

The membership of any self-help group may include not just people concerned with a problem but also their families and friends. Such is often the case in this category of self-help group, especially when the issue in question involves birth defects, such as severe mental retardation, or children who have died ("grieving" groups, such as Compassionate Friends, which aids parents who've lost a child). In such groups, the membership may consist largely or exclusively of parents and perhaps friends, and not the children themselves. A special example of this phenomenon are groups, such as Al-Anon and S-Anon, for families and friends of people with alcoholism and sexual compulsions respectively, which brings us to the second category.

Groups for People with Compulsions and Addictions

The most common are those dealing with alcoholism and other substance abuse, overeating and sexual compulsions. Other, less well-known problems are also addressed by self-help groups of this type, including procrastination, poor domestic hygiene (Messies Anonymous) or self-abuse. In any case, members of such groups are united in a desire to eliminate—or at least control—some type of unwanted behavior.

Many, but not all, of these groups employ the 12-step program adopted from Alcoholics Anonymous. (See Appendix II.) Though the

---

cessful marketing of recovery self-help—both books and services—see the opening section of "Selling Self-Help" by Patricia Braus (1992).

AA program has proven its effectiveness in helping people abstain from self-destructive behavior, the 12-step approach has been rejected by a number of groups because of its explicitly spiritual orientation. Notable among these groups is the highly publicized Rational Recovery.[2] In addition, controversy has arisen when the 12 steps have been applied to problems unrelated to compulsive, self-destructive behavior; note, for example, A.R.T.S. ("Artists Recovering through the Twelve Steps"), Compulsive Stutterers Anonymous, Emphysema Anonymous, or Schizophrenics Anonymous, cataloged in Chapter 2.

Groups for Minorities

The most common are those for the disabled, sexual-orientation minorities (gays, lesbians and bisexuals), members of certain professions (there are numerous groups for profes-

---

[2] In any case, the number of 12-step programs is now in the triple digits. The following partial list assembled nearly two decades ago in *Self-Help in the Human Services* by Gartner and Riessman (1977) will give the reader an idea of the 12-step phenomenon: Cancer Anonymous, Checks Anonymous, Convicts Anonymous, Crooks Anonymous, Delinquents Anonymous, Disturbed Children Anonymous, Divorcees Anonymous, Dropouts Anonymous, Fatties Anonymous, Gamblers Anonymous, Migraines Anonymous, Mothers Anonymous, Narcotics Anonymous, Neurotics Anonymous, Overeaters Anonymous, Parents Anonymous, Parents of Youth in Trouble Anonymous, Prison Families Anonymous, Psychotics Anonymous, Recidivists Anonymous, Relatives Anonymous, Retirees Anonymous, Rich Kids Anonymous, Schizophrenics Anonymous, Sexual Child Abusers Anonymous, Smokers Anonymous, Stutterers Anonymous, Suicide Anonymous and Youth Anonymous.

sionals seeking to recover from codependency), veterans and so forth. The focus of activity for these groups may tend toward advocacy efforts on behalf of their membership (for example, the disabled) or fostering alternative patterns for living (for example, for gays and lesbians). Interestingly, though women today constitute the majority in U.S. and Canadian society, women's groups conceptually may be included in this category due to their focus on advocacy. Where the minorities in question have been the object of scorn, such as blacks or gays, group activities may serve to help members boost their self-esteem through mutual support and consciousness raising, in addition to ameliorating their condition through educational and lobbying efforts.

WHY SELF-HELP?

Whatever the contours of its historical development, and whatever the details of the taxonomies into which today's groups may be categorized, self-help is clearly an idea whose time has come, and for at least two reasons: It is cost effective and it appeals to current ideology.

A Cost-Effective Response to a Human-Services Need

True, self-help has historically inspired some skepticism by professionals. (See "Problems, Potentials, Perspectives" below, as well as Appendix I.) But on balance, today it is regarded as an effective complement to the existing human services system and even patient care. The 1987 Report of the *Surgeon General's Workshop on Self-Help and Public Health* (see U.S. Department of Health & Human Services, 1988), one of the turning points in the history of the phenomenon, marked the recognition of self-help by institutionalized health and human services.[3] The bibliography that follows contains an impressive number of professional studies of self-help's benefits, including *Outsiders U.S.A.: Original Essays on 24 Outgroups in American Society* by David Spiegel et al. (1989) that describes the *medical* benefits of self-help.[4]

In brief, there is consensus among human services professionals that, in the current economic environment, where funding is becoming increasingly scarce even as costs are rising and pressures exist to expand many services, self-help is a beneficial resource. Supplying support and helpful information to people in need, self-help has emerged to fill the gap created by at least two events: *the disappearance of traditional sources of help,* such as the nuclear and extended family, and close-knit traditional societies; and *the noninvolvement of professionals,* such as doctors and other human service providers, who feel that providing such support services is outside their purview.

In some cases, self-help has emerged as the primary service when professionals had, in fact, failed to provide necessary help. One instance is the formation of Alcoholics Anonymous in 1935, the primordial modern self-help group and the first effective treatment for alcoholism, a problem that had baffled medical doctors ever since John Barleycorn first crushed grapes; most physicians regarded it as a character flaw. Another example are peer groups that help people cope with life after ostomy; health care had failed—perhaps through inability, perhaps disinterest, perhaps unwillingness—to address the problems that confront patients after this particularly traumatic type of surgery. As these and many other cases illustrate, throughout its history, self-help—driven by the consumer—has rushed in to fill gaps.

Self-Help Appeals to Current Ideology

Besides fulfilling a need at the right price— essentially, it's free—self-help also fits in well with contemporary culture and society. Today self-help has taken root in an ideological environment that ensures its luxuriant growth well into the foreseeable future. Contemporary self-help responds tit for tat to many key preoccupations of post-'60s American society. Two of the most important are the following:

- *Self-help is informal and nonprofessional,* ensuring its appeal to a participatory, shirt-sleeve society that, especially since the 1960s, is antibureaucratic and antiauthoritarian. Authority in a self-help context is not the result of an institution-granted academic degree, but rather experiences garnered in the "real world," for example, as an alcoholic, as an amputee, as a lesbian. For many, the avuncular, peer-oriented self-help group is an agreeable alternative to the perceived—perhaps real—condescending, paternal tone of professionals.

  However, self-help group members are not antiprofessional. (See Appendix I for a further discussion of this issue.) True, AA meetings often rock with laughter as a member regales fellows with tales of how his ex-shrink failed to diagnose and per-

---

[3] Then Surgeon General C. Everett Koop, M.D., who called the workshop, was himself a member of Compassionate Friends, a bereavement group for parents of children who have died; Dr. Koop had lost a son in a hiking accident.

[4] For excellent annotated bibliographies of self-help, see "The Recent Literature" by David Spiegel (1980) and *Self-Help Groups* by Rubin Todres (n.d.).

haps even, through the prescription of addictive tranquilizers, aggravated his alcoholism. But research has shown that, in fact, participants in self-help groups are more likely to be in professional psychotherapy and be highly satisfied with it. Self-help resources overlap significantly with professional services.

- *Self-help is consumer driven:* One of self-help's salient features is that the consumer is in control, actually producing—through involvement in the group—the beneficial services. In this sense, self-help is the latter-day human services wing of the 1960s consumer rights movement.

Other advantages of such a consumer-driven human service source include its increased accountability, determined not by professional providers and their peer review but by the consumers and their peers. In self-help, the customer is always right.

PROBLEMS, POTENTIALS, PERSPECTIVES

Historically—though perhaps less so in the last decade—human service professionals have raised various caveats about self-help and its problems and dangers, real, imagined or potential. One set of fears relates to the consumer. Will self-help create dependency by encouraging its users to believe that only by continued participation will they remain healthy? Is it possible that users, through participation, will derive satisfaction, but not genuine help? And will participation in self-help steer people away from other, perhaps more potent forms of help? (This is especially a concern for disadvantaged sectors of society, which may be able to afford only self-help and not costly professional services.)

Other concerns relate to self-help and the professional community. Will the continued

growth and success of self-help diminish the size and importance of professional services? And might the success of a consumer-driven system like self-help result in the abrogation by the government health and human services system of any responsibility to the public?

To the extent that these fears are well founded—and some are—it seems likely, given the alliance struck by the professional and self-help communities, that they will be addressed and resolved. To get the flavor of this historic alliance, see, for example, the 16 "Recommendations to the Surgeon General" and Dr. Koop's response (U.S. Department of Health & Human Services, 1988), where Dr. Koop, in "The Surgeon General's Response," pp. 33–38, endorses, for the most part, the workshop's 16 recommendations on the expansion of services and their integration into traditional human services in the U.S. Among them are recommendations to build self-help into the policy and practice of public and private organizations, including health care providers; to establish a structure within the Public Health Service for promoting and developing self-help; to sponsor information campaigns aimed at the general public but also human service professionals; to conduct scientific research into self-help; to identify mechanisms for linking self-help with formal service delivery systems "as equal partners"; to develop a national health policy that recognizes the validity of self-help; to change the attitude of professionals—as well as policy-makers, clergy, school counselors and probation officers—toward self-help; and to increase federal, state, local and private funding for self-help groups and activities.

With minimal qualifications, Dr. Koop seconded the recommendations of the workshop. In doing so, he opened a whole new era of legitimacy for self-help—its coming of age—and tacked up on the wall a blueprint for self-help's development into the next millennium.

Bibliography

Abel, Charles, and Carter, I. "Social Workers and Self-Help Groups for Terminally Ill." *Archives of the Foundation of Thanatology* 5/1 (1975): 94.

Ablon, Joan. "Al-Anon Family Groups." *American Journal of Psychotherapy* 28/1 (1974): 30–45.

————. "Dwarfism and Social Identity: Self-Help Group Participation." *Social Sciences and Medicine* 15B/1 (1981): 25–30.

————. "The Parents' Auxiliary of Little People of America: A Self-Help Model of Social Support for Families of Short-Statured Children." *Prevention in Human Services* 1/3 (1982): 31–46.

Abrahams, R. B. "Mutual Help for the Widowed." *Social Work* 17 (1972): 54–61.

————. "Mutual Helping: Styles of Caregiving in a Mutual Aid Program." In G. Caplan and M. Killilea, eds. *Support Systems and Mutual Help*. New York: Grune & Stratton, 1976.

Adams, Robert. *Self-Help, Social Work, and Empowerment*. Houndmills, Basingstoke, Hampshire, U.K.: Macmillan Education, 1990.

Adler, H. O., and Hammett, V. O. "Crisis, Conversation and Cult Formation: An Examination of a Common Psychosocial Sequence." *American Journal of Psychiatry* 13 (1973): 861–64.

Al-Anon. *Living with an Alcoholic,* 6th ed. rev. New York: Al-Anon Family Groups Headquarters, 1975.

Alexander, N. B. "Self-Help Groups, Part 1." *Clinics in Gastroenterology* 11/2 (1982): 405–15.

Alford, Geary S. "Alcoholics Anonymous: An Empirical Outcome Study." *Addictive Behaviors* 5/4 (1980): 359–70.

Alinsky, S. D. "The Poor and the Powerful." *International Journal of Psychiatry* 4/4 (1967): 308.

Allon, Natalie. "Group Dieting Interaction." *Dissertation Abstracts International* 32 (12-A): 7093, 1972.

————. "Latent Social Services in Group Dieting." *Social Problems* 23/1 (1975): 59–69.

American Hospital Association, Illinois Self-Help Center. *Director of National Self-Help Mutual Aid Resources*. Chicago: American Hospital Association, 1988.

Anderson, W. A., and Anderson, N. D. "The Politics of Age Exclusion: The Adults Only Movement in Arizona." *Gerontologist* 18 (1978): 6–12.

Anonymous. "The Compulsive Gambler." *International Journal of Offender Therapy and Comparative Criminology* 25/1 (1981): 90–92.

Anonymous. "Overeaters Anonymous: A Self-Help Group." *American Journal of Nursing* 81/3 (1981): 560–63.

Antze, P. "The Role of Ideologies in Peer Psychotherapy Organization: Some Theoretical Considerations and Three Case Studies." *Journal of Applied Behavioral Science* 12 (1976): 323–44.

Asp, David R. "A Response to 'Toward a Model for Counselling Alcoholics.' " *Journal of Contemporary Psychotherapy* 10/1 (1978): 39–45.

Back, K. W., and Taylor, R. C. "Self-Help Groups: Tool or Symbol?" *Journal of Applied Behavioral Science* 12 (1976): 295–309.

Bacon, Gertrude M. "Parents Anonymous of New York, New York." *Victimology* 2/2 (1977): 331–37.

Bailey, M. B. "Al-Anon Family Groups as an Aid to Wives of Alcoholics." *Social Work* 10 (1965): 68–74.

Baker, Frank. "The Interface between Professional and Natural Support Systems." *Clinical Social Work* 5/2 (1977): 139–48.

Bankoff, Elizabeth A., Bond, Gary R., and Videka, Lynn. "Who Uses Self-Help Groups?" *Innovations* 7/3 (1980): 39–40.

Barath, A. *Self-Help and Its Support Systems in Europe 1979–1989: A Critical Review.* Zagreb: Department of Health Psychology, Medical School of Zagreb, n.d.

Barish, Herbert. "Self-Help Groups." *Encyclopedia of Social Work* 16/2 (1971): 1163–68.

Bassin, Alexander. "Red, White and Blue Poker Chips: An A.A. Behavior Modification Technique." *American Psychologist* 30/6 (1975): 695f.

Bean, Margaret. "Alcoholics Anonymous." *Psychiatric Annals* 5/2 (1975): 7–61.

Bebbington, Paul E. "The Efficacy of Alcoholics Anonymous: The Elusiveness of Hard Data."*British Journal of Psychiatry* 128 (1976): 572–80.

Beers, C. *A Mind That Found Itself.* New York: Doubleday, 1948.

Bender, Eugene I. "The Citizen as Emotional Activist: An Appraisal of Self-Help Groups in North America." *Canada's Mental Health* 19/2 (1971): 30–37.

Bentley, Stuart. "Harmony: Self-Activity in Multi-Racial Families." *Social Work Today* 8/22 (1977): 17.

Berenson, David. "A Family Approach to Alcoholism." *Psychiatric Opinion* 12/1 (1976); 33–38.

Bernstein, A. D., ed. *Self-Help Groups for People Dealing with AIDS: You Are Not Alone.* Denville, New Jersey: Self-Help Clearinghouse, St. Clares-Riverside Medical Center, 1988.

Beverley, E. V. "Organziations for Seniors— What They Stand for, What They Offer." *Geriatrics* 31/11 (1976): 121f.

Bitley, Raymond Thomas. "The Cancer Experience in an American Cultural Context: A Study of Cancer Clinics and Self-Help Programs." *Dissertaiton Abstracts International* 41 (8): 3641-A, 1981.

Blau, David. "On Widowhood: Discussion." *Journal of Geriatric Psychiatry* 8/1 (1975): 29–40.

Blorsky, Lawrence E. "An Innovative Service for the Elderly." *Gerontologist* 13/2 (1973): 189–96.

Bond, Gary R., and Lieberman, M. A. "The Role and Function of Women's Consciousness Raising: Self-Help, Psychotherapy, or

Political Activism?" In C. L. Heckerman, ed., *Women and Psychotherapy: Changing Emotions in Changing Times*. New York: Human Sciences, n.d.

Bond, Gary R., et al. "Mended Hearts: A Self-Help Case Study." *Social Policy* 9/4 (1979): 50–57.

Borck, Leslie E., and Aronowitz, Eugene. "The Role of a Self-Help Clearinghouse." *Prevention in Human Sciences* 1/3 (1982): 121–29.

Borkman, T. "Experiential Knowledge: A New Concept for the Analysis of Self-Help Groups." *Social Service Review* 50 (1976): 445f.

———. "Self-Help Groups at the Turning Point: Emerging Egalitarian Alliances with the Formal Health Care System?" *American Journal of Community Psychiatry* 18/2 (1990): 321f.

Borman, L. D. *Explorations in Self-Help and Mutual Aid*. Evanston, Illinois: Center for Urban Affairs, Northwestern University, 1975.

———. "Special Issue on Self-Help Groups." *Journal of Applied Behavior Sciences* 12/3 (1976).

Borman, L. D., ed. *Explorations in Self-help and Mutual Aid; Proceedings of the Self-help Exploratory Workshop*. Evanston, Illinois: Northwestern, 1974

Borman, L. D., Borck, L., Hess, R., and Pasquale., F., eds. "Helping People to Help Themselves: Self-Help and Prevention." *Prevention in Human Services* 1/3 (1982): 1–129.

———. "Help Yourself, and Others, Too." *The Rotarian* 143/1 (1983): 12–15.

———. "Self-Help/Mutual Aid Groups: Strategies for Prevention." *Director of Self-Help/ Mutual Aid Groups*. Evanston, Illinois: The Self-Help Center, 1988.

Borman, L. D., and Lieberman, Morton. "Impact of Self-Help Groups on Widows' Mental Health." *National Reporter* 4/7 (1981): 2–5.

Borman, L. D., Pasquale, F., and Davies, J. "Epilepsy Self-Help Groups: Collaboration with Professionals." *Prevention in Human Services* 1/3 (1982): 111–20.

Bradfield, Cecil D., and Myers, R. Ann. "Make Today Count: A Mutual Support Group for the Dying." *Mid-American Review of Sociology* 5/1 (1980): 91–100.

Bradshaw, J., Glendinning, C., and Hatch, S. "Voluntary Organizations for Handicapped Children and Their Families: The Meaning of Membership." *Child Care, Health and Development* (Great Britain) 3 (1977): 247–60.

Branckaerts, Jan, and Nuyens, Yvo. *Self-Help Organizations in Flanders*. Holland: K. V. Leuven, Sociological Research Institute, n.d.

Braus, Patricia. "Selling Self-Help." *American Demographics* (March 1992): 48–53.

Brennan, J. O. "The Welcome Club: Helping Psychiatric Patients to Face the World Outside." *Nursing Times* (Great Britain) 73/11 (1977): 393.

Brieff, R., Hiatt, L. G., Hager, M., and Horwitz, J. "Description of Self-Help Groups of Older People Meeting on Health Topics." In L. G. Hiatt, *Uses of Self-Help*, vol. 1, pp. 1–25. New York: American Foundation for the Blind, 1978.

Brieff, R., Horwitz, J., and Hiatt, L. G. "Self-Help and Mutual Aid for the Elderly: A Literature Review." In L. G. Hiatt, ed. *Uses of Self-Help*. vol. 2, pp. 1–70, Section B. New York: American Foundation for the Blind, 1978.

Brown, Vivian B. "Drug People: Schizoid Personalities in Search of a Treatment." *Psychotherapy* 8/3 (1971): 213–15.

Brugliera, M. "The Self-Help Roots of Northcare." *Journal of Applied Behavioral Sciences* 12 (1976): 397–403.

Buck, S., and Dabrowska, M. "An Introduction to the Work of the Parent Self-Help Groups in the United Kingdom." *Child Abuse and Neglect* 5/4 (1981): 375–82.

Budd, S., et al., eds. *Mental Health Clients Helping Each Other.* Riverside, California: California Network of Mental Health Clients, 1990.

Bumbalo, Judith. "The Self-Help Phenomenon. *American Journal of Nursing* 9 (1973): 1588–91.

Burdett-Finn, Penelope Miller. "Evaluation of a Model for Prevention of Maladjustment in Young Widows." *Dissertation Abstracts International* 40 (11): 5399-B, 1980.

Burdman, Milton. "Ethnic Self-Help Groups in Prison and on Parole." *Crime and Delinquency* 20/2 (1974): 107–18.

Butler, Robert N., et al. "Self-Care, Self-Help, and the Elderly." *International Journal of Aging and Human Development* 10/1 (1980): 95–119.

Cannold, Stuart A. "Investigation of Alcoholics Anonymous and Its Impact on Americans under Thirty-Six." *Dissertation Abstraction International,* 41 (10): 4223-A, 1981.

Cantin L., and Daoust, G. "Les Déprimés anonymes." *Santé mentale au Québec* 6 (1981): 180–82.

Caplan, G. "The Family as Support System." In G. Caplan and M. Killilea, eds. *Support Systems and Mutual Help.* New York: Grune & Stratton, 1976.

———. *Support Systems and Community Mental Health: Lectures on Concept Development.* New York: Behavioral Publications, 1974.

Caplan, G., and Killilea, M., eds. *Support Systems and Mutual Help: Multidisciplinary Explorations.* New York: Grune & Stratton, 1976.

Cardinal, Jani, and Farquharson, Andy. *The Self-Help Resource Kit.* Victoria, British Columbia: School of Social Work, University of Victoria, n.d.

Chamberlin, J. *On Our Own: Patient-Controlled Alternatives to the Mental Health System.* New York: McGraw-Hill, 1978.

Chutis, Laurieann. *Self-Help Mutual Aid Groups and Community Mental Health Centers—Effective Partners.* New York: National Self-Help Clearinghouse, 1980.

Claflin, Bill. "Alcoholics Anonymous: One Million Members and Growing." *Self-Help and Health: A Report.* New York: New Careers Training Laboratory, n.d.

Clayton, Patricia N. "Meeting the Needs of the Single Parent Family." *The Family Coordinator* 20/4 (1971): 327–36.

Coghlan, Allan, and Zimmerman, Roger S. "Self-Help (Daytop) and Methadone Maintenance: Are They Both Failing?" *Drug Forum* 50/3 (1972): 221–25.

Cole, Stephen A. "Evaluation of Self-Help Groups for Chronic Illnesses: A Research Proposal." *Self-Help and Health: A Report.* New York: New Careers Training Laboratory, n.d.

Collins, M. L. *Child Abuser: A Study of Child Abusers in Self-Help Group Therapy.* Littleton, Massachusetts: PSG Publishing Company, 1978.

Comstock, Christine H. "Preventive Processes in Self-Help Groups: Parents Anonymous." *Prevention in Human Services* 1/3 (1982): 47–53.

Corder, M. P., and Anderrs, R. L. "Death and Dying—Oncology Discussion Groups." *Journal of Psychiatric Nursing & Mental Health Service* 12 (1974): 10–14.

Cornstock, C. M. "Preventive Processes in Self-Help Groups: Parents Anonymous." *Prevention in Human Services: Helping People Help Themselves* 1/3 (1982).

Cressey, D. R. "Social Psychological Foundations for Using Criminals in the Rehabilitation of Criminals." *Journal of Research* in *Crime and Deliquency* 2/2 (1965): 49–59.

Cromer, Gerald. "Gamblers Anonymous in Israel: A Participant Observation Study of Self-Help Group." *International Journal of the Addictions* 12/7 (1978): 1069–77.

Crowe, Brenda. "Self-Help Group for Child-rearing Parents." *Child Abuse and Neglect* 3/1 (1979): 335–40.

Cutler, S. "Membership in Different Types of Voluntary Associations and Psychological Well-Being." *Geronologist* 16/4 (1976): 335, 339.

Davis, Donald I. "Alcoholics Anonymous and Family Therapy." *Journal of Marital and Family Therapy* 6/1 (1980): 65–73.

Davis, M. S. "Women's Liberation Groups as a Primary Preventive Mental Health Strategy." *Community Mental Health Journal* 13/3 (1977): 219–28.

Dean, S. R. "The Role of Self-Conducted Group Therapy in Psycho-rehabilitation: A Look at Recovery, Inc." *American Journal of Psychiatry* 127/7 (1971): 934–37.

———. "Self-help Group Psychotherapy: Mental Patients Rediscover Will Power." *International Journal of Social Psychiatry* 17 (1971): 72–78.

DeJohngh, J. F. "Self-Help in Modern Society." In G. R. B. Villimoria and S. D. Patel, eds. *Self-Help in Social Welfare: Processsings of the Seventh International Conference of Social Work*. Toronto: n.o., 1954.

Dentler, R. A., and Erikson, K. R. "The Functions of Deviance in Groups." *Social Problems* 8 (1959): 98–107.

Devall, B. "Gay Liberation: An Overview." *Journal of Voluntary Action Research* 2/1 (1973): 24–35.

Dewar, Tom. "Professionalized Clients as Self-Helpers." *Self-Help and Health: A Report*. New York: New Careers Training Laboratory, n.d.

Dinitz, S., and Beran, N. "Community Mental Health as a Boundary-less and Boundary-busting System." *Journal of Health and Social Behavior* 12 (1971): 99–108.

Dumont, M. P. "Self-help Treatment Programs." *American Journal of Psychiatry* 6 (1974): 631–35.

Durman, E. C. "The Role of Self-help in Service Provision." *Journal of Applied Behavioral Science* 12 (1976): 433–43.

Enomoto, J. J. "Participation in Correctional Management by Offender Self-Help Groups." *Federal Probation* 36/2 (1972): 36f.

Enright, M. F., and Parsons, B. V. "Training Crisis Intervention Specialists and Peer-Group Counselors as Therapeutic Agents in the Gay Community." *Community Mental Health Journal* 12 (1976): 383–91.

Farquason, William A. F. "Peers as Helpers: Personal Change in Members of Self-Help Groups in Metropolitan Toronto." *Dissertation Abstracts International* 38 (10 A): 5848, 1975.

Farris-Kurtz, Linda. "Time in Residential Care and Participation in Alcoholics Anonymous as Predictors of Continued Sobriety." *Psychological Reports* 48/2 (1981): 633f.

Fichter, Manfred. "Kellektive Selbsthilfe: Alternative Modelle in Selbstorganization" ("Collective Self-Help: Alternative Models in Self-Organization.") In G. Sommer, *Gemeindepsychologie*. München: Urban & Schwarzenberg, 1977.

Frankel, Alan, and Sloat, Wilbur E. "The Odyssey of a Self-Help Group." *Psychological Aspects of Disability* 18/1 (1971): 46–51.

Fremouw, William J., and Harmatz, Morton G. "A Helper Model for Behavioral Treatment of Speech Anxiety." *Journal of Consulting and Clinical Psychology* 43/5 (1975): 652–60.

French, G. A. "Self-Help Groups: More than a Band-Aid Treatment?" *Chicago Medicine* 92/18 (1989): 10–13.

Freyberger, Hellmuth. "Psychosomatic Aspects in Self-Help Groups Made up of Medical Patients. Presented on the Example of the Ostomy Group." *Psychotherapy and Psychosomatics* 31/1–4 (1979): 114–20.

Fry, Lincoln J. "Research Grants and Drug Self-Help Programs: What Price Knowledge." *Journal of Health and Social Behavior* 18/4 (1977): 405–17.

Galanter, M., Gleaton, T., Marcus, C. E., and McMillen, J. "Self-Help Groups for Parents of Young Adults and Alcohol Abusers." *American Journal of Psychiatry* 141/7 (1984): 889–91.

Galper, Miriam, and Washburne, Carolyn Knott. "A Women's Self-Help Program in Action." *Social Policy* 6/5 (1976): 46–52.

Garb, J. R., and Stunkard, A. J. "Effectiveness of a Self-help Group in Obesity Control." *Archives of Internal Medicine* 134 (1974): 716–20.

Gartner, A. "Self-Help and Mental Health." *Social Policy* 7/2 (1976): 28–40.

Gartner, A., ed. "Arthritis Self-Help Project." *Self-Help Reporter* 3/4 (1979): 7.

Gartner, A., and Riessman, F. "Health Care in a Technological Age." *Self-Help and Health: A Report.* New York: New Careers Training Laboratory, n.d.

———, eds. *Mental Health and Self-Help Groups.* New York: Human Services Press, n.d.

———. "Self-Help and Mental Health." *Hospital and Community Psychiatry* 33/8 (1982): 631–35.

———. *Self-Help in the Human Services.* San Francisco: Jossey-Bass, 1977.

———. "Self-Help Models and Consumer-Intensive Health Practice." *American Journal of Public Health* 66/8 (1976): 783–86.

Gartner, A., and Riessman, F., eds. *The Self-Help Revolution.* New York: Human Sciences Press, 1984.

Gates, June Collins. "Comparison of Behavior Modification and Self-Help Groups with Conventional Therapy of Diabetes." *Dissertation Abstracts International* 40 (7): 3084-B, 1980.

Glaser, Frederick B. "Gaudenzia, Incorporated: Historical and Theoretical Background of a Self-Help Addiction Treatment Program." *International Journal of Addiction* 6/4 (1971): 615–26.

Glaser, Kristin. "Women's Self-Help Groups as an Alternative to Therapy." *Psychotherapy: Theory, Research and Practice* 13/1 (1976): 77–81.

Glendenning, Frank. "Hands across the Seas: Self-Help and Older People in Britain." *Self-Help Reporter* 2/4 (1978).

Goldwyn, E. N. "Weight Watchers: A Case Study in the Negotiation of Reality." *Dissertation Abstracts International* 31 (12A): 6745, 1970.

Goodman, G., and Jacobs, M. "Psychology and Self-Help Groups: Predictions on a Partnership." *American Psychologist.*

Gordon, R. E., Edmunson, E., and Bedell, J. "Reducing Rehospitalization of State Mental Patients: Peer Management and Support." In A. Jeger and R. Slotnick, eds., *Community Mental Health.* New York: Plenum, 1982.

Gottlieb, Benjamin H. "Mutual Help Groups: Members' Views of Their Benefits and of Roles for Professionals." *Prevention in Human Services* 1/3 (1982): 55–67.

Gottlieb, Benjamin H., ed. *Social Networks and Social Support.* Beverly Hills, California: Sage, 1981.

Gould, Edward, Garrigues, Charles S., and Scheikowitz, Karen. "Interaction in Hospitalized Patient-Led and Staff-Led Psychotherapy Groups." *American Journal of Psychotherapy* 29/3 (1975): 383–90.

Grimmso, A., Helgesen, G., and Borchgreuink, C. "Short-Term and Long-Term Effects of Lay Groups on Weight Reduction." *British Medical Journal* 283 (October 1981): 1093–95.

Guggenheim, F. C., and O'Hara, S. "Peer Counseling in a General Hospital." *American Journal of Psychiatry* 10 (1976): 1197–99.

Gussow, Z., and Tracy, G. S. "The Role of Self-Help Clubs in Adaptation to Chronic Illness and Disability." *Social Science and Medicine* 10 (1976): 407–14.

Hallowitz, E., and Riessman, R. "The Role of the Indigenous Non-Professional in a Community Mental Health Neighborhood Service Center Program." *American Journal of Orthopsychiatry* 7/4 (1967): 766–78.

Hamilton, Alice T. "An Exploration Study of Therapeutic Self-Help Child Abuse Groups for Low-Income Populations." *Dissertation Abstracts International* 41 (21-A): 5245, 1981.

Hardy, A. *Agoraphobia: Symptoms, Causes, and Treatments*. Menlo Park, California: Terrap, Inc., 1976.

Harris, Zelda. "Ten Steps Towards Establishing a Self-Help Group: A Report from Montreal." *Canada's Mental Health* 29/1 (1981): 16, 21.

Hatfield, Agnes B. "Self-Help Groups for the Families of the Mentally Ill." *Social Work* 26/5 (1981): 408–13.

Hawkins, J. David. "Some Suggestions for 'Self-Help' Approaches with Street Drug Abusers." *Journal of Psychedelic Drugs* 12/2 (1980): 131–37.

Hecker, Benson, et al. "Self-Help Therapy Programs: A Model for Correctional Institutions." *Georgia Journal of Corrections* 4/1 (1975): 78–80.

Heckerman, C. L., ed. *Women and Psychotherapy: Changing Emotions in Changing Times*. New York: Human Sciences Press, n.d.

Hedrick, H. L. "Increasing Access to Self-Help Groups." *Journal of Allied Health* 17/3 (1988): 165–69.

———. "Involvement in Mutual Aid/Self-Help Activities." *Journal of Allied Health* 15/3 (1986): 268f.

Henry, S., and Robinson, D. "Understanding Alcoholics Anonymous." *The Lancet* 1/8060 (1978): 372–75.

Hermalin, Jared, et al. "Enhancing Primary Prevention: The Marriage of Self-Help Groups and Formal Health Care Delivery Systems." *Journal of Clinical Child Psychology* 8/2 (1979): 125–29.

Hess, B. "Self-Help Among the Aged." *Social Policy* (November/December 1976): 55–62.

Hess, Robert. " 'Helping Thyself' to Mental Health: Interview." *Innovations* 7/1 (1980): 18–21.

Hinrichsen, G., Revenson, T., and Shinn, M. "Does Self-Help Help? An Empirical Investigation of Scoliosis Peer Support Groups." *Journal of Social Issues* 41/1 (1985): 65–87.

Hirschowitz, R. G. "Groups to Help People Cope with the Task of Transition." In R. G. Hirschowitz and B. Levy, eds., *The Changing Mental Health Scene*. New York: Spectrum Publications, 1976.

Hirschowitz, R. G., and Levy, B., eds. *The Changing Mental Health Scene*. New York: Spectrum Publications, 1976.

Hollister, William G., et al. *Alternative Services in Community Mental Health: Programs and Processes*. Chapel Hill, North Carolina: University of North Carolina Press, 1985.

Holmes, Robert M. "Alcoholics Anonymous as Group Logotherapy." *Pastoral Psychology* 21/3 (1970): 30–36.

Hornstein, F., Downer, C., and Farber, S. "Gynecological Self-Help." *Self-Help and Health: A Report*. New York: New Careers Training Laboratory, n.d.

Houle, Pierre. "L'Alcool et l'homme: alcoolisme et comité d'entraide dans l'industrie des pâtes et papier en Mauricies. *Le médecin du Québec* 14/5 (1979): 74–79.

Huey, K. "Conference Report: Developing Effective Links Between Human Service Providers and the Self-Help System." *Hospital and Community Psychiatry* 28 (1977): 767–70.

Hughes, J. M. "Adolescent Children of Alcoholic Parents and the Relationship of Alateen to These Children." *Journal of Consulting and Clinical Psychology* 45/5 (1977): 946f.

Hurley, D. "Getting Help from Helping Others." *Psychology Today* 21/1 (1988): 63–67.

Hurvitz, N. "The Origins of the Peer Self-Help Psychotherapy Group Movement." *Journal of Applied Behavioral Science* 12 (1976): 283–94.

———. "Peer Self-Help Psychotherapy Groups: Psychotherapy Without Psychotherapists." In Paul M. Roman and Harrison, M., eds., *The Sociology of Psychotherapy*. New York: Jason Aronson, 1974.

———. "Peer Self-Help Psychotherapy Groups and Their Implications for Psychotherapy." *Psychotherapy: Theory, Research and Practice* 7 (1970): 41–49.

Isenberg, Daryl Holtz. "Coping with Cancer: The Role of Belief Systems and Support in Cancer Self-Help Groups." *Dissertation Abstracts International* 42 (9-A): 3914, 1981.

Jackins, H. *Fundamentals of Co-Counseling Manual*. Seattle, Washington: Personal Counselors, 1962.

Jackson, Margery Leithliter. "Actualization of Alcoholics Anonymous Members." *Dissertation Abstracts International* 41 (3): 1091-B, 1980.

Jacobs, M. K., and Goodman, G. "Psychology and Self-Help Groups: Predictions on a Partnership." *American Psychologist* 44/3 (1989): 536–45.

Jacques, M. E., and Patterson, K. M. "The Self-Help Group Model: A Review." *Rehabilitation Counseling Bulletin* 18/1 (1974): 48–58.

Jeger, Abraham A., Slotnick, Robert S., and Schure, Matthew. "Toward a Self-Help/Professional Collaborative Perspective in Mental Health." In David E. Biegel and Arthur J. Naparstek, eds., *Community Support Systems and Mental Health Review: Practice, Policy and Research*. New York: Spring Publishing Company, 1982.

Jensen, P. S. "Risk, Protective Factors and Supportive Interventions in Chronic Airway Obstruction." *Archives of General Psychiatry* 40/11 (1983).

Jertson, James M. "Self-Help Groups." *Social Work* 20/2 (1975): 144f.

Johnson, John E., and Peebles, Otis W. "Use of a Self-Help Community Model in the Treatment of Adolescent Behavior Disorders." *Adolescence* 8/29 (1973): 67–84.

Jones, Robert K. "Sectarian Characteristics of Alcoholics Anonymous." *Sociology* 4/1 (1970): 182–95.

Kagey, J. R., Vivace, J., and Lutz, W. "Mental Health Primary Prevention: The Role of Parent Mutual Support Groups." *American Journal of Public Health* 71/2 (1981): 166f.

Kahana, Ralph J. "On Widowhood: Introduction." *Journal of Geriatric Psychiatry* 8/1 (1975): 5–8.

Kanzler, M., Jaffe, J., and Zeidenberg, P. "Long- and Short-Term Effectiveness of a Large-Scale Proprietary Smoking Cessation Program: A Four-Year Follow-up of Smokenders Participants." *Journal of Clinical Psychology* 32/3 (1976): 661–69.

Katz, A. H. "Application of Self-Help Concepts in Current Social Welfare." *Social Work* 10 (1965): 68–74.

———. *Partners in Wellness*. Los Angeles: California Department of Public Health, 1987.

———. "Self-Help and Mutual Aid: An Emerging Social Movement." *Annual Review of Sociology* 7 (1981): 129–55.

———. "Self-Help Groups." *Social Work* 17/8 (1972): 120f.

———. "Self-Help Groups: Some Clarifications." *Ethics in Science and Medicine* 5 (1978): 109–114.

———. "Self-Help Organizations and Volunteer Participation in Social Welfare." *Social Work* 15/1 (1970): 51–60.

Katz, A. H., and Bender, E. I. *Helping One Another: Self-Help Groups in a Changing World*. Oakland, California: Third Party Publishing, 1990.

———. "Self-Help Groups in Western Society: History and Prospects." *Journal of Applied Behavioral Science* 12 (1976): 265–82.

———, eds. *The Strength in Us: Self-Help Groups in the Modern World*. New York: New Viewpoints, n.d.

Katz, A. H., et al., eds. *Self-Help: Concepts and Applications*. Philadelphia: Charles Press, 1992.

Khantzian, E. J. "Perspectives on the Self-Help–Psychiatry Controversy in Addiction Treatment." *Psychiatric Annals* 6/4 (1976): 8–11, 15.

Killilea, M. "Mutual Help Organizations: Interpretations in the Literature." In G. Caplan and M. Killilia, eds., *Support Systems and Mutual Help*. New York: Grune & Stratton, 1976.

King, B., Bissell, L., and O'Brien, P. "Alcoholics Anonymous, Alcoholism Counseling and Social Work Treatment." *Health and Social Work* 4/4 (1979): 181–98.

Kirshbaum, H. R., Harveston, D. S., and Katz, A. H. "Independent Living for the Disabled." *Social Policy* 7/2 (1976): 59f.

Klass, Dennis. "Self-Help Groups for the Bereaved: Theory, Theology and Practice." *Journal of Religion and Health* 21/4 (1982): 307.

Kleeman, Michael J., and DePree, Janet L. "Self-Help Groups and Their Effectiveness as Agents for Chronic Illness Care: The Case of Kidney Transplant Recipients." *Self-Help and Health: A Report*. New York: New Careers Training Laboratory, n.d.

Kleiman, M. A., Mantell, J. E., and Alexander, E. S. "Collaboration and Its Discontents: The Perils of Partnership." *Journal of Applied Behavioral Science* 12 (1976): 403–10.

Knight, B., et al. "Self-Help Groups: Member's Perspectives." *American Journal of Community Psychology* 8/1 (1980): 53–65.

Kopolow, Louis E. "Client Participation in Mental Health Service Delivery." *Community Mental Health Journal* 17/1 (1981): 46–53.

Kramer, Abe S. "Helping the Gambler Help Himself/Herself: Gamblers Anonymous and Beyond." *American Archives of Rehabilitation Therapy* 28/2 (1980): 10f.

Kropotkin, P. *Mutual Aid: A Factor of Evolution*. New York: New York University Press, 1972.

Kurtz, E. *A.A.: The Story*. Cambridge, Massachusetts: Harper/Hazelden, 1988.

Kurtz, L. F. "Mutual Aid for Affective Disorders: The Manic Depressive and Depressive Association." *American Journal of Orthopsychiatry* 58/1 (1988): 152–55.

———. "The Self-Help Movement: Review of the Past Decade of Research." *Social Work with Groups* 13/3 (1990): 101–5.

Kurtz, L. F., Mann, K. B., and Chambon, A. "Linking Between Social Workers and

Mental Health Mutual-Aid Groups." *Social Work in Health Care* 13/1 (1987): 69–78.

Kurtz, L. F., and Powell, T. J. "Three Approaches to Understanding Self-Help Groups." *Social Work with Groups* (Fall 1987): 69–80.

Ladas, Alice K. "Information and Social Support in the Outcome of Breastfeeding." *Journal of Applied Behavioral Science* 8/1 (1972): 110–14.

Lamb, Richard H., and Oliphant, Eve. "Empathy and Advice: Counseling Families of the Mentally Ill." *Behavioral Medicine* 6/9 (1979): 35–38.

Lasogga, Frank, and Kondrign, Irmgard. "Stotterer in Selbsthilfegruppen und in Einzeltherapie" ("Stutterers in Self-Help Groups and in Individual Therapy"). *Zeitschrift für Psychologies: Forschung und Praxis* 11/3 (1982): 201–14.

Lavoie, Francine. "Action Research: A New Model of Interaction between the Professional and Self-Help Groups." In A. Gartner and F. Reissman, eds., *Mental Health and Self-Help Groups.* New York: Human Services Press, n.d.

———. "Citizen Participation in Health Care." In D. L. Pancoast, ed. *Rediscovering Self-Help.* Newbury Park, California: Sage Publishers, 1983.

———. "Elaboration d'une méthode d'analyse descriptive des procédés interactifs dans les groupes d'entraide." *Revue québecoise de psychologie* 3/1 (1982): 106–9.

———. "Les groupes d'entraide." In J. Arseneau et al., *Psychothérapies: Attention!* Sillery, Québec: Québec Science, 1983.

———. "Modes d'évaluation des groupes d'entraide." *Revue québecoise de psychologie* 4 (1982).

———. "Social Atmosphere in Self-Help Groups: A Case Study." *Canada's Mental Health* 29/1 (1981): 13–15.

Lee, Donald T. "Recovery, Inc.: Aid in the Transition from Hospital to Community." *Mental Hygiene* 55/2 (1971): 194–99.

———. "Therapeutic Type: Recovery, Inc." In A. H. Katz and Bender, E. I., eds., *The Strength in Us.* New York: New Viewpoints, 1976.

Lee, Judith A., and Park, Danielle N. "A Groups Approach to the Adolescent Girl in Foster Care." *American Journal of Orthopsychiatry* 48/3 (1978): 516–27.

Lenrow, P. B., and Burch, R. W. "Mutual Aid and Professional Service: Opposing or Complementary?" In B. J. Gottlieb, ed., *Social Networks and Social Support.* Beverly Hills, California: Sage, 1982.

Leventhal, G. S., Maton, K. I., and Madara, E. J. "Systemic Organizational Support for Self-Help Groups." *American Journal of Orthopsychiatry* 58/4 (October 1988): 592–603.

Levine, I. S., and Spaniel, L. "The Role of Families of the Severely Mentally Ill in the Development of Community Support Services." *Psychosocial Rehabilitation Journal* 8/4 (1985): 83–94.

Levitz, L. S., and Stunkard, A. J. "A Therapeutic Coalition for Obesity: Behavior Modification and Patient Self-Help." *American Journal of Psychiatry* 34 (1974): 423–27.

Levy, L. H. "The National Schizophrenia Fellowship: A British Self-Help Group." *Social Psychiatry* 16/3 (1981): 129–35.

———. "Self-help Groups: Types and Psychological Processes." *Journal of Applied Behavioral Science* 12 (1976): 310–32.

———. "Self-Help Groups Viewed by Mental Health Professionals: A Survey and Comments." *American Journal of Community Psychiatry* (August 1978): 305–313.

Lieberman, M. "The Role of Self-Help Groups in Helping Patients and Families Cope with

Cancer." *CA: A Cancer Journal for Clinicians* 38/3 (1988): 162–68.

———. "Self-Help Groups and Psychiatry." *American Psychiatric Annals Review* 5 (1986): 744–60.

Lieberman, M., and Bond, G. R. "The Problem of Being a Woman: A Survey of 1,700 Women in Consciousness-Raising Groups." *Journal of Applied Behavioral Sciences* 12 (1976): 363–79.

———. "Self-Help Groups: Problems of Measuring Outcome." *Small Group Behavior* 9/2 (1978): 221–41.

Lieberman, M., and Borman, L. "The Impact of Self-Help Groups on Widows' Mental Health." *The National Reporter* (The National Research and Information Center, Illinois Self-Help Clearinghouse) 4/7 (1981).

———. "Self-help and Social Research." *Journal of Applied Behavioral Science* 12 (1976): 455–46.

———. *Self-Help Groups for Coping with Crisis: Origins, Members, Processes, and Impact.* San Francisco: Jossey-Bass, 1979.

Lieberman, M. A., Solow, N., Bond, G. R., and Reibstein, J. "The Psychotherapeutic Impact of Women's Consciousness-Raising Groups." In E. Howell and M. Bayes, eds., *Women and Mental Health.* New York: Basic Books, 1981.

Lieberman, M., and Videka-Sherman, L. "The Impact of Self-Help Groups on the Mental Health of Widows and Widowers." *American Journal of Orthopsychiatry* 56/3 (1976): 435–49.

Lipson, Juliene G. "Caesarian Support Groups: Mutual Aid and Education." *Women in Health* 6/3–4 (1981): 27–39.

———. "Effects of a Support Group on the Emotional Impact of Caesarean Childbirth." *Prevention in Human Services* 1/3 (1982): 17–29.

Low, A. A. "Mental Health through Will-Training: A System of Self-help." *Psycho-*therapy as Practiced by Recovery, Inc.* Boston: Christopher Publishing House, 1950.

Lusky, Richard A., and Ingman, Stanley R. "The Pros, Cons and Pitfalls of 'Self-Help' Rehabilitation Programs." *Social Science and Medicine* 13A/1 (1979): 113–21.

Mack, John E. "Alcoholism, A.A., and the Governance of the Self." In Margaret Bean and Norman E. Zinberg, eds., *Dynamic Approaches to the Understanding and Treatment of Alcoholism.* New York: Free Press, 1981.

Madara, E. J. "A Comprehensive Systems Approach to Promoting Self-Help Groups: The New Jersey Self-Help Clearinghouse Model." *Journal of Voluntary Action Research* 15/2 (April–June, 1986): 57–63.

———. "MASH in Its Newest and Most Futuristic Form: The Computer Networks." *Exchange Systems* (Summer 1984): 7f.

———. "Maximizing the Potential for Community Self-Help through Clearinghouse Approaches." *Prevention in the Human Services* 7/1 (1990): 109–38.

———. "The Primary Value of a Self-Help Clearinghouse." In A. H. Katz, et al., eds., *Self-Help: Concept and Applications.* Philadelphia: Charles Press, 1992.

———. The Self-Help Clearinghouse Operation: Tapping the Resource Development Potential of I & R Services." *Information and Referral: The Journal of the Alliance of Information and Referral Systems* 12/1 (Summer, 1985): 42–57.

———. "Supporting Self-Help: A Clearinghouse Perspective." *Social Policy* 18/2 (Fall 1987): 28f.

———. "Twelve Functions of a Clearinghouse in Support Self-Help." *Report of the Conference on Self-Help/Mutual Aid* (March 20–21, 1987). Ottawa: Canadian Council on Social Development, 1987, pp. 18–22.

Madara, E. J., Kalafat, J. and Biller, B. "The Computerized Self-Help Clearinghouse: Using 'High Tech' to Promote 'High Touch' Support Networks." *Computers in Human Services* 3/3 (1988): 39–54.

Madara, E. J., and Neigher, W. D. "Hospitals and Self-Help Groups: Opportunity and Challenge." *Health Progress* 67/3 (April, 1986): 42–45.

Madara, E. J., and Peterson, B. A. "Clergy and Self-Help Groups: Practical and Promising Relationship." *Journal of Pastoral Care* 41/3 (September 1987): 213–20.

Madison, P. "Have Grouped, Will Travel." *Psychotherapy: Theory, Research and Practice* 9 (1972): 324–27.

Maeda, Daisaku. "Growth of Old People's Clubs in Japan." *Geronologist* 15/3 (1975): 254–56.

Maisaik, R., Caine, M., Yarbro, C. H., and Josof, L. "Evaluation of 'Touch': An Oncology Self-Help Group." *Oncology Nursing Forum* 8/3 (1981).

Mantell, J. E., Alexander, E. S., and Kleiman, M. A. "Social Work and Self-help Groups." *Health and Social Work* 1 (1976): 87–101.

Marieskind, Helen I. "Helping Oneself to Health." *Social Policy* 7/2 (1976): 63–66.

Martins, Maria Christina. "Towards an Understanding of the Therapeutic Work of Alcoholics Anonymous." *Jornal Brasileiro de Psiquiatria* 29/4 (1980): 271–74.

Maton, K. I., Leventhal, G. S., Madara, E. J. and Julien, M. "The Birth and Death of Self-Help Groups: A Population Economy Perspective." In A. H. Katz and E. I. Bender, eds., *Self-Help Groups in a Changing World*. Oakland, California: Third Party Associates, 1990.

———. "Factors Affecting the Birth and Death of Mutual-Help Groups: The Role of National Affiliation, Professional Involvement, and Member Focal Problem." *American Journal of Community Psychiatry* 17/5 (1989): 643–71.

McAfee, Raymond Mack. "Male and Female Abstainers Attending Alcoholics Anonymous." *Dissertation Abstracts International*. 41 (5): 2020-A, 1980.

McAnany, Patrick D., and Tromanhauser, Edward. "Organizing the Convicted: Self-Help for Prisoners and Ex-Prisoners." *Crime and Delinquency* 23/1 (1977): 68–74.

McCall, R. J. "Group Therapy with Obese Women of Varying M.M.P.I. Profiles." *Journal of Clinical Psychology* 30 (1974): 466–70.

———. "M.M.P.I. Factors that Differentiate Remediably from Irremediably Obese Women." *Journal of Community Psychology* 1 (1973): 34–36.

McCall, R. J., Siderits, M. A., and Fadden, T. F. "Differential Effectiveness of Information Group Procedures in Weight Control." *Journal of Clinical Psychology* 2 (1977): 351–55.

McCarthy, Dennis. "Parents Anonymous Self-Help Groups for Abusive Parents: A Safe Place to Talk." *The Harrisburg Challenge* 19/2 (1976): 13–15.

McGennis, A., Hartman, M., and Nolan, G. "The Role of a Self-Help Association in Agoraphobia: One Year's Experience with 'Out and About.'" *Irish Medical Journal* 70/1 (1977): 10–13.

Meier, C. A. "Sudden Infant Death Syndrome: Death without Apparent Cause." *Life-Threatening Behavior* 3 (1973): 298–304.

Mellor, Joanna M., Rzetelny, Harriet, and Hudis, Iris E. "Self-Help Groups for Caregivers of the Aged." In New York Community Service Society, eds. *Strengthening Information Support for the Aged: Theory, Practice, and Policy Implications*. New York: New York Community Service Society, 1981.

Menning, B. E. "Resolve: A Support Group for Infertile Couples." *American Journal of Nursing* 76/2 (1976): 258f.

Mental Health Policy Resource Center. "The Growing Mental Health Self-Help Movement." *Policy in Perspective* (May, 1991): 1–7.

Miller, L. K. "Self-Help and the Patient/Professional Partnership. *Social Policy* (Fall, 1987): 26–28.

Miller, L. K., and Miller, O. L. "Reinforcing Self-help Group Activities of Welfare Recipients." *Journal of Applied Behavior Analysis* 3 (1970): 57–64.

Minde, K., et al. "Self-Help Groups in a Premature Nursery: A Controlled Evaluation." *Journal of Pediatrics* 96/5 (1980): 933–40.

Moeller, Michael Lukas. "Self-Help Groups in Psychotherapy." *Praxis der Psychotherapie* 20/4 (1975): 181–93.

Moline, R. A. "The Therapeutic Community and Milieu Therapy: A Review and Current Assessment." *Community Mental Health Review* 2/5 (1977): 1–13.

Moore, Peter. "People as Lawyers: Lay Advocacy and Self-Help in the Legal System." *British Journal of Law and Society* 5/1 (1978): 121–32.

Morrow, Deborah. "Neurotics Anonymous: When You're Sick and Tired of Being Sick and Tired." *Journal of Mental Health* 12/10 (1976): 1–4.

Mowrer, O. Hobart. "Integrity Groups: Basic Principles and Objectives." *Counseling Psychologist* 3/2 (1972): 7–32.

———. "Integrity Groups: Principles and Procedures." *The Counselling Psychologist* 3/2 (1972): 7–32.

———. "The 'Self-Help' or Mutual Aid Movement: Do Professionals Help or Hinder?" *Self-Help and Health: A Report.* New York: New Careers Training Laboratory, n.d.

Mowrer, O. Hobart, and Vattano, Anthony J. "Integrity Groups: A Context for Growth in Honesty, Responsibility, and Involvement." *Journal of Applied Behavioral Science* 12 (1976): 419–31.

Murphy, Adele Davis. "The Perceptions of Family Environment by Couples Who Are Members of Parents Anonymous." *Dissertation Abstracts International* 41 (6): 2389-B, 1980.

Nessman, Donald George. "The Effects of Patient-Operated Hypertension Groups on Compliance in Hypertension Treatment." *Dissertation Abstracts International* 39 (9): 4590-B, 1979.

"Neurotics Anonymous: 'I Am Well.' " *Journal of Mental Health* 12/1 (1976): 1–3.

Newmark, Gerald, and Newmark, Sandy. "Older Persons in a Planned Community: Synanon." *Social Policy* 7/3 (1976): 93–99.

Nichols, Keith A. *Leading a Support Group.* London: Chapman and Hall, 1991.

Nix, Helen. "Why Parents Anonymous." *Journal of Psychiatric Nursing and Mental Health Services* 18/10 (1980): 23–28.

Norman, J. "Consciousness-Raising: Self-Help in the Women's Movement." In A. H. Katz and E. I. Bender, eds., *The Strength in Us.* New York: New Viewpoints, 1976.

Norman, William Howard. "A Field Study of Weight-Loss Groups." *Dissertation Abstracts International* 42 (1): 396-A, 1981.

Norris, John. "Alcoholics Anonymous." In Elizabeth Whitney, ed., *World Dialogue on Alcohol and Drug Dependence.* Boston: Beacon Press, 1970.

Nurco, D. N., and Makofsky, A. "The Self-Help Movement of Narcotics Addicts." *American Journal of Drug and Alcohol Abuse* 8/2 (1981): 139–51.

Nuttal, E. V., Nuttal, R. L., Polit, D., and Clark, K. "Assessing Adolescent Mental Health Needs: The Views of Consumers, Providers and Others." *Adolescence* 12 (1977): 277–85.

Omark, Richard C. "The Dilemma of Membership in Recovery, Inc., A Self-Help Ex-

Mental Patients' Organization." *Psychological Reports* 44/3 (1979): 1119–25.

Pancoast, Diane, Parker, P., and Froland, C. *Rediscovering Self-Help: Its Role in Social Care.* Beverly Hills, California: Sage, 1983.

Paquette, D. "Les habilités d'aide chez les membres d'un service d'entraide pour veuves." Master's thesis, École de psychologie, Université de Laval, 1983.

Parcell, S., and Tagliareni, E. M. "Cancer Patients Help Each Other." *American Journal of Nursing* 74 (1974): 650f.

Park, Clara Claiborne, and Shapiro, Leon N. "The Lord Helps Those Who Help Themselves." In Clara Park, ed., *You Are Not Alone.* New York: Little, Brown, 1976.

Paskert, C. J., and Madara, E. J. "Introducing and Tapping Self-Help Mutual Aid Resources." *Health Education* 16/4 (August–September 1985): 25–29.

Peterman, Phylis J. "Parenting and Environmental Considerations." *American Journal of Orthopsychiatry* 51/2 (1981): 351–55.

Peterson, Barrie Alan. "Self-Help Mutual Aid: An Idea Whose Time Has Come Again." *Journal of Volunteer Administration* 1/1 (Fall 1982): 35–41.

Petrillo, Robert. "Rap Room: Self-help at School." *Social Policy* 7/2 (1976): 54–58.

Petrunik, Michael S. "Seeing the Light: A Study of Conversion to Alcoholics Anonymous." *Journal of Voluntary Action Research* 1/4 (1972): 30–36.

Pierce, Robert A., and Schwartz, Alan J. "Student Self-Help Group in a College Mental Health Program." *Journal of College Student Personnel* 19/4 (1978): 321–24.

Piven, F. F., and Cloward, R. A. "Social Advocacy Type: The National Welfare Rights Organization." In A. H. Katz and E. I. Bender, eds., *The Strength in Us.* New York: New Viewpoints, 1976.

Plummer, E., Thorton, J. F., Seeman, M. V., and Littmann, S. "Living with Schizophrenia: A Group Approach with Relatives." *Canada's Mental Health* 29/1 (1981): 17.

Politser, Peter E. "Social Climates in Community Groups: Toward a Taxonomy." *Community Mental Health Journal* 16/3 (1980): 87–200.

Potasznik, H., and Nelson, G. "Stress and Social Support: The Burden Experienced by the Family of a Mentally Ill Person." *American Journal of Community Psychology* 12/5 (1984).

Powell, Thomas J. "Comparisons Between Self-Help Groups and Professional Services." *Social Casework* 60/9 (1979): 651–56.

———. "Impact of Social Networks on Help-Seeking Behavior." *Social Work* 26/4 (1981): 335–37.

———. "Interpreting Parents Anonymous as a Source of Help for Those with Child Abuse Problems." *Child Welfare* 58/2 (1979): 105–14.

———. *Self-Help Organizations and Professional Practice.* Silver Spring, Maryland: National Association of Social Workers, 1987.

———. "The Use of Self-Help Groups as Supportive Reference Communities." *American Journal of Orthopsychiatry* 45/2 (1975): 756–64.

Powell, Thomas J., ed. *Working with Self-Help Organizations.* Silver Spring, Maryland: National Association of Social Workers, 1990.

President's Commission on Mental Health. "Report of the Task Panel on Community Support Systems." (February 15, 1978): 139–235.

Raiff, Norma Radol. "Recovery, Inc.: A Study of Self-Help Organization in Mental Health." *Dissertation Abstracts International* 40 (2): 1085-A, 1979.

———. "Self-Help Participation and Quality of Life: A Study of the Staff of Recovery,

Inc." *Prevention in Human Services* 1/3 (1982): 79–89.

Rappaport, J., et al. "Collaborative Research with Mutual Help Organization." *Social Policy* 15 (1985): 12–24.

Rau, N., and Rau, M. *My Dear Ones*. Englewood Cliffs, New Jersey: Prentice-Hall, 1971.

Raubolt, Richard R. "Adolescent Peer Networks: An Alternative to Alientation." *Corrective and Social Psychiatry and Journal of Behavior Technology* 21/4 (1975): 1–3.

Recovery, Inc., National Headquarters. " 'Helping Thyself' to Mental Health, Rediscovering Recovery." *Innovations* 7/1 (1980): 21f.

Ricker, George A. "The Little People of America." *Personnel and Guidance Journal* 48/8 (1970): 663f.

Riessman, Frank. "The Helper-Therapy Principle." *Social Work* 10 (1965): 27–32.

———. "How Does Self-Help Work?" *Social Policy* 7/2 (1976): 41–45.

———. "Restructuring Help: A Human Services Paradigm for the 1990s." *American Journal of Community Psychology* 18/2 (1990): 221–30.

———. "Self-Help/Mutual Aid and Social Change." *Perception* 15/4: 56–59.

Riessman, Frank, and Gartner, Audrey. "The Surgeon General and the Self-Help Ethos." *Social Policy* (Fall 1987): 23–33.

Riordan, R. J., and Beggs, M. S. "Counselors and Self-Help Groups." *Journal of Counseling Development* 65 (1987): 427–29.

Robinson, David. "The Self-Help Component of Primary Health Care." *Social Science and Medicine* 14A/5 (1980): 415–21.

———. "Self-Help Groups in Primary Health Care." *World Health Forum* 2/2 (1981): 185–91.

———. "The Self-Help Process of Alcoholics Anonymous." *British Journal of Alcohol and Alcoholism* 12/4 (1977): 143–46.

Robinson, David, and Henry, Stuart. *Self-Help and Health: Mutual Aid for Modern Problems*. London: Martin Robinson, 1977.

Robinson, David, and Robinson, Yvonne. *From Self-Help to Health*. London: Concord, 1979.

Rodolfa, Emil R., and Hungerford, Lynn. "Self-Help Groups: A Referral Resource for Professional Therapists." *Professional Psychology* 13/3 (1982): 345–53.

Rogers, Joy, et al. "A Self-Help Program for Widows as an Independent Community Service." *Hospital and Community Psychiatry* 31/12 (1980): 844–47.

Rogers, T. F., Bauman, L. J., and Metzger, L. "An Assessment of the Reach-to-Recovery Program." *CA: A Cancer Journal for Clinicans* 35/2 (1985).

Romeder, Jean-Marie. "Self-Help Groups and Mental Health: A Promising Avenue." *Canada's Mental Health* 29/1 (1981): 10–12.

———. *Self-Help Groups in Canada*. Ottawa: Health and Welfare Canada, 1982.

Romeder, Jean-Marie, ed. With contributions from Hector Balthazan, Andrew Farquharson and Francine Lavoie. *The Self-Help Way*. Ottawa: Canadian Council on Social Development, 1990.

Rouse, S. Denise. "One Health Professional's Experience with Self-Help." *Social Policy* (Fall 1987): 31.

Ryback, Ralph S. "Schizophrenics Anonymous: A Treatment Adjunct." *Psychiatry in Medicine* 2/3 (1971): 247–53.

Sagarin, E. *Odd Man in: Societies of Deviants in America*. New York: Quadrangle Books, 1969.

Sale, June Solnit. "Family Day Care Mothers Work Together to Improve Services." *Children Today* 4/5 (1975): 22–24.

———. *A Self-Help Organization of Family Day-Care Mothers: Means of Quality Control*. Arlington, Virginia: Education Resource Information Centre, 1974.

Scanlon-Schilpp, Ann M., and Levesque, Jeffry. "Helping the Patient Cope with the Sequelae of Trauma through the Self-Help Group Approach." *Journal of Trauma* 21/2 (1981): 135.

Schnall, Sandra Joy. "An Interpersonal Approach to Alcoholism: The Transformation of Self through Alcoholics Anonymous." *Dissertation Abstracts International* 41 (8): 3197-B, 1981.

Schwartz, L. H., Marcus, R., and Condon, R. "Multidisciplinary Group Therapy for Rheumatoid Arthritis." *Psychosomatics* 19 (1978): 289–93.

"Self-Help and How We Teach Tomorrow." *What's New in Home Economics* 17/4 (December, 1983): 1, 4.

Sharing Caring: A Communications Kit to Assist Hospitals in Their Involvement with Self-Help Groups. Chicago: American Hospital Association, 1987.

Shatan, C. F. "The Grief of Soldiers: Vietnam Combat Veterans Self-Help Movement." *American Journal of Orthopsychiatry* 43/4 (1973): 648f.

Shearn, M. A., and Fireman, B. H. "Stress Management and Mutual Support Groups in Rheumatoid Arthritis." *American Journal of Medicine* 78/5 (1985): 771–76.

Shosenberg, Nancy. "Self-Help Groups for Parents of Premature Infants." *Canadian Nurse* 76/7 (1980): 30–34.

Sidel, Victor W., and Sidel, Ruth. "Beyond Coping." *Social Policy* 7/2 (1976): 67–69.

Silcott, Ernie J. "The Correspondence Between Alcoholics Anonymous and the Adaptive Capacities of Its Members." *Dissertation Abstracts International* 23 5348, 1972.

Silverman, Phyllis R. "Mutual Help." In R. G. Hirschowitz and B. Levy, eds., *The Changing Mental Health Scene*. New York: Spectrum Publications, Inc., 1976.

———. *Mutual Help: An Alternative Network*. Washington, D.C.: U.S. Government Printing Office, 1978, Select Committee on Aging Publication No. 95-170: 254–70.

———. *Mutual Help Groups: Organization and Development*. Newbury Park, California: Sage Publications, 1980.

———. "The Role of the Professional in a Mutual Help Organization: Some Informal Thoughts on This Subject." In Silverman, Phyllis R., et al., eds. *Helping Each Other in Widowhood*. New York: Meihan Press, 1974.

———. "The Widow as a Caregiver in a Program of Preventative Internation with Other Widows." *Mental Hygiene* 54/4 (1970): 540–47.

———. "The Widow as a Caregiver in a Program of Preventative Internation with Other Widows." In G. Caplan and M. Killilea, eds., *Support Systems and Mutual Help*. New York: Grune & Stratton, 1976.

———. "Widowhood and Preventive Intervention." *The Family Coordinator* 20 (1970): 95–102.

Silverman, Phyllis R., and Cooperband, Adele. "Mutual Help and the Elderly Widow." *Journal of Geriatric Psychiatry* 8/1 (1975): 9–27.

Silverman, Phyllis R., and Murrow, H. G. "Mutual Help During Critical Role Transitions." *Journal of Applied Behavioral Science* 12 (1976): 410–18.

Silverman, Phyllis R., and Smith, Diane. " 'Helping' in Mutual Help Groups for the Physically Disabled." In Alan Gartner and Frank Riessman, eds., *The Self-Help Revolution*. New York: Human Science Press, 1982.

Small, Rona, and Goldhamer, Paul. "The Professional Role within a Self-Help Model: A 'Widow-to-Widow' Project." *Journal of Jewish Communal Service* 56/2 (1980): 176–80.

Smith, L. "Operation Bootstrap." In A. H. Katz and E. I. Bender, eds., *The Strength in Us*. New York: New Viewpoints, 1976.

Snowdon, J. "Self-Help Groups and Schizophrenia." *Australian and New Zealand Journal of Psychiatry* 14/4 (1980): 265–68.

———. "Special Self-Help Issue." *Social Policy* 7/2 (September/October 1976).

Spicuzza, Frank J., and DeVoe, Marianne W. "Burnout in the Helping Professions: Mutual Aid Groups as Self-Help." *Personnel and Guidance Journal* 61/2 (1982): 95–99.

Spiegel, David. "Going Public and Self-Help" In G. Caplan and M. Killilea, eds., *Support Systems and Mutual Help*. New York: Grune & Stratton, 1976.

———. "The Psychiatrist as a Consultant to Self-Help Groups." *Hospital and Community Psychiatry* 28/10 (1977): 771f.

———. "The Recent Literature: Self-Help and Mutual Support Groups." *Community Mental Health Review* 5/1–4 (1980): 14–25.

Spiegel, David. "Self-Help and Mutual Support Groups: A Synthesis of the Recent Literature." In David E. Spiegel and Arthur J. Naparstek, eds., *Community Support Systems and Mental Health: Practice, Policy and Research*. New York: Springer Publishing Company, 1982.

Spiegel, David, Bloom, J. R., and Yalom, I. "Groups Support for Patients with Metastitic Cancer: A Randomized Prospective Outcome Study." *Archives of General Psychiatry* 38/5 (1981): 527–33.

Spiegel, David, and Keith-Spiegel, P., eds. *Outsiders U.S.A.: Original Essays on 24 Outgroups in American Society*. San Francisco: Rinehart Press, 1973.

Spiegel, David, et al. "Effect of Psychosocial Treatment on Survival of Patients with Metastatic Breast Cancer." *The Lancet* 8668 (1989, vol. II): 888–91.

Squires, S. "A Group for All Reasons: Why Millions Are Turning to Self-Help Organizations." *Washington Post* (May 17, 1988): 14–17.

St.-Amand, Nere, and Clavette, Huguette. *Self-Help and Mental Health: Beyond Psychiatry*. Ottawa: Canadian Council on Social Development, 1991.

Staver S. "AIDS MDs Cope with Frustrations in Support Groups." *American Medical News* (June 5, 1987): 34f.

Stead, Peter, and Viders, Judith. A 'SHARP' Approach to Treating Alcoholism." *Social Work* 24/2 (1979): 144–49.

Steinman, R., and Traunstein, D. M. "Redefining Deviance: The Self-Help Challenge to the Human Services." *Journal of Applied Behavioral Science* 12 (1976): 347–61.

Stern, R. A. "A Peer Self-Help Group of Homosexuals on the North Side of Chicago." *Psychotherapy: Theory, Research and Practice* 12 (1975): 418–24.

Strupp, H. *Psychotherapy: Clinical Research and Theoretical Issues*. New York: Aronson, 1973.

Stuart, Henry. "The Dangers of Self-Help Groups." *New Society* 44 (1978): 654–65.

Stuart, Richard B., and Mitchell, Christene. "Self-Help Weight Control Groups: A Professional and a Consumer Perspective." *Psychiatric Clinics of North America* 1/3 (1978): 697–711.

Stunkard, A. "The Success of T.O.P.S., a Self-Help Group." *Postgraduate Medicine* 51 (1972): 143–47.

Stunkard, A., Levine, H., and Fox, S. "The Management of Obesity, Patient Self-Help, and Medical Treatment." *Archives of Internal Medicine* 124 (1970): 1067–72.

Taietz, P. "Two Conceptual Models of the Senior Center." *Journal of Gerontology* 31/2 (1976): 219–22.

Takahashi, T. "A Social Club Spontaneously Formed by Ex-Patients Who Had Suffered from Anthropophobia (Taijin Kyofu). *International Journal of Social Psychiatry* 21/1 (1975): 137–40.

Tavris, C. "Self-Help or Therapy?" *Vogue* (February 1987).

Tax, S. "Self-Help Groups: Thoughts on Public Policy." *Journal of Applied Behavioral Science* 12 (1976): 448–54.

Taylor, Mary Catherine. "Alcoholics Anonymous: How It Works, Recovery Processes in Self-Help Groups." *Dissertation Abstracts International* 39 (12): 7532-A, 1979.

Taylor, S. E., Falke, R. L., Shoptaw, S. J., and Lichtman, R. R. "Social Support, Support Groups, and the Cancer Patient." *Journal of Consulting and Clinical Psychology* 54/4 (1986): 608–15.

Thiers, N. "Self-Help Movement Gains Strength, Offers Hope." *Guidepost* 30/9 (1987): 1f.

Todres, Rubin. "Professional Attitudes, Awareness and Use of Self-Help Groups." *Prevention in Human Services* 1/3 (1982): 91–98.

———. *Self-Help Groups: An Annotated Bibliography 1970–1982/Les groupes d'entraide: Une bibliographie anotée 1970–1982.* New York: National Self-Help Clearinghouse, n.d.

Torjman, Sherri Resin. "Self-Help: An Association for Relatives and Friends of the Mentally Ill." *Canada's Mental Health* 28/1 (1980): 2–4.

Torrey, E. F. *Surviving Schizophrenia.* New York: Harper & Row, 1983.

Toseland, Ronald W., and Hacker, Lynda. "Self-help Groups and Professional Involvement." *Social Work* 27/4 (1982): 314–17.

Tracy, G. S., and Gussow, Z. "Self-Help Health Groups: A Grass-roots Response to a Need for Services." *Journal of Applied Behavioral Science* 12 (1976): 381–96.

Trainor, Mary A. "Acceptance of Ostomy and the Visitor Role in Self-Help Groups for Ostomy Patients." *Nursing Research* 31/2 (1981): 102–06.

———. "Self-Help Groups, Part Two." *Clinics in Gastroenterology* 11/2 (1982): 415–19.

Traunstein, Donald M., and Steinman, Richard. "Voluntary Self-Help Organizations: An Exploratory Study." *Journal of Voluntary Action Research* 2/4 (1973): 230–39.

Trela, J. E. "Social Class and Association Membership: An Analysis of Age-Graded and Non-Age-Graded Voluntary Participation." *Journal of Gerontology* 31/2 (1976): 198–203.

Trice, Harrison M., and Roman, Paul M. "Delabeling, Relabeling and Alcoholics Anonymous." *Social Problems* 17/4 (1970): 538–46.

Trojan, A. "Groupès de santé: The User's Movement in France." In S. Hatch and I. Kickbusch, eds. *Self-Help and Health in Europe: New Approaches in Health Care.* Copenhagen: W.H.O., 1983.

Tyler, R. W. "Social Policy and Self-Help Groups." *Journal of Applied Behavioral Science* 12 (1976): 444–48.

U.S. Department of Health & Human Services, Public Health Service, Health Resources and Services Administration, Bureau of Maternal and Child Health and Resource Development. *Report of the Surgeon General's Workshop on Self-Help and Public Health.* Rockville, Maryland: U.S. Public Health Service, 1988.

Vachon, M. J., et al. "A Controlled Study of Self-Help Intervention for Widows." *American Journal of Psychiatry* 137/11 (1980): 1380–84.

Vattano, A. J. "Power to the People: Self-help Groups." *Social Work* 17 (1972): 7–15.

Videka-Sherman, L. "Effects of Participation in a Self-Help Group for Bereaved Parents: Compassionate Friends." *Prevention in Human Service* 1/3 (1982): 69–77.

Videka-Sherman, L., and Lieberman, M. "The Effects of Self-Help and Psychotherapy Intervention on Child Loss: The Limits of Recovery." *American Journal of Orthopsychiatry* 55 (January 1985): 70–82.

Vinokur-Kaplan, Diane. "The Relevance of Self-Help Groups to Social Work Education." *Contemporary Social Work Education* 2/1 (1978): 79–86.

Wagonfield, S., and Wolowitz, H. M. "Obesity and the Self-Help Groups: A Look at T.O.P.S." *American Journal of Psychiatry* 2 (1968): 145–48.

Walley, William V., and Stokes, Joseph P. *Self-Help Support Groups for Teachers under Stress*. Bethesda, Maryland: National Institutes of Mental Health, 1981, number R01-MH 33761.

Wasserman, Harry. *The Human Bond: Support Groups and Mutual Aid*. New York: Springer, 1988.

Wechsler, H. "The Ex-Patient Organization: A Survey." *Journal of Social Issues* 16 (1960): 47–53.

———. "The Self-Help Organization in the Mental Health Field: Recovery, Inc., A Case Study." In G. Caplan and M. Killilea, eds., *Support Systems and Mutual Help*. New York: Grune & Stratton, 1976.

Weiner, M. F., and Caldwell, T. "The Process and Impact of an ICU Nurse Support Group." *International Journal of Psychiatry in Medicine* 13/1 (1983–4).

Weiss, R. S. "The Contributions of an Organization of Single Parents to the Well-Being of Its Members." In G. Caplan and M. Killilea, eds., *Support Systems and Mutual Help*. New York: Grune & Stratton, 1976.

———. "The Fund of Sociability." *Transaction* 6 (1969): 26–43.

———. "Transition States and Other Stressful Situations: Their Nature and Programs for Their Management." In G. Caplan and M. Killilea, eds., *Support Systems and Mutual Help*. New York: Grune & Stratton, 1976.

Weiss, R. S., and Bergen, B. J. "Social Support and the Reduction of Psychiatric Disability." *Psychiatry: Journal of the Study of Interpersonal Processes* 31 (1968): 107–15.

Weppner, Robert S. "Some Characteristics of an Ex-Addict Self-Help Therapeutic Community and Its Members." *British Journal of Addictions* 68/1 (1973): 73–79.

Wilbur, Sandra Styron. "Coping with Cancer: Self-help to Parents of Leukemic Children." *Smith College Studies in Social Work* 47/1 (1976): 55f.

Williams, Ann. "The Student and the Alcoholic Patient." *Nursing Outlook* 27/1 (1979): 470–72.

Williams, Lola Janet. "A Comparative Study of Self-Actualization in Female Alcoholics in Alcoholics Anonymous." *Dissertation Abstracts International* 41 (1): 337-B, 1980.

Williams, R. M. "The Wave of Self-help." *Foundation News* (July–August, 1988): 28–32.

Wilson, Ann, and Soule, Douglas J. "The Role of a Self-Help Group in Working with Parents of a Stillborn Baby." *Death Education* 5/2 (1981): 175–86.

Wiltshaw, E., Buckman, R., and Mitchell, D. "The Oncology Club." *The Lancet* 1 (1977): 699f.

Withorn, Ann. "Helping Ourselves: The Limits and Potential of Self-Help." *Radical America* (May–June 1980): 25–40.

Wittenberg, R. M. "Personality Adjustment through Social Action." *American Journal of Orthopsychiatry* 14/2 (1948): 219.

Wolcott, Nancy Dunn. "Alchemy and Alcoholism Based on the Psychology of C. G. Jung." *Dissertation Abstractions International* 39 (12): 6105-B, 1979.

Wollert, R. W. "Human Services and the Self-Help Clearinghouse Concept." *Canadian*

Journal of Community Mental Health 6/1 (1987): 79–90.

———. "Psychosocial Helping Processes in a Heterogeneous Sample of Self-Help Groups." *Canadian Journal of Community Mental Health* 5/1 (1986): 63–76.

Wollert, R. W., et al. *A Model for the Establishment of Productive Relationships between Mental Health Professionals and Self-Help Groups.* Arlington, Virginia: Education Resource Information, 1978.

Wollert, R. W., et al. "Parents United of Oregon: A Natural History of a Self-Help Group for Sexually Abusive Families." *Prevention in Human Services* 1/3 (1982): 99–109.

Wollert, R. W., Knight, Bob, and Levy, Leon H. "Make Today Count: A Collaborative Model for Professionals and Self-Help Groups." *Professional Psychology* 11/1 (1980): 130–38.

Wollert, R. W., Levy, Leon H., and Knight, Bob. "Help-Giving in Behavioral Control and Stress Coping Self-Help Groups." *Small Group Behavior* 13/2 (1982): 204–18.

Wong, Martin R. "Males in Transition and the Self-Help Group." *Counselling Psychologist* 7/4 (1978): 46–50.

Wright, Eric M. "Self-Help Groups in the Rehabilitation Enterprise." *Psychological Aspects of Disability* 18/1 (1971): 43–45.

Yalom, I. D. *The Theory and Practice of Group Psychotherapy.* New York: Basic Books, 1975.

Yalom, I. D., Bloch, S., et al. "Alcoholics in Interactional Group Therapy." *Archives of General Psychiatry* 35 (1978): 419–25.

Yoder, Barbara. *The Recovery Resource Book.* New York: Simon & Schuster, 1990.

Zola, Irving Kenneth. "The Politicization of the Self-Help Movement." *Social Policy* (Fall 1987): 32f.

2

Directory of Self-Help Groups and Clearinghouses in the United States and Canada

This chapter—a list of self-help groups and clearinghouses in the United States and Canada—contains the information necessary for a two-pronged search for help for a particular problem: via the directory itself and via the list of self-help clearinghouses that follows it.

SEARCHING VIA THE SELF-HELP DIRECTORY

First, look in the index under the name of the problem for which you need help—for example, "alcoholism"—to find the page reference for the section that lists citations for self-help organizations that address this particular problem.

Note that all groups are divided into two categories, "national" (or, occasionally, "regional" or "international") or "model." (If "National" appears in the name of the group, it is not repeated in the citation.)

"National"—or "Regional" or "International"—indicates a self-help organization that has one or more centralized offices that you can contact to learn about affiliated groups meeting in your particular geographic area. Some such groups are very large and have numerous affiliated groups; Alcoholics Anonymous, for example, has nearly 100,000 groups worldwide. In addition to information about group meetings, the national office also may be able to advise you about other related activities—such as pen-pal programs or con-

ferences—that are also described in the citation.

"Model" indicates a one-of-a-kind self-help organization. If there's a model group for your problem but you live too far away to participate in its meetings, you may wish to contact the group anyway to get advice on starting a similar group in your own area. (Eventually, this may result in a network of groups large enough to warrant a national organization. In any case, to learn about starting a group, be sure to read Chapter 3.)

Be aware, however, that model groups usually have no administrative apparatus, that is, no support staff, infrastructure or funding to handle volume telephone or mail inquiries. (The telephone numbers and mailing addresses listed here are home contacts for model group members.) So you should contact these groups only if you are seriously interested. As a courtesy, always be willing to accept the burden—financial or otherwise—that the contact entails.

- *When you write* to a model group, always include a stamped self-addressed envelope for a response. Be aware that model groups—and even some national organizations—may take weeks or even months to respond.
- *When you call* a model group, remember that it's probably someone's home you're calling. Call at a reasonable hour, be aware of differences in time zones, be extra courteous, and, if you have to leave a message, offer to pay for the return call.

Searching via a Local Self-Help Clearinghouse

Second, contact the nearest of the 50-odd self-help clearinghouses in the United States and Canada, which are listed by state, province and geographic area at the end of this chapter. The clearinghouse may have up-to-the-minute information on local groups affiliated with the national organizations listed in this directory as well as obscure model groups not listed. In addition, should you decide to start your own self-help group, the clearinghouse may be able to offer you assistance and advice in setting up, administering and spreading the word about your new group.

While every attempt was made to make this reference volume as comprehensive as possible within certain practical guidelines for inclusion, important self-help groups and organizations—both national and model—may well have been overlooked. In addition, the on-going, even accelerating, phenomenon of self-help in the U.S. and Canada means that new groups will undoubtedly have appeared after publication of this work.

If you are a member—or if you know of—a self-help organization that would like to be listed in a possible future edition of this directory, please send a description of it to:

Joe Donovan
THE SELF-HELP DIRECTORY
P. O. Box 602
New York, New York 10025

Please model the description of your group after the citations in this volume; that is, be sure to include: the name of the group; whether it is national or model; a definition of the problem it addresses, especially if it is a medical condition; services it provides members (for example, medical, legal or other referrals, pen-pal programs, lending libraries of audio-visual materials, speakers bureaus, and so forth); any publications it produces; whether or not it is involved in advocacy and public education efforts; when it was established; and, if it is a national organization, how many affiliated groups there are under its aegis. Most importantly, be sure to include contact information, including name, address, telephone, and fax. Also include any additional published materials—such as pamphlets, brochures, and clippings—that will aid in describing your group.

Self-Help Groups

ABORTION

Genetic Pregnancy Termination Support Group _____

Model. For women who have terminated their pregnancies because of a fetal abnormality. Led by a professional. Fosters networks among members for exchange of support, information. Established 1987. Call: (203) 384-3049. Write: Sharon Suntag, 267 Grant Street, Bridgeport, Connecticut 06610.

ADDISON'S DISEASE

National Addison's Disease Foundation _____

For people who suffer from Addison's disease, a disease characterized by deficient secretions of the adrenal glands, causing extreme weakness, weight loss, low blood pressure, gastrointestinal disturbances and brownish pigmentation of the skin. Coordinates area support groups to put patients and their families in touch with others to discuss common concerns. Supplies educational information to patients, the general public and physicians. Advocates research into the causes and treatment of the disease. Organizes fund-raising event, solicits grants to underwrite research. Publishes chapter development guidelines. Established 1984. Call: (516) 487-4992. Write: Renee Grabiner, Lewis Road, Irvington, New York 10533.

ADOPTION: ADOPTIVE FAMILIES

Adoptive Families of America, Inc. _____

National. Problem-solving assistance and information for adoptive and prospective adoptive families. Creates opportunities for successful adoptive placement. Publishes *Ours,* a bimonthly magazine. Free group development guidelines. $35 group membership fee. Pen-pal program, phone network. 300 groups. Established 1968. Call: (612) 535-4829. Write: 3333 Highway 100 N., Minneapolis, Minnesota 55422.

Adoptive Single Parents of New Jersey

Model. For single adults who've adopted children or are contemplating doing so. Discussion groups, telephone networking, other opportunities to exchange support, information. Maintains speakers' bureau, publishes newsletter, holds social events, provides referrals and other assistance by telephone. Established 1978. Call: (201) 766-6281. Write: 79 Old Army Road, Bernardsville, New Jersey 07924.

Committee for Single Adoptive Parents

International. For prospective and actual single adoptive parents. Helps locate sources of adoptable children and support groups, provides information and referrals, list of support groups, networking for individuals. Publishes handbook for single people who have adopted. Established 1973. Write: P.O. Box 15084, Chevy Chase, Maryland 20825.

F.A.C.T. (Forgotten & Abused Children & Teens)

Regional. For current and former (now adult) foster children who have suffered abuse; also for their families and friends and interested professionals. Primarily an advocacy group, but also seeks to connect F.A.C.T.'s for networking to exchange support, information. Runs speakers' bureau, special events. Literature available. Established 1992. Call: (508) 677-0218. Write: P.O. Box 6333, South Station, Fall River, Massachusetts 02724.

International Families Adoptive Information Service

Model. For prospective adoptive families interested in adopting children from foreign countries. Services include information and referrals, phone support. Established 1977.

Call: (314) 631-6910. Write Carol Mees, 9264 Coral Drive, St. Louis, Missouri 63123

Latin-American Parents Organization

National. For prospective and current adoptive parents of children from Latin America. Distributes information regarding adoption and naturalization requirements to interested prospective parents. Also offers support before, during and after the adoption process through monthly meetings and social events. Publishes quarterly newsletter, *Que Tal*. Established 1975. Call: (718) 236-8689. Write: P.O. Box 339, Brooklyn, New York 11234.

National Foster Parent Association

For foster families. Serves a "coalition of all parties in the foster care" community. Publishes bimonthly newsletter. Maintains comprehensive resource center on foster-care issues. Advocates on behalf of membership. Sponsors annual training conference. 44 state associations, "100s" of local ones. Established 1970. Call: (713) 467-1850. Write: 226 Kilts Drive, Houston, Texas 77024.

Open Door Society of Massachusetts

Model, active in Massachusetts. For families who have adopted or are thinking of doing so. Provides information and support through a variety of activities, including meetings held by local chapters, an annual conference, various other networking possibilities. Publishes newsletter, maintains audio- and videotape library. Advocacy efforts on behalf of membership. 17 chapters throughout Massachusetts. Call: (800) 932-3678. Write: P.O. Box 1158, Westborough, Massachusetts 01581.

ADOPTION: REUNITING BIOLOGICAL FAMILIES

Adoptees in Search (A.I.S.) _____

National. Established 1976. Comprised of adult adoptees, adoptive and birth parents; provides support, advocacy and search services for adult adoptees seeking to locate birth parents. Services include a quarterly newsletter, the *Mid-Atlantic States Search Registry*. Activities include support groups. Established 1976. Call: (301) 656-8555. Write: Joanne Small, P.O. Box 41016, Bethesda, Maryland 20824.

Adoption Connection, The _____

Model. For adoptees, adoptive parents and birth parents. Dedicated to "the belief that every one of America's five million adoptees has a right to know his or her biological history." Activities include monthly support groups and workshops to deal with the search process, reunions and post-search issues. Publishes monthly newsletter. Maintains reunion registries. Provides referral information, private office consultations, research staff, bibliographic information. Outreach activities include speakers' bureau, media presentations. Established 1976. Call: (508) 532-1261. Write: Susan Darke, 11 Peabody Square, Peabody, Massachusetts 01960.

A.L.M.A. Society (Adoptee's Liberty Movement Association) _____

National. Support for adults separated from their biological families through adoption; help in locating families. Maintains an "international reunion registry" of adoptees and families seeking to reunite. $60 initial registration fee, $40 annual renewal. Publishes quarterly newsletter. 65 chapters. Established 1971. Call: (212) 581-1568. Write: P.O. Box 727, Radio City Station, New York, New York 10101.

Birth Parent & Relative Group of Canada _____

U.S. and Canada. For families separated through adoption. Provides support to members, helps reunite them with birth parents, biological children. Maintains birth registry. Established 1982. Call: (403) 473-4552. Write: 5317-145 Avenue, Edmonton, Alberta, Canada T5A 4E9.

Concerned United Birthparents, Inc. (CUB) _____

National. Support and various services for people whose lives have been affected by adoption, including birth parents, adoptees and adoptive parents as well as interested professionals. Provides assistance to people searching for family members separated by adoption. Seeks to prevent unnecessary separations. Maintains a reunion registry, where members can register vital statistics of their searches in the hope that the people they are searching for have also registered. Publishes monthly newsletter as well as various pamphlets and booklets. Activities include a pen-pal program and telephone network. Branches in nine states plus the District of Columbia. Established 1976. Call: (515) 263-9558. Write: 2000 Walker Street, Des Moines, Iowa 50317.

Operation Identity _____

International. Mutual aid, self-help organization for all three parts of the adoption triad: biological and adoptive parents and adoptees. Provides information and counseling for adult adoptees searching for biological parents. Services include a newsletter, referrals and phone network. Established 1979. Call: (505) 293-3144. Write: 13101 Black Stone Road, Northeast, Albuquerque, New Mexico 87111.

Orphan Voyage _____

National. For people separated from biological families through adoption. Provides information (including educational materials), guidance and referrals to individuals and groups for peer counseling. Established 1953. Write: 2141 Road 2300, Cedaredge, Colorado 81413.

ADULTERY

(See also "Marriage.")

W.A.T.C.H. (Women and Their Cheating Husbands) _____

Model. For women whose husbands commit adultery. Self-help to deal with feelings of anger, low self-esteem caused by a partner's infidelity. Chapter development guidelines available. Established 1988. Write: P.O. Box 682, Olathe, Kansas 66051.

W.E.S.O.M. (We Saved Our Marriage) _____

National. For married couples troubled by adultery. Seeks to help couples save their marriages by dealing with infidelity openly. Provides assistance to individuals interested in starting new groups. Approximately 12 affiliated groups. Established 1986. Call: (312) 792-7034. Write: P.O. Box 46312, Chicago, Illinois 60646.

AGING

American Association of Retired Persons (AARP) _____

National. Oldest and largest organization of people—retired or not—age 50 and over "dedicated to helping older Americans achieve lives of independence, dignity and purpose." Activities include insurance, financial investment, pharmaceutical, educational programs.

Legal counsel. Local group activities may include self-help groups, such as widows' and widowers' support groups. Over 4,000 chapters. Established 1958. Call: (202) 434-2560. Write: 601 E Street, N.W., Washington, D.C. 20049.

Older Women's League _____

National. Addresses problems and concerns of women in midlife and women senior citizens. Provides self-help and mutual support for dealing with problems including social security, pension rights, health insurance, employment-related problems and caregiving. Activities include support groups and advocacy efforts. Publishes newsletter, chapter development guidelines. 110 chapters. Established 1980. Call: (202) 783-6686. Write: 666 11th Street, N.W., Washington, D.C. 20001.

Phenix Society _____

Members seek to explore meaning and potential of later years of life through discussions and readings. Orientation is spiritual and holistic. Publishes quarterly newsletter, *Mind Expander,* and handbook, *The Club of Life.* Call: (203) 387-6913. Write: Box 351, Cheshire, Connecticut 06410.

Supportive Older Women's Network, The (S.O.W.N.) _____

Regional. For women age 60 and over who need help in dealing with problems of their age group. Activities include discussion groups, networking opportunities, outreach efforts and leadership training. Publishes group development guidelines, quarterly newsletter, *The Sounding Board.* Over 30 groups in the Philadelphia area. Established 1982. Call: (215) 477-6000. Write: 2805 North 47th Street, Philadelphia, Pennsylvania 19131.

AIDS/HIV

ACT-UP (AIDS Coalition to Unleash Power)

National. For people whose lives have been affected by the AIDS (acquired immune-deficiency syndrome) crisis, including AIDS patients, their families and friends, members of the gay community and any other interested parties. Activities involve direct action—including demonstrations and protests against the government, church and medical individuals within the establishment and institutions—that will call attention to the AIDS crisis and the perceived failure to hasten its solution. Distributes current medical information. Fosters informal networks by which members can exchange information, support. Publishes newsletter, *ACT-UP Report*. Approximately 45 affiliated groups. Established 1987. Call: (212) 564-2437. Write: 135 West 29th Street, 10th Floor, New York, New York 10001.

BEBASHI (Blacks Educating Blacks about Sexual-Health Issues)

Model. For African-American and Latino people and other people of color. Seeks to educate members of those communities about sexual health issues, especially HIV (human immunodeficiency virus). Sponsors workshops; provides assistance, including peer counseling by phone, and testing. Established 1985. Call: (215) 546-4140. Write: 1233 Locust Street, Suite 401, Philadelphia, Pennsylvania 19107.

Bethany Place AIDS Service Organization

Model. Active in the greater Chicago area. For people with HIV (human immunodeficiency virus) disease and their families and friends. Various groups including: Caregivers Support Group, for families, friends, significant others of persons living with AIDS (acquired immune-deficiency syndrome); HIV Support Group, for people living with HIV, not yet progressed to full-blown AIDS; People Living with AIDS Support Group, for people with full-blown AIDS; Bereavement Support Group, for persons who have lost someone to AIDS. Discussion groups, telephone networking, other opportunities to exchange support, information. Established 1989 and later. Call: (618) 234-0291. Write: 224 West Washington Street, Belleville, Illinois 62220.

Body Positive of New York

Model. Serves the greater New York area. For people affected by—and especially people who've tested positive for—HIV (human immunodeficiency virus). Also for their friends and families. Provides information and referral by phone; sponsors workshops, various public forums on HIV-related topics, social activities; conducts an 8-to-12-week peer-support program for people who've tested positive for HIV to help them adjust to their status. Publishes *The Body Positive Magazine*. Established 1987. Call: Body Positive: (212) 721-1618 or 1619; hotline: (212) 721-1346. Write: 2095 Broadway, Suite 306, New York, New York 10023.

Gay Men's Health Crisis

National. For people with AIDS (acquired immune-deficiency syndrome), their families, friends and interested others. Organizes support groups for people with AIDS (PWAs) and people with ARC (AIDS-related condition) (PWARCs). Provides counseling on medical, legal, insurance and other matters by phone and printed materials. Sponsors educational outreach efforts. Call: (212) 807-6655.

Write: 129 West 20th Street, New York, New York 10011.

Hemophilia and AIDS/HIV Network for the Dissemination of Information (HANDI)

Model. For people with hemophilia, family members and caregivers and others in need of information. Makes referrals, disseminates resources, materials. Maintains growing collection of materials on hemophilia and AIDS/HIV (acquired immune-deficiency syndrome/human immunodeficiency virus). Publishes *HANDI Quarterly,* 23-page resource listing, various other publications, including video and audio tapes, posters. Established 1990. Call: (212) 431-8541 or (800) 42-HANDI, 24 hours daily; fax: (212) 966-9247. Write: 110 Greene Street, Suite 303, New York, New York 10012.

HIVIES (HIV Information and Exchange Support Group)

Model. For people recovering from addiction who are infected with HIV (human immunodeficiency virus) or think they might be. 12-step program. "Only requirement for attending is a desire to live with the HIV." HIVIES manual available to help guide group; includes sample meeting formats, the Twelve Steps and Traditions, personal stories. Established 1987. Call: Dan, (708) 724-3832. Write: 610 Greenwood, Glenview, Illinois 60025.

National Association of People with AIDS

For people with AIDS (acquired immune-deficiency syndrome), associated with an infection by HIV (human immunodeficiency virus), characterized by a breakdown in the body's immune system and the consequent appearance of life-threatening diseases, such as viral pneumonia, cancers and opportunistic infec-

tion. Helps establish networks by phone, mail and meetings to share information. Speaks on behalf of the AIDS patient community in political, health care and other forums (sponsors speakers bureau). Publishes bimonthly newsletter. Over 100 affiliated groups. Established 1986. Call: (202) 898-0414. Write: 1413 K Street, N. W., #10, Washington, D.C. 20005.

We the People Living with AIDS/HIV of the Delaware Valley

Regional. For people with HIV (human immunodeficiency virus) infections. Discussion groups help members familiarize themselves with various medical, social and legal services available to them; seek to empower members through realization that they are not alone with their problem. Publishes newsletter, group development guidelines. Established 1987. Call: (215) 545-6868. Write: David Fair, 425 South Broad Street, Philadelphia, Pennsylvania 19147.

ALBINISM

NOAH (National Organization for Albinism & Hypopigmentation)

For people with albinism and other forms of hypopigmentation, a deficiency or lack of pigmentation in the skin, hair and eyes; also for their families and friends and for interested professionals. Support and information for members. Advocates research into diagnosis of and treatments for hypopigmentation. Publishes semiannual newsletter, chapter development guidelines. Sponsors national conferences. 12 chapters. Established 1982. Call: (800) 473-2310. Write: 1500 Locust Street, Suite 1816, Philadelphia, Pennsylvania 19102.

ALCOHOLISM, SUBSTANCE ABUSE

(See also "Fetal Alcohol Syndrome," "Jews.")

Adult Children of Alcoholics

International. A 12-step program for people with alcoholic parents. Believes that the behavior patterns they developed as children in alcoholic, "dysfunctional" families helped them survive then but prevent them from fully experiencing life now, as adults. Publishes groups development guidelines, other materials. Nearly 2,000 chapters. Established 1984. Call: (310) 534-1815. Write: P.O. Box 3216, Torrance, California 18951.

Al-Anon Family Groups

International. Self-help for relatives and friends of alcoholics, whether in recovery or not. "A fellowship for relatives and friends of alcoholics, who share their experience, strength and hope in order to solve their common problems, and to help others do the same. Al-Anon believes alcoholism is a disease that is devastating to all involved and that changed attitudes can aid recovery." 12-step program. Publishes a wide variety of literature, including books, pamphlets and films in 29 different languages as well as Braille and on tape. Over 27,000 groups. Established 1951. Call: (800) 356-9996; for meeting information: (800) 344-2666; Canada: (800) 443-4525. Write: P.O. Box 862 Midtown Station, New York, New York 10018.

Alateen

International. For younger members of Al-Anon (see entry), usually teenagers. Adult member of Al-Anon serves as sponsor for each group. 12-step program. Publishes group de-velopment guidelines. Over 3,000 chapters. Established 1957. Call: (212) 302-7240 or (800) 344-2666 (meeting information only). Write: P.O. Box 862 Midtown Station, New York, New York 10018.

Alcoholics Anonymous

International. The original 12-step program for people who abuse alcohol. Local groups regularly sponsor both closed (alcoholics only) and open discussion meetings. Publishes newsletters and a variety of literature. Group development guidelines available. Approximately 96,500 affiliated groups. Established 1935. Call: (212) 686-1100. Write: Box 459 Grand Central Station, New York, New York 10163.

A.R.T. ("Academics Recovering Together")

Model. For faculty and nonfaculty employees of colleges and universities in recovery from various addictions. Mutual support through newsletter and activities proposed by individual members. Established 1990. Write: Box 1865, Brown University, Providence, Rhode Island 02912.

Calix Society

National. For Roman Catholics in recovery in Alcoholics Anonymous. Publishes bimonthly newsletter and group development guidelines. 58 chapters. Established 1947. Call: (612) 546-0544 (mornings only). Write: Bill Fox, 7601 Wayzata Boulevard, Minneapolis, Minnesota 55426.

Cocaine Anonymous

International. For people who wish to recover from an addiction to cocaine. 12-step program of recovery. Offers group starter kit. Publishes various brochures, including "Self Test for Cocaine Addiction." Nearly 1,000 groups in the U.S. and Canada. Established 1982. Call: (310) 559-5833; fax: (310) 559-2554. Write: 3740 Overland Avenue, Suite H, Los Angeles, California 90034.

Dentists Concerned for Dentists

National. For dentists who suffer from alcoholism or chemical dependency. Adopts certain activities from 12-step program including "12-step calls" and "interventions," whereby dentists already in recovery intervene with a colleague who needs help. Discussion groups, telephone networking, pen-pal program, conferences, other opportunities to exchange support, information. Established 1977. Call: (612) 641-0730. Write: 450 North Syndicate, Suite 117, St. Paul, Minnesota 55104.

Dual Disorders Anonymous

Model. For men and women who suffer from both mental illness and alcoholism and/or drug addiction. 12-step program. Publishes group development guidelines. Over 12 groups active in Illinois. Established 1978. Call: (708) 462-3380. Write: P.O. Box 3147, Chicago, Illinois 60631.

Elderly Alcohol Support Groups

Regional. For men and women over 60 who suffer from alcoholism, and their spouses. Call: Noel Gardner, (203) 747-6801. Write: 91 Northwest Drive, Plainville, Connecticut 06062.

Families Anonymous

International. 12-step program for families and friends of people who abuse drugs or alcohol or who have drug-related behavioral problems; also for young people with behavior problems, not necessarily drug or alcohol related. 12-step meetings for exchange of sup-

port, information. Publishes bimonthly newsletter, pamphlets, booklets. Annual convention. Over 500 affiliated groups. Established 1971. Call: (800) 736-9805 or (818) 989-7841. Write: 14553 Delano Street, Suite 316, Van Nuys, California 91411.

International Nurses Anonymous

Fellowship of nurses—registered, licensed-practical and students—in any 12-step program for recovery from any problem, such as alcoholism, overeating, codependency. Publishes quarterly newsletter. Call: (913) 842-3893. Write: 1020 Sunset Drive, Lawrence, Kansas 66044.

"Just Say No" International

For parents, children, educators and others who wish to form chapters of "Just Say No," a program of activities for children to encourage them not to drink or take drugs. Includes educational and social events and outreach efforts. Provides training, materials and other assistance. 15,000 clubs. Established 1985. Call: In California: (510) 451-6666; elsewhere: (800) 258-2766. Write: 2101 Webster Street, Suite 1300, Oakland, California 94612.

Lawyers Assistance Program of Connecticut, Inc.

Model. For lawyers who wish to recover from dependency on alcohol and/or drugs. Established 1989. Call: (203) 245-3530. Write: P.O. Box 927, Madison, Connecticut 06443.

Nar-Anon, Inc.

International. 12-step program for families and friends of drug addicts, whether or not in recovery, analogous to Al-Anon (see entry). Offers a group development information packet. Established 1967. Call: (310) 547-

5800. Write: P.O. Box 2562, Palos Verdes, California 90247.

Narcotics Anonymous

International. 12-step fellowship for people seeking recovery from drug addiction. Publishes *Narcotics Anonymous,* the program's basic text, *The NA Way,* a monthly magazine, telephone directory of groups, group development guidelines, other literature is available in Braille and various languages as well as on audiotape and large-type editions. Over 22,000 affiliated groups in over 50 countries. Established 1953. Call: (818) 780-3951. Write: P.O. Box 9999, Van Nuys, California 91409.

Overcomers Outreach, Inc.

International. For Christians who participate in 12-step programs of recovery, such as Alcoholics Anonymous. Sponsors meetings, retreats, conventions, conferences. Publishes newsletter, *Overcomers Outreach News* as well as various books and pamphlets. Over 950 affiliated groups in 47 U.S. states and six foreign countries. Established 1985. Call: (310) 697-3994. Write: 2290 West Whittier Boulevard, Suite A/D, La Habra, California 90631.

Pill Addicts Anonymous

International. 12-step program for people recovering from drugs, especially mood-altering pills. Offers group development guidelines. Activities include a pen-pal program. Approximately six affiliated groups. Established 1979. Call: (215) 372-1128. Write: P.O. Box 278, Reading, Pennsylvania 19603.

Rational Recovery Systems

International. For people who have developed a dependency on alcohol, drugs or food that they wish to recover from. A nonspiritual program, unlike Alcoholics Anonymous and other 12-step programs such as Drugs Anon-

ymous and Narcotics Anonymous. Uses a system based on Rational Emotive Therapy (RET) and Addictive Voice Recognition Training (AVRT). Publishes bimonthly journal, chapter development guidelines. Groups are run by members, but advised by professionals. 500 affiliated groups. Established 1986. Call: (916) 621-4374. Write: Lois Trimpey, P.O. Box 800, Lotus, California 95651.

Secular Organizations for Sobriety (Save Ourselves)

Regional. For alcoholics and addicts who wish to remain clean and sober, but in a program that does not include a spiritual component, as do Alcoholics Anonymous and other 12-step programs. Publishes newsletter, group development guidelines. 1,000 groups. Established 1986. Call: (716) 834-2922. Write: P.O. Box 5, Buffalo, New York 14215.

Women for Sobriety

National. For female alcoholics. Local chapters sponsor discussion groups. Administers pen-pal network, national conferences. Publishes monthly newsletter and group development guidelines. 250 groups. Established 1976. Call: (215) 536-8026. Write: Box 618, Quakertown, Pennsylvania 18951.

ALPHA 1 ANTITRYPSIN

Alpha 1 Antitrypsin Support Group

National. For people (estimated at approximately 40,000 in the United States) with alpha 1-antitrypsin deficiency (AAT), a hereditary condition in which the blood lacks enough of a certain enzyme, alpha 1-antitrypsin, that normally helps protect lung tissue from breakdown; often leads to severe emphysema. Also for family, friends and interested professionals. Facilitates exchange of support and information (medical, health care, etc.) among members. Maintains AAT Support Network, which helps in the creation of informal networks of AAT patients. Publishes *A1 News,* a quarterly newsletter. Administers pen-pal program. Makes referrals. Advocates on behalf of membership. Holds conferences. 25 affiliated groups. Established 1988. Call: (612) 871-7332. Write: 1829 Portland Avenue, Minneapolis, Minnesota 55404.

ALS (AMYOTROPHIC LATERAL SCLEROSIS)

ALS Association ————————————
National. For people with ALS (amyotrophic lateral sclerosis), sometimes referred to as "Lou Gehrig's disease," a progressive fatal neuromuscular disease that attacks nerve cells and pathways in the brain and spinal cord. Helps ALS patients and families through referrals for counseling, training and support groups for aid in coping with the disease. Promotes research into prevention, causes and cure for ALS. Educates public about disease. Seeks to stimulate public support for research. Over 100 affiliated support groups. Established 1972. Call: (800) 782-4787; fax: (818) 340-2060. Write: 21021 Ventura Boulevard, Suite 321, Woodland Hills, California 91364.

ALZHEIMER'S DISEASE

(See also "Aging," "Caregivers.")

Alzheimer's Disease & Related Disorders Association ————————————
National. For caregivers of patients with Alzheimer's disease, a degenerative disease of the central nervous system marked by premature mental deterioration. Provides referrals to local sources of help, including discussion groups for exchange of support, information. Publishes quarterly newsletter and chapter development guidelines. Over 200 chapters. Established 1980. Call: (312) 335-8700; (800) 272-3900; TDD: (312) 335-8882; fax: (312) 335-1110. Write: 919 North Michigan Avenue, Suite 1000, Chicago, Illinois 60611.

AMPUTATION, LIMB DEFICIENCY

American Amputee Foundation, Inc. ————————————
National. Provides information, referrals and counseling; visits and counsels recent amputees in hospitals. Publishes directory, group development guidelines. 15 chapters. Established 1975. Call: (501) 666-2523. Write: P.O. Box 250218, Little Rock, Arkansas 72225.

Amputees in Motion (AIM) ————————————
Model. For amputees and their families and friends. Provides discussion groups, rehabilitation advice and assistance, outreach to recent amputees while still in the hospital through visitation program. Facilitates creation of networks of people with similar amputations. Sponsors social and sports activities and administers a speakers' bureau. Publishes newsletter, group development guidelines. Established 1973. Serves San Diego County. Call: (619) 454-9300. Write: P.O. Box 2703, Escondido, California 92033.

LEAPS across the Heartland ("Lower-Extremity-Amputees Providing Support") ————————————
Regional. Affiliated with American Amputee Foundation (see entry). For people who have

undergone or who are about to undergo amputation surgery of a lower extremity. Serves the Midwest. Provides peer group support, counseling and patient visitation in hospital and home. Organizes monthly discussion groups. Publishes newsletter. Assists in group development. Established 1987. Call: (816) 361-3206. Write: Lou Keyes, P.O. Box 15961, Lenexa, Kansas 66215.

National Amputation Foundation, Inc.

For people with one or more amputated limbs. Administers "Amp to Amp" program that links persons with similar amputations. Publishes newsletter, *The Amp,* and a variety of other literature. Maintains library of pertinent information. Provides vocational guidance, referrals and other information by phone. Organizes advocacy efforts. Established 1919. Call: (718) 767-0596; fax: (718) 767-3103. Write: 12-45 150th Street, Whitestone, New York 11357.

ANXIETY, PANIC, PHOBIA

(See also "Mental Health.")

Agoraphobics in Motion (AIM)

National. For people who suffer from agoraphobia—the fear of open or public places—and other anxiety disorders that cause panic attacks. Members meet and work on a "10-tool program, which is behavioral and cognitive." Publishes newsletter, group development guidelines and sponsors trips to help members overcome fear of going out in public. Administers pen-pal club. 22 groups. Established 1983. Call: (313) 547-0400. Write: 1729 Crooks, Suite 106, Royal Oak, Michigan 48067.

Anxiety Disorders Association of America

National. For people with phobias and related anxiety disorders. Also encourages participation by health care professionals and other concerned individuals. The ADAA serves as an advocate for its members vis-à-vis the health care industry and promotes their welfare in general. Maintains a *National Professional Membership Directory* of resources for treatment of anxiety disorders, publishes a quarterly newsletter. Established 1980. Call: (800) 737-3400. Write: 6000 Executive Boulevard #513, Rockville, Maryland 20852.

Council on Anxiety Disorders

Model. Works to educate the public about anxiety disorders, including general anxiety, panic disorder, phobias, obsessive-compulsive disorder and post-traumatic stress. Provides assistance in forming support groups and sponsors educational seminars for the public and professionals. Publishes quarterly newsletter. Distributes educational materials by mail. Provides nationwide phone service about support groups, treatment professionals and medications. Established 1988. Call: (919) 722-7760. Write: P.O. Box 17011, Winston-Salem, North Carolina 27116.

APNEA

A.W.A.K.E. Network (Alert, Well and Keeping Energetic)

National. For individuals who suffer from sleep apnea (abnormal breathing during sleep). Discussion groups for exchange of support, information. Publishes newsletter, *The Awake Network,* and other educational materials. Seeks to inform public about sleep apnea.

Over 100 affiliated groups. Established 1988. Call: (412) 647-3464. Write: P.O. Box 534, Bethel Park, Pennsylvania 15102.

ARTHRITIS

American Juvenile Arthritis Organization _____

National. For families of children with arthritis. Provides support and advocacy on behalf of membership. Publishes quarterly newsletter. Holds annual national conference. Offers workshops on self-help. A council of the Arthritis Foundation (see entry). Established 1981. Call: (404) 872-7100. Write: Patricia Harrington, 1314 Spring Street, N.W., Atlanta, Georgia 30303.

Arthritis Foundation _____

National. For people with arthritis and their families and friends. Offers support and educational outreach and social programs. Publishes guidelines for forming new groups, including group-leader manual. 72 chapters. Established 1948. Call: (404) 872-7100. Write: 1314 Spring Street, N.W., Atlanta, Georgia 30309.

ARTHROGRYPOSIS

Avenues: A National Support Group for Arthrogryposis _____

For families in which there is a child with arthrogryposis, a congenital limb defect. Helps connect member families to exchange support, information. Educational outreach to health care and social service professionals. Publishes semiannual newsletter. Established 1980. Call: (209) 928-3688. Write: P.O. Box 5192, Sonora, California 95370.

ARTISTS

A.R.T.S. Anonymous (Artists Recovering through the Twelve Steps) _____

International. For artists encountering life problems that are preventing them from achieving their artistic potential. Problems might include procrastination in pursuing artistic goals; inability to balance amount of time devoted to artistic vs. nonartistic activities, such as relationships; and financial problems. Discussion groups, telephone networking to exchange support, information. Publishes various brochures. Uses 12-step format. Over 100 affiliated groups. Established 1984. Call: (212) 969-0144. Write: P.O. Box 175, Ansonia Station, New York, New York 10023.

ASTHMA

Parents of Asthmatic Kids

Model. For parents with children who suffer from asthma. Discussion groups, telephone networking, other opportunities to exchange support, information. Established 1980. Call: (617) 272-2866. Write: P.O. Box 265, Burlington, Massachusetts 01803.

ATAXIA

National Ataxia Foundation _____

For families in which a member suffers from ataxia, the inability to coordinate the muscles in the execution of voluntary movement. Facilitates formation of support groups. Educational outreach to members, professionals and the general public. Provides referrals to members. Promotes research into causes and treatments. Encourages prevention of hereditary ataxia through genetic screening. 13 groups. Established 1957. Call: (612) 473-7666. Write: 15500 Wayzata Boulevard, Wayzata, Minnesota 55391.

ATTENTION-DEFICIT DISORDERS

ADAPPT (Attention Disorders Association of Parents and Professionals Together) _____

Regional (Illinois). For people—especially children—dealing with attention disorders, a condition, now believed to be neurologically based, marked by poor regulation of attention, impulsivity and, sometimes, hyperactivity. Discussion groups, telephone networking, social activities, other opportunities to exchange support, information. Provides referrals, publishes newsletter and other informational materials, administers speakers' bureau. Library of materials. Established 1988. Call: Liz Zavodny, (708) 361-3387. Write: P.O. Box 293, Oak Forest, Illinois 60452.

C.H.A.D.D. (Children with Attention-Deficit Disorders) _____

National. For children with attention deficit disorders, now believed to be neurologically based, marked by poor regulation of attention, impulsivity and, sometimes, hyperactivity; also for families, friends and interested professionals. Provides support, advocacy, and public and professional education, encourages scientific research. Monthly meetings with guest speakers. Publishes semiannual magazine, monthly newsletter, various brochures. Over 340 local chapters throughout the U.S. Established 1987. Call: (305) 587-3700; fax: (305) 587-4599. Write: 499 Northwest 70th Avenue, Suite 308, Plantation, Florida 33317.

AUTISM

Autism Society of America _____

National. For children and adults with autism, a severely incapacitating, lifelong developmental disability; symptoms include slow development or lack of physical, social and learning skills; abnormal responses to sensations; and abnormal ways of relating to people, objects and events. Provides information and referral services. Hosts annual convention. Public education about and research into autism; advocacy on behalf of autistic people. Publishes newsletter. Over 200 chapters. Established 1965. Call: (301) 565-0433; fax: (301) 565-0834. Write: 1234 Massachusetts Avenue, N.W., Suite 1017, Washington, D.C. 20005.

BALDNESS

AARF-HAIR (Alopecia Areata Research Foundation-Help Alopecia International Research) _____

National. For people with alopecia areata, an uncommon form of baldness, unrelated to male pattern baldness. Also for interested professionals. Fund-raises for research projects to find cause, cure for condition. Mounts educational outreach efforts to patients, professionals. Established 1983. Call: (805) 494-4903. Write: P.O. Box 1875, Thousand Oaks, California 91358.

Bald-Headed Men of America _____

National. For bald-headed men. Seeks to engender a positive mental attitude among its members vis-à-vis their baldness. Activities include support groups and an annual conference held the second week of September. Established 1973. Call: (919) 726-1855; fax: (919) 726-6061. Write: 203 Bald Drive, Morehead City, North Carolina 28557.

National Alopecia Areata Foundation

For people with alopecia areata, an uncommon form of baldness, unrelated to male pattern baldness. Provides support and information to members. Funds major research worldwide. Promotes public awareness of problem. Publishes bimonthly newsletter, support group development guidelines. 45 chapters. Established 1981. Call: (415) 456-4644. Write: P.O. Box 150760, San Rafael, California 94915.

BATTERERS

Batterers Anonymous

National. For men who wish to stop their abusive behavior toward women. 12-step program seeks to help men control the anger that leads to such behavior. Women affected by battering may attend. Group development manual available. 30 chapters. Established 1979. Call: (714) 355-1100. Write: 8485D Tamarind Avenue, Fontana, California 92335.

BECKWITH-WIEDEMANN SYNDROME

Beckwith-Wiedemann Support Network

International. For families with a child with Beckwith-Wiedemann syndrome, also known as EMG syndrome ("exomphalos, macroglossia, gigantism," the condition's characteristics), a syndrome of congenital birth defects. Also for interested professionals. Encourages formation of groups and phone networks whereby families can exchange support and information. Provides referrals. Publishes newsletter. Established 1989. Call: (313) 973-0263. Write: Susan Fettes, 3206 Braeburn Circle, Ann Arbor, Michigan 48108.

BENIGN ESSENTIAL BLEPHAROSPASM

Benign Essential Blepharospasm Research Foundation, Inc.

National. For people who suffer from benign essential blepharospasm (spasmodic winking). Encourages formation of support groups and helps connect people with BEB. Promotes education and research. Provides referrals. Publishes newsletter, group development guidelines. Over 170 affiliated groups. Established 1981. Call: (409) 832-0788. Write: P.O. Box 12468, Beaumont, Texas 77726.

BEREAVEMENT: CHILD (HOMICIDE)

Parents of Murdered Children

National. Support groups, telephone networking, other opportunities to exchange support and information. Members accompany each other to subsequent court appearances. Publishes newsletter. 300 chapters or contact persons in the U.S. and Canada. Established 1978. Call: (513) 721-5683. Write: 100 East Eighth Street, B-41, Cincinnati, Ohio 45202.

Parents of Murdered Children of New York State, Inc. _____

Model. For family and friends of a murdered child. Members help each other deal with the experience, assist each other during criminal proceedings. Seeks to be a medium for exchange of information about the civil rights of families and friends of murdered children and the social services available to them. Publishes newsletter. Established 1982. Call: (212) 873-3361 or (212) 227-9544. Write: 26 West 84th Street, New York, New York 10024.

S.O.S.A.D. (Save Our Sons and Daughters) _____

National. For families of children killed in urban street violence. Holds weekly discussion group meetings for exchange of support; workshops on "the stages of grief" and "children who hurt"; stress-management classes. Provides individual and group counseling, assistance to families to help them deal with the judicial system. Services for children to help them escape dangerous street environment include peer support groups, various workshops and special programs, including summer camps. Established 1987. Call: (313) 361-5200. Write: 2441 West Grand Boulevard, Detroit, Michigan 48208.

BEREAVEMENT: CHILD (NEONATAL DEATH)

AMEND (Aiding Mothers & Fathers Experiencing Neonatal Death) _____

National. For parents who have lost a child during pregnancy, birth or infancy. Offers private peer counseling with trained volunteers and opportunities to exchange support, information. Established 1977. Call: (314) 487-

7582. Write: Maureen Connelly, 4324 Berrywick Terrace, St. Louis, Missouri 63128.

Bereaved Parents _____

Model. For parents and other family members grieving the loss of a child. Discussion groups, telephone networking, other opportunities to exchange support, information. Established 1989. Call: (203) 372-8250. Write: Walter H. Everett, 25 Flat Rock Road, Easton, Connecticut 06612.

Center for Loss in Multiple Birth (C.L.I.M.B.), Inc. _____

International. "By and for parents who have experienced the death of one or more children during a multiple birth (twins or more) pregnancy, at birth or in infancy or childhood. Peer support, pen pals and phone contacts, information and resources, other opportunities for exchanging support and information. Offers assistance and resources to twin clubs, infant loss support groups, health care professionals and the public. Publishes quarterly *Our Newsletter*. Established 1987. Call: (907) 746-6123. Write: Jean Killantai, P.O. Box 1064, Palmer, Alaska 99645.

Compassionate Friends _____

National. Self-help support group for parents and siblings grieving the death of a child or sibling, respectively. Discussion group meetings, telephone networking for exchange of support and information on grieving. Publishes national newsletter for parents and special newsletter for siblings of the deceased child. 600 chapters. Established 1969. Call: (708) 990-0010. Write: P.O. Box 3696, Oak Brook, Illinois 60522.

National Sudden Infant Death Syndrome Foundation _____

For families of victims of sudden infant death syndrome (SIDS), also known as crib death, a recognized, unpredictable medical disorder in which an apparently healthy infant suddenly and unexpectedly dies; the death remains unexplained after a complete postmortem investigation, an examination of the scene of death and a review of the child's medical history. The cause of SIDS is still unknown but is thought to be determined by more than one factor. Discussion groups, telephone networking, other opportunities for exchange of support and information. Promotes research, public education about SIDS. Publishes newsletter, chapter development guidelines. 82 chapters. Established 1962. Call: In Maryland, (301) 459-3388; elsewhere, (800) 221-SIDS. Write: 10500 Little Patuxent Parkway, #420, Columbia, Maryland 21044.

SHARE (Sources of Help in Airing & Resolving Experiences): Pregnancy & Infant Loss Support, Inc. _____

National. For parents who have lost a child in pregnancy, birth or infancy, for exchanging support, information. Publishes newsletter, chapter development guidelines. 280 chapters. Established 1977. Call: (314) 947-6164. Write: Catherine A. Lammert, 300 First Capitol Drive, St. Charles, Missouri 63301.

Unite, Inc. _____

National. For parents grieving the loss of a child by stillbirth, sudden infant death syndrome (a recognized, unpredictable medical disorder in which an apparently healthy infant suddenly and unexpectedly dies) and miscarriage. Discussion groups, telephone networking, an annual conference, other opportunities for exchange of support, information, especially during pregnancies subsequent to ones where the child died. Professionals retained in advisory roles. Administers training program for group leaders. Publishes quarterly news-

letter. 10 groups. Established 1975. Call: (215) 728-2082 or (215) 728-3777. Write: Janis Heil, 7600 Central Avenue, Philadelphia, Pennsylvania 19111.

BEREAVEMENT: HOMICIDE VICTIMS

Families of Homicide Victims Support Group _____

Model. For parents and siblings of homicide victims. Individual, family and group counseling. Various discussion groups for parents and siblings for exchange of support. Assists victim's families in obtaining funeral benefits; applying for compensation for loss of income; in obtaining social security and welfare benefits. Provides referrals for child care, vocational training, medical care, other services. Acts as liaison between family and police and district attorney. Advocates for family, keeps survivors apprised of criminal proceedings, assists family in court. Call: (718) 834-6688 (9 A.M.–5 P.M.); 24-hour hotline: (212) 577-7772. Write: 2 Lafayette Street, New York, New York 10007.

Survivors of Homicide _____

Model. For families and friends of murder victims. Discussion groups, other opportunities to exchange support, information. Call: (203) 384-3325. Write: Diana Tomlin, 267 Grant Street, Bridgeport, Connecticut 06610.

BEREAVEMENT: SPOUSE

Concerns of Police Survivors (COPS) _____

National. For families of law-enforcement officers killed while on duty. Discussion groups, other opportunities for exchange of support, information. Yearly grief seminar. 14 chapters. Established 1984. Call: (301) 599-0445. Write: 9423A Marlboro Pike, Upper Marlboro, Maryland 20772.

National Association of Military Widows

Provides immediate assistance to members through referrals but also advocates legislative change to ameliorate their situation in the long term. Established 1976. Write: 4023 25th Road, North Arlington, Virginia 22207.

Society of Military Widows

National. For widows and widowers of members of the U.S. military. Various activities for exchange of support. Also engaged in public-information outreach. Publishes newsletter, chapter development guidelines. Over 20 chapters. Established 1968. Call: (703) 750-1342. Write: 5535 Hempstead Way, Springfield, Virginia 22151.

THEOS (They Help Each Other Spiritually)

National. For widowed men and women grieving the deaths of their spouses. Discussion groups, other networking opportunities for exchange of support, information. Publishes newsletter, chapter development guidelines, magazine, brochures. 110 chapters. Established 1962. Call: (412) 471-7779. Write: 1301 Clark Building, 717 Liberty Avenue, Pittsburgh, Pennsylvania 15222.

Widowed Persons Service

National. For widowed persons. Helps form one-to-one peer relationships between members and also discussion groups for exchange of support and information. Administered jointly by the American Association of Retired Persons (see AARP entry) and local commu-

nity groups. Other activities include referral services and public education outreach efforts. Publishes quarterly newsletter and group development guidelines. 230 chapters. Established 1973. Call: (202) 434-2260. Write: 601 E Street, N.W., Washington, D.C. 20049.

BEREAVEMENT: SUICIDE

Heartbeat

Model. For families and friends of suicides. Discussion groups, telephone networking, other opportunities for exchange of support, information. Publishes chapter development guidelines. 15 chapters. Established 1981. Call: (719) 596-2575. Write: 2015 Devon Street, Colorado Springs, Colorado 80909.

Ray of Hope, Inc.

Model. For families and friends of persons who have died by suicide. Discussion groups, telephone networking, other opportunities for exchange of support and information. Assists in developing new groups. Publishes informational book, booklet and video. 5 affiliated groups. Established 1977. Call: (319) 337-9890. Write: P.O. Box 2323, Iowa City, Iowa 52244.

Survivors of Suicide (S.O.S.)

National. For families and friends of suicides. Discussion groups, telephone networking, other opportunities for exchange of support and information. Seeks to increase public awareness of problem of suicide. Maintains speakers' bureau. Provides assistance for developing new chapters. Over 300 groups. Established 1980. Call: (414) 442-4638. Write: Sharry Schaefer, 3251 North 78th Street, Milwaukee, Wisconsin 53222.

BIRACIAL

See "Interracial."

BLINDNESS, VISUAL IMPAIRMENT

(See also "Usher's Syndrome.")

American Council of the Blind

National. For blind and visually impaired people, their families, friends and interested professionals and others. Advocacy, education and support for blind and visually impaired people. Provides information and referrals. Sponsors annual national conference. Publishes bimonthly magazine, *The Braille Forum*, and chapter development guidelines. 72 affiliated organizations. Established 1961. Call: (202) 467-5081 or (800) 424-8666; fax: (202) 467-5085. Write: 1155 15th Street, N.W., Washington, D.C. 20005.

Association for Macular Diseases, Inc.

National. For persons who suffer loss of vision due to macular degeneration (degeneration of the macular lutea), the leading cause of legal blindness in people over 50 years of age. The macula lutea is the point of the retina upon which the light rays meet as they are focused by the cornea and the lens of the eye. Damage to it causes the central portion of visual images to be blocked as if a blurred area had been placed in the center of the picture, while the images around the blurred area may be clearly visible. Membership also includes families and friends of people with macular degeneration. Provides support groups and telephone networks for members. Helps disseminate information on research into causes and treatments for these diseases and on vision aids for people who suffer from them. Working on establishing an eye bank devoted solely to macular disease research. Publishes quarterly, large-type newsletter for members. Established 1978. Call: (212) 605-3719. Write: 210 East 64th Street, New York, New York 10021.

Blinded Veterans Association

National. For blinded veterans. Provides support for members and information on various topics, including benefits and rehabilitation programs. Assistance in career planning and job placement. Sponsors regional meetings. Publishes bimonthly newsletter and group development guidelines. Approximately 40 groups. Established 1945. Call: (800) 605-3719 or (202) 371-8880. Write: 477 H Street, N.W., Washington, D.C. 20001.

Council of Citizens with Low Vision

National. For persons with low vision, impaired vision with significant reduction in visual function that is not correctable by conventional eyeglasses but improvable through special assistive technology. Goal is to help members make the fullest possible use of their vision through various services and technologies. Sponsors educational and advocacy efforts. Provides referrals to members. Publishes newsletter and group development guidelines. Chapters in seven states, with numerous local groups. Established 1978. Call: (616) 381-9566. Write: 1400 North Drake Road, #218, Kalamazoo, Michigan 49006.

Lighthouse National Center for Vision and Aging

For people who are concerned with problems of vision, especially as they relate to older people. Provides various resources and referrals. Publishes newsletter and *Self-help/Mutual Aid Support Groups For Visually Impaired Older People: A Guide and Directory.* N.B.: Beginning 1994, address for Lighthouse will be 111 East 59th Street, New York, New York 10022; telephone number will remain the same. Established 1906. Call: (800) 334-5497; fax: (212) 808-0110. Write: 800 Second Avenue, New York, New York 10017.

National Federation of the Blind

For blind people who seek "complete integration . . . into society on a basis of equality." Variety of activities and services to the blind. Outreach to people who have just become blind, advising them on available services, legal rights and protection due them. Advocacy efforts on behalf of membership. Employment-related activities include special job training for the nonsighted. Provides scholarships to blind students. Publishes various literature, including magazine. Organizes monthly meetings of members. 51 chapters. Established 1940. Call: (410) 659-9314. Employment hotline: (800) 638-7518. Write: 1800 Johnson Street, Baltimore, Maryland 21230.

R.P. Foundation Fighting Blindness (Retinitis Pigmentosa)

National. For people with retinitis pigmentosa, a degenerative disease of the retina that causes loss of vision. Supports research into causes and treatments for retinitis pigmentosa and related conditions. Provides information and referrals to patients. Sponsors conferences. Maintains confidential registry of af-fected individuals. Administers a retina donor program. Publishes newsletter. Established 1971. Call: Maryland: (800) 683-5555; elsewhere: (410) 225-9400; TDD: (410) 225-9409. Write: 1401 Mount Royal Avenue, 4th Floor, Baltimore, Maryland 21217.

Sight-Loss Support Group of Central Pennsylvania, Inc.

Model. For people of all ages with any degree of sight loss. Provides information and referrals. Promotes formation of support groups, encourages telephone networking. Publishes monthly newsletter and group development guidelines. Provides reader/scanner equipment for demonstration. Administers "Art through Touch" programs. Established 1982. Call: (814) 238-0132. Write: 111 Sowers Street, Suite 310, State College, Pennsylvania 16801.

Vision Northwest

Regional. For people with vision loss and their families and friends. Outreach efforts to potential new members. Promotes formation of support groups and networks. Provides information and referrals. Publishes quarterly newsletter. Over 40 groups in the Northwest. Established 1983. Call: (503) 284-7560 or (800) 448-2232. Write: 4370 Northeast Halsey, Portland, Oregon 97213.

Vision Foundation, Inc.

National. For blind and visually impaired people. Conducts support groups headed by peers. Seeks to establish networks among members. Other activities include outreach efforts, career-mentor program, program in survival skills for elderly members. Publishes bimonthly newsletter, group development guidelines. Established 1970. Call: In Massachusetts, (800) 852-3029; elsewhere: (617) 926-4232. Write: 808 Mt. Auburn Street, Watertown, Massachusetts 02172.

BLOOD DISEASE

(See also AIDS/HIV, "Cooley's Anemia," "Leukemia.")

Aplastic Anemia Foundation of America

National. For people with aplastic anemia, a blood disorder caused by a failure of cell production in the bone marrow; also for families and friends. Activities include support groups and counseling services. Promotes public awareness of the disease and research into its causes and treatment. Publishes quarterly newsletter and group development guidelines. 15 chapters. Established 1983. Call: (800) 747-2820. Write: P.O. Box 22689, Baltimore, Maryland 21203.

Hemochromatosis Research Foundation, Inc.

National. For people who suffer from hemochromatosis, a disorder of iron metabolism in which iron accumulates in body tissues; also for families and friends and interested professionals. Educational efforts to promote public awareness of disease. Sponsors genetic screening of families in which the disease is likely to occur. Other activities include fund-raising for research into hemochromatosis, conferences. Publishes quarterly newsletter and other educational materials. Established 1982. Call: (518) 489-0972. Write: P.O. Box 8569, Albany, New York 12208.

National Association for Sickle Cell Disease

National. For persons with sickle-cell anemia, a hereditary blood disease occurring mostly in blacks and characterized by anemia. Members also include families and friends and interested professionals. Activities include support groups for people affected by the disease; phone networks to connect members. Promotes public awareness of the disease through various educational outreach efforts (films available) and fund-raises for research into its causes and cures. Publishes quarterly newsletter, group development guidelines. Approximately 100 chapters. Established 1971. Call: (213) 736-5455 or (800) 421-8453. Write: 3345 Wilshire Boulevard, Suite 1106, Los Angeles, California 90010.

National Hemophilia Foundation

For persons with hemophilia and their families and friends. Promotes research into and public awareness of hemophilia. Publishes quarterly newsletter and group development guidelines. Sponsors annual meeting for patients and professionals. 48 chapters. Established 1948. Call: (212) 219-8180. Write: The SoHo Building, 110 Greene Street, #303, New York, New York 10012.

BONE-MARROW TRANSPLANT

Bone Marrow Transplant Family Support Network

An international telephone network providing information about transplant centers and resources available to patients. Members in the network are bone-marrow transplant patients, donors, partners and spouses of patients and parents of children who have had bone marrow transplants. Members share support and strategies for coping during the pre- and post-transplant period. Coordinates contact between patients, partner and parents. Established 1988. Call: (203) 646-2836. Write: Sandra Connell, P.O. Box 845, Avon, Connecticut 06001.

BREAST CANCER

Reach to Recovery _____

National. The Reach to Recovery Program, administered by local chapters of the American Cancer Society, often includes self-help groups of women with breast cancer. Contact local chapters of the American Cancer Society.

SHARE: Self Help for Women with Breast Cancer _____

Model. For women with breast cancer. Sponsors support groups. Other activities include telephone hotlines (English, Spanish and Chinese) and educational meetings. Established 1976. Call: (212) 719-0364. Write: 19 West 44th Street, New York, New York 10036.

BROWN LUNG

(See also "Lung Disease.")

Brown Lung Association _____

National, but especially active in textile-industry states, such as South Carolina. For people with byssinosis ("brown lung disease" or "mill fever"), an occupational respiratory disease associated with inhalation of cotton, flax or hemp dust, characterized initially by chest tightness, shortness of breath and coughing, and eventually by irreversible lung disease; also for friends and family members and interested professionals. Provides support for and advocacy on behalf of membership, especially in seeking workman's compensation for this occupation-related illness. Seeks to educate general public and textile workers in particular about dangers of byssinosis. Publishes monthly newsletter; group development guidelines available. Over 12 chapters. Established 1975. Call: (803) 269-8048. Write: La-

mar Case, P.O. Box 7583, Greenville, South Carolina 29611.

BURN VICTIMS

Burns United Support Group _____

National. For burn survivors and their families and friends. Provides support through discussion groups, telephone networking, pen-pal program, visits to burn victims during and after hospitalization. Publishes newsletter. Offers assistance in starting new groups. 2 affiliated groups. Established 1986. Call: (313) 881-5577. Write: 441 Colonial Court, Grosse Pointe Farms, Michigan 48236.

National Burn Victim Foundation _____

For burn victims and their families and friends. Provides education, mental health services and referrals to members after hospitalization. Promotes formation of support groups. Sponsors visits to recent burn victims during hospitalization. Organizes advocacy efforts on behalf of members. Established 1974. Call: (210) 731-3112. Write: 308 Main Street, Orange, New Jersey 07050.

The Phoenix Society for Burn Survivors, Inc. _____

International. For severely burned people and their families and friends. Recovered members provide support, information and other assistance to burn victims during and after hospitalization. Activities include phone and pen-pal networks, national and international conferences. Advocates on behalf of membership. Runs fire safety and burn prevention programs. Burn-survivor speakers' bureau. Publishes quarterly newsletter and other materials. Books, audiovisual, other materials available for educational efforts. 265 chapters. Established 1977. Call: (215) 946-BURN or (800) 888-BURN. Write: 11 Rust Hill Road, Levittown, Pennsylvania 19056.

CANCER

(See also "Breast Cancer," "Colorectal Cancer," "Ostomy.")

Cancer Support Network

Model. For people whose lives have been affected by cancer. Activities include peer support groups, including a bereavement group, community awareness and education programs, art therapy for cancer survivors. Makes referrals to medical, other services. Publishes newsletter. Established 1988. Call: (412) 361-8600. Write: Barbara Seltman, 5850 Ellsworth Avenue, Suite 303, Pittsburgh, Pennsylvania 15232.

Candlelighters Childhood Cancer Foundation

International. Umbrella organization for self-help, mutual aid groups for children and adolescents with cancer and their families. Facilitates information exchange, networking. Services include quarterly newsletter, youth newsletter, bibliography. Ombudsman program for health insurance problems, second opinions, employment issues. Advocacy efforts on behalf of membership. Also operates an information clearinghouse, speakers' bureau. Over 400 groups. Established 1970. Call: (800) 366-2223. Write: 7910 Woodmont Avenue, Suite 460, Bethesda, Maryland 20814.

National Coalition for Cancer Survivorship

National. Information clearinghouse for programs and publications that relate to cancer survivorship. Advocacy services on behalf of cancer survivors. Assists in establishing new support and networking systems for cancer survivors. Publishes newsletter; sponsors conferences. 180 member organizations. Established 1986. Call: (301) 585-2616. Write: 1010 Wayne Avenue, Suite 300, Silver Spring, Maryland 20910.

CAREGIVERS

(See also "Alzheimer's Disease," "Stroke," "Tube Feeding.")

Caregivers of Patients with Memory Loss

Model. For family caregivers of persons with memory loss; affiliated with Alzheimer's Association—Chicago Area Chapter. Discussion groups to share support and information about coping with Alzheimer's Disease and related disorders. Sponsors other, educational programs. Established 1984. Call: (708) 441-7775. Write: Seven Happ Road, Northfield, Illinois 60093.

Children of Aging Parents (CAPS)

National. Provides self-help, mutual aid for caregivers of the aged. Fosters formation of support groups. Publishes quarterly newsletter. Furnishes an information packet for those interested in starting new chapters. Established 1977. Call: (215) 945-6900; fax: (215) 945-8720. Write: 1609 Woodbourne Road, Suite 302A, Levittown, Pennsylvania 19057.

Concerned Relatives of Nursing Home Patients

National. Established 1976. Provides information to families of the elderly about a variety of relevant topics, including nursing homes, Medicaid and patients' rights. Bimonthly newsletter, *Insight*. Call: (216) 321-0403. Write: P.O. Box 18820, Cleveland, Ohio 44118.

DEBUT (Daughters of Elderly Bridging the Unknown Together)

Model. Support group for women responsible for the care of aging parents. Publishes *Daughters of the Elderly: Building Partnerships in Caregiving* (Indiana University Press, 1988). Established 1981. Write: Area 10 Agency Aging, 2129 Yost Avenue, Bloomington, Indiana 47401.

Friends and Relatives of Institutionalized Aged, Inc. (F.R.I.A.)

Model. A consumer organization offering free assistance with nursing and adult home placement, including how to get financial help and protect your assets, how to evaluate care, how to advocate for your loved one. F.R.I.A. also serves as a watchdog over private providers and government regulators to ensure quality care. Publishes newsletter and comprehensive consumer guide, *Eldercare in the '90s*. Established 1975. Call: (212) 732-4455. Write: 11 John Street, Suite 601, New York, New York 10038.

Well Spouse Foundation

International. Self-help, mutual aid for people married to a chronically ill person. Supports and sponsors advocacy efforts for improved long-term health care. Publishes bimonthly newsletter. Services and activities include pen-pal program, annual conference, and guidelines and assistance for starting new support groups. Established 1988. 75 active support groups. Call: (619) 673-9043. Write: P.O. Box 28876, San Diego, California 92198.

CEREBRAL PALSY

United Cerebral Palsy Associations, Inc.

National. For people with cerebral palsy, a nonprogressive, noncommunicable, incurable condition (not disease) caused by damage to the brain during pregnancy, labor or shortly following birth and characterized by an inability to fully control motor function. Services and activities include medical assistance, special education, career development, social and recreation programs, counseling, advocacy and public education. Advocates on behalf of membership at national level. Administers various research efforts into causes and treatments for CP. Established 1949. Call: (202) 842-1266 or (800) 872-5827. Write: 1522 K Street, N.W., #1112, Washington, D.C. 20005.

CHARCOT-MARIE-TOOTH (CMT) DISEASE

Charcot-Marie-Tooth Association

International. For people with CMT also called peroneal muscular atrophy, a disease (usually genetic) that causes progressive wasting of muscles in the extremities; also for their families and friends, and professionals. Discussion groups, telephone networking for exchange of support and information. Provides physician referrals and information. Sells informational videotapes. Publishes newsletter and "CMT Facts," a special, occasional series on CMT topics. Sponsors regional conferences. Assists in generic research on CMT. Established 1983. 32 affiliated groups in U.S.; members in 28 other countries. Call: (215) 499-7486. Write: Pat Dreibellois, 601 Upland Avenue, Upland, Pennsylvania 19015.

CHEMICAL HYPERSENSITIVITY

National Foundation for the Chemically Hypersensitive

For people with a chemically induced immune system disorder. Discussion groups, pen-pal program, conferences and other networking opportunities for exchange of support and information. Advocates research into and education about problem. Provides referrals to members. Assists in development of local chapters. 40 chapters. Established 1986. Call: (517) 697-3989. Write: P.O. Box 222, Ophelia, Virginia 22530.

CHILD ABUSE

Believe the Children

National. For parents of children who have been abused or victimized by people who are not members of the family. Parents and professionals meet to discuss problems and issues surrounding sexual and ritualistic exploitation of young children. Publishes quarterly newsletter and chapter development guidelines. 4 chapters. Established 1986. Call: (310) 379-3514. Write: P.O. Box 77, Hermosa Beach, California 90254.

Grandparents Raising Grandchildren

Model. For grandparents or other relatives raising a child or concerned about an abusive environment in which a child in their extended family is being raised. Members provide mutual aid and exchange information at meetings. Provides guidelines for starting new groups. Established 1986. Call: (619) 223-0344. Write: 3851 Centraloma Drive, San Diego, California 92107.

Parents Anonymous

National. For parents who abuse their children, or fear they might. Provides self-help, mutual aid. Each support group retains a trained professional to serve as facilitator for meetings, other activities. Publishes manuals for group leaders and new chapter development. Many groups also offer meetings where members' children can meet, discuss their experiences and feelings, form friendships. Approximately 1,121 groups. Established 1970. Call: (800) 421-0353. Write: 520 South Lafayette Park Place, #316, Los Angeles, California 90057.

VOCAL (Victims of Child Abuse Laws)

National. Seeks to protect civil rights of persons wrongly or falsely accused of child abuse and to increase protection for children from their abusers within the children's services system. Publishes a newsletter and chapter development guidelines. Approximately 40 chapters. Established 1984. Call: (800) 745-8778. Write: 7485 East Kenyon Avenue, Denver, Colorado 80237.

CHILD SEXUAL MOLESTATION

(See also "Incest.")

Molesters Anonymous

Model. For men who molest children and who wish to stop doing so. Confidential, anonymous self-help, mutual support groups set up by a professional, ultimately run by members. Group development manual available. Approximately 12 groups. Established 1985. Call: (714) 355-1100. Write: Dr. Jerry Goffmann, 8485 Tamarind Avenue, #D, Fontana, California 92335.

Parents Against Molesters, Inc. _____

Model. For parents of children who were victims of sexual molestation. Discussion groups, telephone networking to exchange support, information. Seeks to educate public at large about the problem of sexual molestation. Speakers' bureau. Maintains approved referral list of counselors and clinicians. Monitors legal action against accused molesters; provides support for families during such court action. Sponsors various legislative advocacy efforts. Maintains statistics on child molestation. Publishes bimonthly newsletter, group development guidelines. Established 1983. Call: (804) 363-2549. Write: Barbara Barker, P.O. Box 3557, Portsmouth, Virginia 23701.

SARA (Sexual Assault Recovery Anonymous) _____

National in Canada. For adults and teens who were sexually abused as children. Discussion groups, other opportunities for exchange of support, educational information. Provides group development assistance. 50 affiliated groups. Established 1983. Call: (604) 584-2626; fax: (604) 584-2888. Write: P.O. Box 16, Surrey, B.C., Canada V3T 4W4.

CHILDBIRTH AND CHILD CARE

See also "Bereavement: Child (Neonatal Death)," "Fetal Alcohol Syndrome," "Multiple Birth," "Teen Pregnancy," "Premature, High-Risk, Sick Infants," "Sick, Disabled Children."

ASPO/Lamaze (American Society for Psychoprophylaxis in Obstetrics) _____

National. For parents, childbirth educators and health care providers interested in family-centered maternity care. Seeks to educate expectant and new parents regarding proper pre- and postnatal baby care and to increase public awareness of the need for broader education in these areas through advocacy and reform. Espouses a childbirth method called psychoprophylaxis, developed in the 1950s by French obstetrician-gynecologist Dr. Fernand Lamaze, who based the method on previous work by Soviet scientists, including Pavlov. Instructs approximately 3.5 million expectant and new parents annually; ongoing membership is approximately 4,500 members. Publishes a variety of materials, including *The Journal of Perinatal Education* and *Lamaze Parents Magazine*. Established 1960. Call: (800) 368-4404 or (202) 857-1128. Write: 1101 Connecticut Avenue, N.W., Suite 700, Washington, D.C. 20036.

Depression After Delivery _____

National. For women who have suffered from postpartum depression. Activities include discussion groups, telephone networking, pen-pal program, conference, other opportunities to exchange support, information. Publishes newsletter, group development guidelines. 90 chapters. Established 1985. Call: (215) 295-3994; messages: (800) 944-4773. Write: P.O. Box 1282, Morrisville, Pennsylvania 19067.

International Childbirth Education Association, Inc. _____

For people who are interested in "family-centered maternity care (FCMC)"—maternity care that is "appropriate for each family's needs, where there is freedom of choice in childcare based on knowledge of alternatives." Examples of alternative child care procedures that many people are ignorant of, but may wish to explore, include rooming in, where the newborn sleeps in the mother's hospital room, not in the nursery; and demand feeding vs. scheduled feeding, which is standard operating procedure in most maternity wards. Promotes FCMC through their publication, the *International Journal of Childbirth Education*, and other books and pamphlets, sponsorship of conventions and conferences. Administers ICEA Teacher Certification Program. 300 groups. Established 1960. Call: (612) 854-8660. Write: P.O. Box 20048, Minneapolis, Minnesota 55420.

La Leche League

International. For breast-feeding mothers. Discussion groups, peer counseling, classes, conferences, telephone networking, other opportunities for exchange of support and information. Workshops and seminars for health care providers as well as access to a "comprehensive" collection of professional studies that reflect breast-feeding trends. Publishes bimonthly newsletter, literature on breast-feeding and parenting, quarterly abstracts. Over 40,000 members. Established 1956. Call: (800) LA-LECHE between 9 A.M.–3 P.M. Central Time or (708) 455-7730. Write: P.O. Box 1209, Franklin Park, Illinois 60131.

MELD (Minnesota Early Learning Design)

National. For parents, from the last trimester of pregnancy through the child's second year. Discussion groups for the exchange of support and information, parent materials and curriculum. Special programs for first-time parents, parents of children with special needs, young mothers and fathers, single mothers with older children, parents who are deaf and hard of hearing, Latino families, and Hmong families. Over 75 affiliated groups. Established 1975. Call: (612) 337-7563; fax: (612) 337-5468. Write: 123 North Third Street, Suite 507, Minneapolis, Minnesota 55401.

NAPSAC (National Association of Parents and Professionals for Safe Alternative in Childbirth)

For parents and professionals interested in "alternative birthing" modalities, such as home birth, family-centered maternity care and midwifery. Maintains directory of alternative-birth practitioners. Publishes newsletter, childbirth activist handbook, group development guidelines. Call: (314) 238-2010. Write: Route 1, Box 646, Marble Hill, Missouri 63764.

National Association of Mothers' Centers

For parents and professionals who are involved in pregnancy, childbirth and parenting. Discussion groups, telephone networking, peer counseling, other opportunities for exchange of support and information. Research and advocacy efforts on behalf of members and their interests. Sponsors annual conference. Publishes yearbook, manual, other literature. 85 sites. Established 1981. Call: (800) 645-3828; in New York (516) 486-6614. Write: 336 Fulton Avenue, Hempstead, New York 11550.

CHILD CUSTODY

Mothers Without Custody

Statewide in Illinois. For women without custody of one or more of their children. Facilitates networking among membership for exchange of support, information. Activities include social events, fund-raising and public education efforts. Provides referrals. Publishes newsletter. Established 1981. Call: (815) 455-2955. Write: Jennifer Isham, President, 609 North Avenue, Crystal Lake, Illinois 60014.

CHRONIC-FATIGUE SYNDROME

CFIDS Association, Inc. _____
International. For people affected by CFS, formerly called chronic Epstein-Barr virus syndrome, which is characterized by debilitating fatigue and a group of related symptoms, including headaches, sore throat, fever, weakness, lymph node pain, muscle and joint pain, memory loss and difficulty in concentrating. Activities include education, advocacy and research funding. Publishes journal, *The CFIDS Chronicle*. Administers public policy programs. Call: (800) 442-3437 or (900) 988-2343. Write: P.O. Box 220398, Charlotte, North Carolina 28222.

National Chronic Fatigue Syndrome Association, Inc. _____
International. For people who suffer from chronic fatigue syndrome (CFS; debilitating fatigue and a group of related symptoms, including headaches, sore throat, fever, weakness, lymph node pain, muscle and joint pain, memory loss and difficulty in concentrating) and related disorders, and for families and friends and interested professionals. Specializes in disseminating the results of research into CFS by the medical establishment. Discussion groups, telephone networking, other opportunities for exchange of support, information; facilitates communications between support groups, individuals worldwide. Pub-

lishes numerous brochures and quarterly newsletter, audio- and videotapes. Maintains speakers' bureau. 800 affiliated groups. Established 1985. Call: (816) 931-4777 (24 hours daily). Write: Janel C. Bohanon, 3521 Broadway, Suite 222, Kansas City, Kansas 64111.

CHRONIC ILLNESS

US (Uncommon Survivors) _____
Model. For "anyone grappling with the challenge of recovering or maintaining their health" through diet, exercise and stress management. Established 1989. Call: (708) 492-3040. Write: 1800 Sherman Avenue, Suite 515, Evanston, Illinois 60201.

CLEFT PALATE, CLEFT LIP

Cleft Palate Association _____
National. For people with cleft lip, cleft palate and other craniofacial anomalies, and for their families and friends. Provides information and referrals to local cleft-palate/craniofacial teams for treatment; also, referrals to local parent discussion groups, for exchange of support, information. Publishes newsletter. Established 1984. Call: (412) 481-1376; 24-hour hotline: (800) 24-CLEFT: fax: (412) 481-0847. Write: 1218 Grandview Avenue, Pittsburgh, Pennsylvania 15211.

COCHLEAR IMPLANT

(See also "Deafness Hearing Impairment.")

Cochlear Implant Club International _____
For people who have had or are going to have a cochlear implant, an implantable inner-ear

prosthesis that provides a degree of hearing for profoundly deaf individuals; developed to assist selected hearing-impaired children and adults who cannot benefit significantly from conventional hearing aids. Also for their families and friends and for interested professionals. Over 30 local groups. Established 1985. Call: (716) 838-4662 (voice or TDD). Write: P.O. Box 464, Buffalo, New York 14223.

CODEPENDENCY

Co-Dependents Anonymous

National. 12-step program for people who wish to recover from "codependency," loosely defined by CoDA as an inability to form and maintain healthy relationships with others and with oneself; typical codependent living patterns involve trying to please and control others. Publishes newsletter, group development guidelines. Over 200 official and unofficial groups in the U.S. and abroad. Established 1986. Call: (602) 277-7991. Write: P.O. Box 33577, Phoenix, Arizona 85067.

Codependents Anonymous for Helping Professionals (CoDAHP)

International. 12-step program for professionals in human services (such as social workers) who are themselves in recovery from codependency (an inability to form and maintain healthy relationships with others and with oneself). Publishes quarterly newsletter, group development guidelines. Over 20 affiliated groups. Established 1985. Call: (602) 468-1149. Write: P.O. Box 42253, Mesa, Arizona 85274.

Love-N-Addiction

International. Support for women suffering from "romantic obsessions," addictive love affairs. Seeks to help women build a support network that will help them recover from addictive love, learn to have healthy, nonaddictive, nonobsessive relationships. Uses ideas from Robin Norwood, *Women Who Love Too Much*. Offers chapter development guidelines. Over 30 chapters. Established 1986. Call: (203) 423-2344. Write: Carolyn Meister, P.O. Box 759, Willimantic, Connecticut 06226.

Support Group for People Who Love Too Much

Model. For men and women in codependent relationships (who are unable to form and maintain healthy relationships with others). Discussion groups lasting six weeks, telephone networking, other opportunities to exchange support. Theoretical basis for group is Robin Norwood's *Women Who Love Too Much*. Call: Laurieann Chutis, (312) 878-4300, x1455. Write: Ravenswood CMHC, 455 N. Winchester Avenue, Chicago, Illinois 60640.

COLITIS

See "Inflammatory Bowel Disease."

COLORECTAL CANCER

IMPACC (Intestinal Multiple Polyposis and Colorectal Cancer)

Model. For people with intestinal multiple polyposis (a condition characterized by numerous polyps on the colon) or colorectal cancer. Discussion groups, telephone networking, other opportunities to exchange peer support, information. Publishes quarterly newsletter. Established 1986. Call: (301) 791-

7526. Write: Dolores Boone, 1008-101 Brinker Drive, Hagerstown, Maryland 21740.

COLOSTOMY

See "Ostomy."

COMA

Coma Recovery Association _____
National. Support for families of coma victims and advocacy on their behalf. Services include information, referrals, socialization programs for recovering coma victims. Publishes quarterly newsletter. 3 chapters. Established 1980. Call: (516) 486-2847. Write: 377 Jerusalem Avenue, Hempstead, New York 11550.

COOLEY'S ANEMIA (THALASSEMIA)

Cooley's Anemia Foundation _____
National. For families in which a member has Cooley's anemia (thalassemia major or homozygous beta thalassemia), a hereditary form of anemia, in which the bone marrow does not produce enough hemoglobin. If untreated, death may result as early as age three. Facilitates creation of networks to connect members. Seeks to educate general public about Cooley's anemia. Fund-raises on behalf of research. Administers discussion groups—called Thalassemia Action Groups (TAGs)—for young adults with the disease. Conducts annual seminars. Provides medical hardware and drugs to people with Cooley's anemia. Publishes newsletter and chapter development guidelines. Approximately 30 chapters. Established

1957. Call: (212) 598-0911 or (800) 221-3571. Write: 105 East 22nd Street, Suite 911, New York, New York 10010.

CORNELIA DE LANGE SYNDROME

(See also "Mental Retardation.')

Cornelia de Lange Syndrome Foundation, Inc. _____
National. For families who have a child with Cornelia de Lange syndrome, a rare birth defect that results in mental retardation, distinctive physical characteristics, delayed psychomotor development and gastrointestinal problems. Network of regional coordinators provides system for exchange of support, information. Supports research into and seeks to increase public awareness about the syndrome. Publishes bimonthly newsletter, *Reaching Out.* Sponsors annual convention. Over 3,400 members; founded 1981. Call: In Connecticut: (203) 693-0159; elsewhere: (800) 753-CDLS or (800) 223-8355; fax: (203) 693-8355. Write: 60 Dyer Avenue, Collinsville, Connecticut 06022.

CRIME VICTIMS

National Organization for Victim Assistance _____
Provides support for crime victims, pursues advocacy efforts on their behalf. Publishes newsletter, provides information and referrals, sponsors conferences, provides guidelines for developing new groups. Established 1975. Call: (202) 232-6682; fax: (202) 877-3355. Write: 1757 Park Road, N.W., Washington, D.C. 20010.

National Victim Center

For crime victims. Provides information and resources to help deal with the trauma of being victimized. Encourages victims to form self-help groups and provides them with advice and guidelines on how to do so; also refers victims to existing groups. Publishes quarterly newsletter. Sponsors conferences. Established 1986. Call: (817) 877-3355. Write: 307 West Seventh Street, Suite 705, Fort Worth, Texas 76102.

CRIMINALS

Forensic Committee of N.A.M.I. (National Alliance for the Mentally Ill)

National. Advocacy for mentally ill persons in prison or the court system and support for their families and friends. Publishes quarterly newsletter. Coordinators in 38 states. Established 1984. Call: (606) 887-2851. Write: Sue Dickinson, 2101 Wilson Boulevard, Arlington, Virginia 22201.

Fortune Society

Model. For ex-offenders who wish to "break out of the destructive cycle of crime and incarceration." Also seeks to help young people avoid committing crimes. Activities and services include support groups, counseling, tutoring, job placement and advocacy on behalf of members in the court system. Counselors are themselves ex-offenders. Group development assistance available. Established 1967. Call: (212) 206-7070. Write: 39 West 19th Street, New York, New York 10011.

Kleptomaniacs/Shoplifters Anonymous

Model. For people who want to stop compulsive stealing. Modified 12-step program.

At support group meetings held in New York, members exchange information, strategies and tips on how to overcome their addiction to stealing. Call: Michele Gitlin, (212) 724-4067. Write: 114 West 70th Street, New York, New York 10023.

Shoplifters Anonymous

Model. For people who want to recover from an addiction to shoplifting. 12-step program. Group development assistance available. Established 1980. Call: (612) 925-4860. Write: P.O. Box 24515, Minneapolis, Minnesota 55424.

CROHNS DISEASE

See "Inflammatory Bowel Disease."

CROSSDRESSING

See "Transvestites."

CULTS

Cult Awareness Network (CAN)

National. For former members—and their families and friends—of "destructive" cults. CAN includes among this group the Unification Church and the Church of Scientology. By "destructive cult," CAN means a "closed system whose followers have been unethically and deceptively recruited through the use of manipulative techniques of thought reform or mind control. The system is imposed without the informed consent of the recruit and is designed to alter personality and behavior." Discussion groups, telephone networking, other opportunities to exchange support, information. Retains legal and social service professionals. Publishes newsletter, group development guidelines. Over 25 affiliated groups. CAN is affiliated with similar organizations throughout the world, including Denmark, England, France, Germany, Spain, Israel, Australia and Canada. Established 1979. Call: (312) 267-7777. Write: 2421 West Pratt Boulevard, Suite 1173, Chicago, Illinois 60645.

Focus

National. For people formerly associated with "high-demand," "cultic," "totalistic" groups, such as the Unification Church, the Church of Scientology, Children of God, est (Forum), Rajneesh, Jehovah's Witnesses and so on, that "systematically employ manipulative techniques of persuasion." Fosters networking among members by telephone, discussion groups, conferences and correspondence in order to exchange support, referrals. Seeks to help members readjust to life outside cults. Publishes newsletter. Affiliated with Cult Awareness Network (CAN) (see entry). Established 1982. Call: (312) 267-7777. Write: 2421 West Pratt Boulevard, Suite 1173, Chicago, Illinois 60645.

CYSTIC FIBROSIS

Parents of Children with Cystic Fibrosis

Model. For people with cystic fibrosis, a congenital metabolic disorder usually appearing in childhood that is characterized by a variety of symptoms, including respiratory problems. Also for their families and friends and interested professionals. Discussion groups, other networking opportunities, support, information. Call: Leona Zarin, M.S.W. (908) 870-5216, or Phyllis Wolff (908) 870-5211. Write:

Phyllis Wolff, 307 Third Avenue, Long Branch, New Jersey 07740.

DEAFNESS/HEARING IMPAIRMENT

(See also "Cochlear Implant," "Ear Anomalies," "Usher's Syndrome.")

American Society for Deaf Children

National. For deaf and hard-of-hearing children and their families. Discussion groups, telephone networking for exchange of support, information. Publishes quarterly newsletter. Over 120 affiliates. Established 1967. Call: (800) 942-ASDC (voice and TDD). Write: 814 Thayer Avenue, Silver Spring, Maryland 20007.

American Tinnitus Association

National. For people who suffer from tinnitus (noises, such as ringing or whistling, in the ears); also for their families and friends and interested professionals. Discussion groups, telephone networking, clinics, other opportunities for exchange of support and information. Supports research into causes, treatments and cures. Publishes quarterly newsletter, *Tinnitus Today,* and self-help group development guidelines. Approximately 110 groups. Established 1971. Call: (503) 248-9985; fax: (503) 248-9076, extension 329. Write: P.O. Box 5, Portland, Oregon 97207.

Association of Late-Deafened Adults (ALDA)

National. For people who became deaf later in childhood, "after the development of speech and language." Discussion groups, telephone networking, social events, annual convention, other opportunities for exchange of support, information. Publishes bimonthly newsletter. Provides referrals, assistance in developing new chapters. 15 affiliated groups. Established 1987. Call: (312) 604-4190; TDD: (312) 604-4192. Write: P.O. Box 641763, Chicago, Illinois 60664.

Children of Deaf Adults (C.O.D.A.)

International. For hearing children of deaf adults. Discussion groups, social events, local retreats, annual conferences, other opportunities to exchange support, information. Advocacy on behalf of membership. Publishes newsletter, conference proceedings, various resource materials. Established 1983. Call: (805) 682-0997. Write: P.O. Box 30715, Santa Barbara, California 93130.

International Parent's Organization of the Alexander Graham Bell Organization for the Deaf

For parents of deaf children. Discussion groups, telephone networking, conferences, other opportunities for exchange of information and support. National organization represents interests and concerns of membership in public education, advocacy, other efforts and serves as information clearinghouse. Publishes newsletter, group development guidelines. 29 affiliated groups. Established 1958. Call: (202) 337-5220. Write: 3417 Volta Place, N.W., Washington, D.C. 20007.

National Association of the Deaf

For deaf and hard-of-hearing individuals, their families and friends and interested professionals. Provides information, referrals and training programs for membership, as well as advocacy, support and education. Administers

a junior organization for deaf youth. Publishes newsletter, magazine. 50 chapters. Established 1880. Call: (301) 587-1788; TDD: (301) 587-1789. Write: 814 Thayer Avenue, Silver Spring, Maryland 20910.

National Fraternal Society of the Deaf

For deaf and hearing-impaired people, their families and friends and professionals. Provides information, referrals and a variety of special services, including low-cost life insurance, scholarships. Various advocacy efforts on behalf of membership. Chapters in U.S. and Canada. Established 1901. Call: (800) 676-NFSD (voice or TDD) or (708) 392-9282. Write: 1300 West Northwest Highway, Mount Prospect, Illinois 60056.

Self-Help for Hard-of-Hearing People, Inc. (S.H.H.H.)

International. For hard-of-hearing people who wish to participate successfully in society; also for their families and friends. Advocates for improved services, research. Seeks to promote public awareness. Publishes bimonthly newsletter, monthly magazine, as well as books, pamphlets, reports, video- and audiotapes. Sponsors annual convention, outreach and other programs, workshops. Provides special support and guidance for parents of children with hearing loss. Acts as liaison with other organizations and institutions in the hearing-loss field. Over 250 chapters. Established 1979. Call: (301) 657-2248; TDD: (301) 657-2249. Write: 7800 Wisconsin Avenue, Bethesda, Maryland 20814.

DEBT, OVERSPENDING

Debtors Anonymous

International. For people who wish to stop using any form of unsecured credit. 12-step program. Support through discussion groups and telephone networking. Publishes newsletter. Approximately 375 groups internationally. Established 1976. Call: To hear recorded message or leave message: (212) 642-8222. Write: P.O. Box 400, Grand Central Station, New York, New York 10163.

DERMATOMYOSITIS

National Support Group for Polymyositis/ Dermatomyositis —————————

For people with dermatomyositis and polymyositis, two related degenerative, inflammatory diseases of certain muscles and skin; also for families and friends of sufferers. Discussion groups, pen-pal programs, telephone networking, other opportunities for exchange of support, information. Publishes newsletter. Call: (704) 456-8207. Write: Route 3, Box 80, Clyde, North Carolina 28721.

DES

DES-Action/USA ——————————

National. For women who took the drug DES (diethylstilbestrol), a synthetic estrogen given to pregnant women from 1941 to 1971 that, as a side effect, caused reproductive abnormalities in female children as well as various medical problems in children of both sexes. Support groups, medical and legal referrals to victims, outreach to health care professionals. Publishes quarterly newsletter. Over 40 groups. Established 1978. Call: (510) 465-4011. Write: 1615 Broadway, Suite 510, Oakland, California 94612.

DEVELOPMENTAL DISABILITIES

People First International ——————

For people with developmental disabilities, a category of emotional, physical or other handicaps appearing in infancy or childhood that cause delay in normal development. Through various activities, provides support for and advocacy on behalf of membership. Assists in establishing new chapters. Publishes newsletter. Established 1977. Call: (503) 362-0336. Write: P.O. Box 12362, Salem, Oregon 97309.

Speaking for Ourselves ——————

Model. For people with developmental disabilities (emotional, physical or other handicaps appearing in infancy or childhood that cause delay in normal development). Provides support for and advocacy on behalf of membership. Goals for members include problem resolution and leadership skills, and development of self confidence. Advocates for public policy changes. 6 affiliated groups. Established 1982. Call: (215) 825-4592. Write: 1 Plymouth Meeting, Suite 530, Plymouth Meeting, Pennsylvania 19462.

DIABETES

American Diabetes Association ——————

National. For people with diabetes, their families and friends. Support, information, advocacy, public education through a variety of activities. Publishes monthly magazine. 54 state affiliates, 800 chapters. Established 1941. Call: (800) 232-3472. Write: 1660 Duke Street, Alexandria, Virginia 22314.

Juvenile
Diabetes Foundation _____

National. For people with diabetes, their families and friends and interested professionals. Operates education programs aimed at the health care community and the general public. Raises funds to support diabetes research to find better treatments and a cure. Provides referrals. Members exchange support, information. Publishes quarterly magazine with latest information on diabetes research and treatment. 115 chapters. Established 1970. Call: (800) JDF-CURE or (212) 889-7575. Write: 432 Park Avenue South, New York, New York 10016.

DISABILITY

American Society of
Handicapped Physicians _____

National. For handicapped people in the health care profession. Discussion groups, telephone networking, other opportunities to exchange support and information, especially about job opportunities. Advocates increased employment opportunities for disabled health care workers. Publishes quarterly newsletter. Established 1981. Call: Will Lambert, (318) 281-4436. Write: 105 Morris Drive, Bastrop, Louisiana 71220.

Catholics United for Spiritual Action
(C.U.S.A.) _____

National. For persons of all faiths who are handicapped or chronically ill. Members exchange mutual support and form networks by means of "group letters," letters circulated seriatim among the members of eight-member subgroups. Emphasis is on spiritual values.

Interested parties are requested to contact C.U.S.A. by mail rather than by phone. Publishes semiannual magazine, written and edited by C.U.S.A. members. Established 1947. Call: (201) 437-0412. Write: 176 West 8th Street, Bayonne, New Jersey 07002.

Disabled Journalists
of America _____

National. Established 1988. For disabled writers in the communications industry, including print and broadcast journalism, public relations and advertising. Members exchange support, information—especially about employment—through a variety of activities. Established 1988. Call: (404) 228-6491. Write: 484 Hammond Drive, Griffin, Georgia 30223.

National Council on
Independent Living _____

For physically disabled people who wish to live as independently as possible. Maintains "independent living centers" that provide a variety of services, including technical, referrals and advocacy, for members. Sponsors conferences. Publishes newsletter. Nearly 100 affiliated centers. Established 1982. Call: (415) 849-1243. Write: 2539 Telegraph Avenue, Berkeley, California 94704.

Siblings for
Significant Change _____

National. For siblings of people with a wide variety of disabilities and illnesses, such as cancer or mental retardation, or who have been victims, as of incest. Helps members serve as caregivers to their disabled siblings. Fosters networks between members with similarly disabled siblings, to facilitate exchange of support, information. Publishes newsletter, group development guidelines. Sponsors monthly, quarterly meetings. 3 chapters. Established 1981. Call: (212) 420-0776. Write: Gerri Zatlow, 105 East 22nd Street, Room 710, New York, New York 10010.

DISORDERED LIFESTYLE

Messies Anonymous _____
National. For "disorganized homemakers." Discussion groups, telephone networking, other opportunities to exchange information on improving members' control over their homes and lives by improving their self-esteem, among other things. Available from Messies Anonymous: organization products, quarterly newsletter, and books, including *The Messies Manual, Messy No More* and *Meditations For Messies*. Approximately 20 groups. Established 1981. Call: (305) 271-8404. Write: 5025 S.W. 114th Avenue, Miami, Florida 33165.

DIVORCE

See "Separation, Divorce, Custody."

DOWN SYNDROME

National Down Syndrome Congress _____
For families in which there is a member with Down syndrome, a congenital illness marked by mental deficiency and a variety of physiological characteristics. Discussion groups, telephone networking, pen-pal program for exchange of support, information. Promotes research into and public awareness about Down syndrome. Various advocacy efforts on behalf of membership. National office serves as a clearinghouse for information and an umbrella for regional and local groups. Publishes chapter development guidelines, newsletter, 10 issues per year. 500 chapters. Established 1974. Call: (800) 232-NDSC or (708) 823-7550. Write: 1800 Dempster Street, Park Ridge, Illinois 60068.

DPT VACCINE VICTIMS

Dissatisfied Parents Together (D.P.T.) _____
National. For parents of children who suffered adverse side effects—including medication-resistant seizure disorders, mental retardation, physical handicaps, learning disability, other chronic illnesses or death—from a routine vaccination with DPT (diphtheria, pertussis, tetanus) vaccine, caused by the pertussis (whooping cough) portion of the vaccine, or from other vaccines, including MMR (measles, mumps, rubella) or OPV (oral polio). Telephone networking, other opportunities for support, exchange of information. Lobbies for reform in large-scale vaccination programs. 10 chapters. Established 1982. Call: (703) 938-DPT3. Write: 204-F Mill Street, Vienna, Virginia 22180.

DRUNKEN-DRIVING VICTIMS

M.A.D.D. (Mothers Against Drunk Driving) _____
National. For victims of drunken-driving accidents, their families and friends. Promotes

public awareness and prevention of drunken driving, emphasizing that it is a serious crime, insisting offenders be held accountable for their acts. Advocates tougher anti-drunken-driving laws, public policies, sentences. Publishes newsletters and victim assistance brochures providing guidelines for developing new chapters. More than 400 chapters. Established 1980. Call: (214) 744-6233. Write: 511 East John Carpenter Freeway, Irving, Texas 75062.

R.I.D. (Remove Intoxicated Drivers)

National. Promotes public awareness of the problem of drunken driving, lobbies for tougher laws and sentences for offenders. Aids victims of drunken drivers. Activities include discussion groups, telephone networking, hospital and home visitations. Maintains speakers bureau, library of video- and audiotapes. Sponsors conferences and public education programs. Publishes quarterly newsletter, brochures, group development guidelines. Send self-addressed stamped envelope for descriptive pamphlet. Over 150 chapters in 41 states. Established 1978. Call: (518) 372-0034; fax: (518) 370-4917. Write: Doris Aiken, P.O. Box 520, Schenectady, New York 12301.

Students Against Driving Drunk (S.A.D.D.)

International. (U.S.A., Canada, Europe, New Zealand and Australia). For all people—including students, parents, educators—interested in solving the problems of students driving drunk. Discussion groups for students; educational outreach programs. Speakers' bureau. Publishes newsletter, group development guidelines. 16,000 groups. Established 1982. Call: (508) 481-3568; fax: (508) 481-5759. Write: P.O. Box 800, Marlboro, Massachusetts 01752.

DYSAUTONOMIA

Dysautonomia Foundation, Inc.

International. For people who suffer from familial dysautonomia, a genetic disease common in Jewish babies, primarily causing dysfunction of the nervous system; also for their families and friends. Maintains the Dysautonomia Treatment and Evaluation Center in New York and Jerusalem. Funds research. Provides information to members and interested professionals. Facilitates creation of networks among membership for exchange of information and support. 16 chapters. Established 1951. Call: (212) 949-6644. Write: 20 East 46th Street, Room #302, New York, New York 10017.

DYSLEXIA

See "Learning Disabilities."

DYSMOTILITY

Chronic Dysmotility Support Group

National. For people who suffer from chronic dysmotility, a loss of the motility (movement) in the function of the gastrointestinal tract, resulting in, among other problems, an inability to have normal bowel movements; also for their families and friends. Networking by phone and mail to exchange information, peer support. Call: (609) 829-0377. Write: Sandra Domask, 114 West 4th Street, Palmyra, New Jersey 08065.

DYSTONIA

Dystonia Medical Research Foundation (U.S.A.)

International. For people who suffer from dystonia, a neurological disorder characterized by powerful, involuntary muscle spasms that cause repetitive movements, twisting and abnormal postures; also for their families and friends. Fund-raises for research. Sponsors educational outreach efforts, especially to health care providers, and conferences. Provides referrals. Discussion groups, telephone networking, other opportunities for exchange of peer support and information. Established 1976. Call: (312) 755-0918. Write: 1 East Wacker Drive, Suite 2900, Chicago, Illinois 60601.

DYSTROPHIC EPIDERMOLYSIS BULLOSA

Dystrophic Epidermolysis Bullosa Research Association (D.E.B.R.A.)

National. For people with epidermolysis bullosa, a genetic, progressive and sometimes lethal skin disease; also for their families and friends and interested professionals. Telephone networking for exchange of support among members. Telephone referrals and information from national office. Fund-raises for research into a cure for the disease. Mounts public information efforts. Publishes newsletter. Established 1980. Call: Miriam Feder (212) 995-2220. Write: 141 Fifth Avenue, Suite 7-S, New York, New York 10010.

EAR ANOMALIES

(See also "Deafness-Hearing Impairment.")

Ear Anomalies Reconstructed (EAR): Atresia/Microtia Support Group

International. For people who suffer from ear deformities. Provides telephone networking, visitations to homes and hospitals, conferences. Established 1986. 3 affiliated groups. Call: Betsy Old, (201) 761-5438 or Jack Gross, (212) 947-0770. Write: Betsy Old, 72 Durant Road, Maplewood, New Jersey 07040.

EATING DISORDERS

(See also "Overweight, Overeating.")

American Anorexia/Bulimia Association, Inc.

National. For people who suffer from anorexia nervosa (an abnormal psychological condition marked by a lack of appetite, usually caused by a pathological fear of weight gain) and bulimia (an abnormal, chronic desire to eat) and for their families, friends and interested professionals. Groups are run by members who are professionals, or by recovered members or family members. Activities include support group meetings, conferences, various education programs. Provides information, referrals. Publishes quarterly newsletter and group development guidelines. Administers speakers' bureau. Approximately 12 affiliated groups. Established 1978. Call: (212) 734-1114. Write: 418 East 76th Street, New York, New York 10021.

Anorexia Nervosa and Related Eating Disorders (ANRED)

International. For people who suffer from anorexia nervosa (an abnormal psychological condition marked by a lack of appetite, usually caused by a pathological fear of weight gain) and bulimia (an abnormal, chronic desire to eat) and for their families, friends and interested professionals. Provides support groups for people recovering from anorexia and bulimia and other eating disorders. Disseminates information about these problems among professionals and the general public. Conducts public education presentations at schools, civic and professional organizations. Publishes newsletter, pamphlets, brochures and resource materials. Established 1979. Call: (503) 344-1144. Write: Dr. J. Bradley Rubel, P.O. Box 5102, Eugene, Oregon 97405.

National Association of Anorexia Nervosa & Associated Disorders (A.N.A.D.)

For people who suffer from anorexia nervosa (an abnormal psychological condition marked by a lack of appetite, usually caused by a pathological fear of weight gain) and bulimia (an abnormal, chronic desire to eat) and for their families, friends and interested professionals. Provides information, including information about support groups, and referrals to professionals. Support groups are led by members assisted by professionals. Publishes newsletter. Over 200 affiliated groups. Established 1976. Call: (708) 831-3438. Write: P.O. Box 7, Highland Park, Illinois 60035.

ECTODERMAL DYSPLASIAS

National Foundation for Ectodermal Dysplasias

For people who suffer from ectodermal dysplasia, a genetic disease characterized by abnormalities of two or more ectodermal structures, such as skin, hair, nails, teeth, nerve cells, and for their families and friends. Discussion groups, family conferences, telephone networking, other activities for exchange of peer support, information. Maintains directory of member families to facilitate informal networking. Disseminates information. Members often participate in research projects. Publishes monthly newsletter. Established 1981. Call: (618) 566-2020. Write: Mary Kaye Richter, 219 East Main Street, Box 114, Mascoutah, Illinois 62258.

EHLERS-DANLOS SYNDROME

Ehlers-Danlos National Foundation

For people who suffer from Ehlers-Danlos syndrome, a hereditary connective tissue disorder. Seeks to provide updated information and support to sufferers. Provides physician referrals; maintains a computerized database that allows members to communicate with one another; publishes a quarterly newsletter. Sponsors annual conferences. Serves as an information link to and from the medical community. Established 1985. Call: (313) 282-0180; fax: (313) 282-2793. Write: Nancy Rogowski, P.O. Box 1212, Southgate, Michigan 48195.

EMPHYSEMA

(See also "Lung Disease.")

Emphysema Anonymous

National. For people with emphysema, a lung disease marked by progressive loss of tissue elasticity and characterized by labored breathing, a husky cough and frequently by impairment of heart action. Also for other respiratory disorders, such as asthma. Not a 12-step program. Publishes bimonthly newsletter, *Batting the Breeze*. Established 1965. Call: (813) 391-

9977. Write: William E. Jaeckle, Director, P.O. Box 3224, Seminole, Florida 34642.

EMPLOYMENT

Employment Support Center _____

Model. For the unemployed, underemployed and those in job transition. Provides weekly self-help support groups, networking programs, employment workshops, fund-raising, speakers' bureau, clearinghouse of employment materials and an extensive "Job Bank." Trains leaders for and provides technical assistance for self-help support groups. Promotes and assists in the creation of similar such groups in other cities. Publishes a variety of materials, including *The Self-Help Bridge to Employment,* a group development guidelines manual; a portfolio of publicity and program materials. Established 1984. Call: (202) 783-4747; (703) 790-1469. Write: Ellie Wegener, 900 Massachusetts Avenue, N.W., Room 444, Washington, D.C. 20001.

Extra Effort (X.E.) _____

Model. For persons who gain satisfaction working 50 or more hours per week, but don't want to be perceived as workaholics. Call: (316) 263-0371. Write: Hugh Riordan, Box 47494, Wichita, Kansas 67201.

Forty Plus of New York _____

New York chapter of national chain of organizations. For unemployed executives, managers and professionals, 40 years old and above whose previous salary level was at least $40,000. Provides career counseling and training in all aspects of job search, including resume preparation, PC skills, networking, interviewing. Publishes newsletter, brochures. Established 1939. Call: (212) 233-6086. Write: 15 Park Row, New York, New York 10038.

Forty Plus of Philadelphia _____

Philadelphia chapter of national chain of organizations. For managers, executives and professionals currently unemployed who pool their time and effort to find jobs. Members are 40 years of age and older and have earned $30,000 or more annually. Discussion groups, other networking opportunities for exchange of information. Established 1939. Call: (215) 923-2074. Write: 1218 Chestnut Street, Philadelphia, Pennsylvania 19107.

Job Transition Support Group _____

Model. For people between jobs, new graduates seeking jobs and those changing careers. Activities include weekly meetings year-round, small discussion groups, focus group workshops, biweekly speakers panels. Provides support, information and materials. Established 1977. Call: (612) 925-2711. Write: Joe Oliver, 6200 Colonial Way, Edina, Minnesota 55436.

National Federation of Business & Professional Women _____

Oldest and largest organization of working women. Seeks to improve status of working women. Activities include lobbying efforts. Publishes quarterly magazine and other periodical items. Maintains resource center. Holds annual convention. 3,000 chapters. Established 1919. Call: (202) 293-1100. Write: 2012 Massachusetts Avenue, N.W., Washington, D.C. 20036.

W.A.J.E. (Women's Alliance for Job Equality) _____

Model. Membership organization for women in western Pennsylvania interested in improving their working conditions. Workshops on topics including legal rights on the job, pay equity, sexual harrassment prevention and career development. These and other activities provide opportunities for exchange of peer support for victims of unfair and illegal work conditions. Publishes bimonthly newsletter. Established 1979. Call: (215) 561-1873; fax: (215) 561-7112. Write: 1422 Chestnut Street, Suite 1100, Philadelphia, Pennsylvania 19102.

Women Employed

National. Sponsors advocacy and education efforts to promote economic equity for women. Offers career development services and networking procedures and opportunities, including conferences. Established 1973. Call: (312) 782-3902. Write: 22 West Monroe Street, Suite 1400, Chicago, Illinois 60603.

ENDOMETRIOSIS

U.S.-Canadian Endometriosis Association

International. For women with endometriosis, a painful condition in which tissue from the endometrium (lining of the uterus) appears outside the uterus, commonly on the ovaries or Fallopian tubes. The disorder affects 5 million American women. Provides support, education and assistance to members, their families and friends. Publishes a variety of literature, including a newsletter on the disease and information on current research. 26 chapters. Established 1980. Call: (800) 992-ENDO or (414) 355-2200. Write: 8585 North 76th Place, Milwaukee, Wisconsin 53223.

ENVIRONMENTAL ISSUES

Citizen's Clearinghouse for Hazardous Wastes

National. For people affected by toxic waste, including those who own homes in an area polluted by local industry. Provides members with information and referrals and opportunities for networking. Assists in organization of discussion groups, in which people can exchange support, information. Publishes newsletter. Sponsors conferences. Established 1981. Call: (703) 237-2249. Write: P.O. Box 6806, Falls Church, Virginia 22040.

H.E.A.L. (Human Ecology Action League, Inc.)

International. Serves those whose health has been adversely affected by chemicals in the environment. Provides information to those who are concerned about the health effects of chemicals and alerts general public about their potential dangers. Publishes *The Human Ecologist* quarterly. Distributes resource lists, reading lists, fact sheets, travel guides and an index of back issues and articles. Over 60 chapters. Established 1977. Call: (404) 248-1898; fax: (404) 248-0162. Write: P.O. Box 49126, Atlanta, Georgia 30359.

EPILEPSY

Epilepsy Foundation of America

National. For people with epilepsy (an estimated 2 million Americans), an episodic disorder resulting from temporary brain dysfunction that produces convulsive or non-convulsive seizures. Also for families and friends of people with epilepsy. Kit for developing new affiliated chapters available. Publishes a newsletter. Provides information and support and makes referrals to local affiliates, which often can advise members on employment problems and opportunities. Pharmaceutical program. Fund-raises for research. Maintains National Epilepsy Library, the largest cross-disciplinary collection of epilepsy-related materials in the world. Provides legal advocacy on behalf of people with epilepsy. Educates health care workers. Approximately 90 affiliates. Established 1967. Call: (301) 459-3700. Write: 4351 Garden City Drive, Landover, Maryland 20785.

FACIAL DISFIGUREMENT

AboutFace

International. For facially disfigured people and their families and friends. Discussion groups, other means for exchange of peer support, information. Sponsors various public education efforts. Helps start new chapters. Publishes newsletter. Approximately 40 affiliated groups. Established 1985. Call: (416) 944-FACE. Write: 99 Crowns Lane, Third Floor, Toronto, Ontario, Canada M5R 3P4.

Faces

National. For children and adults through the United States who have severe craniofacial (both face and skull) disfigurements as a result of birth, accident or disease. Assists members with travel expenses to go to major medical centers for surgery evaluation and facial reconstruction. Provides information and referrals by phone. Mounts advocacy efforts in social, medical and political communities. Promotes networking and support systems among families who share craniofacial problems. Publishes newsletter, brochure. Established 1969. Call: (800) 332-2373. Write: Carolyn Keesey P.O. Box 11082, Chattanooga, Tennessee 37401.

Forward Face

Model. For people with craniofacial (both face and skull) disfigurement, their families and friends, with a special group for adoles-

cents. Provides information, referrals, telephone networking, other opportunities to exchange peer support, information. Acts as liaison between members and medical and educational communities. Publishes newsletter, videotapes. Established 1978. Call: Patricia Chibbaro, (212) 263-5205 or (800) 422-FACE. Write: 560 First Avenue, New York, New York 10016.

National Foundation for Facial Reconstruction

For children and other people with facial disfigurements as a result of birth defects, accidents and illness, and for their families. Helps provide facilities for the treatment and assistance of individuals unable to afford private reconstructive surgical care; assists in the training and education of personnel for reconstructive plastic surgery; promotes research in this field; educates the public about facial disfigurement. Publishes semiannual newsletter. Established 1951. Call: (800) 422-FACE or (212) 263-6656. Write: Arlyn S. Gardner, 317 East 34th Street, New York, New York 10016.

FANCONI'S ANEMIA

Fanconi Anemia Support Group

National. For families whose child or children have Fanconi anemia, a rare, inherited disorder marked by progressive bone marrow failure (aplastic anemia). Activities include annual "Family Meeting," telephone and letter networking among members for exchange of support, information. Family members raise funds to support medical research. Publishes a semiannual newsletter and has produced a fundraising brochure and film. Established 1985. Call: (503) 687-4658; fax: (503) 484-0892.

Write: Linda Solin, 66 Club Road, Suite 390, Eugene, Oregon 97401.

FARM FAMILIES

American Farm Family Foundation ⎯⎯⎯⎯⎯
National. For farm and ranch families. Primarily an information clearinghouse and referral service, helps people deal with life problems related to the American agriculture and animal husbandry industries, especially downturns in those industries. Provides referrals to services—including support groups—in its directory, *The National Rural Crisis Response Center Directory*. Call: (202) 547-6767. Write: 100 Maryland Avenue, N.E. Suite 500, Box 65, Washington, D.C. 20002.

Farmers Assistance, Counseling, & Training Service (F.A.C.T.S.) ⎯⎯⎯⎯⎯
Model, acting in state of Kansas only. For farmers, ranchers and their families. Clearinghouse, referral service for farm family support groups. Group development guidelines, materials and advice available. Write: Nine Leasure Hall, Kansas State University, Manhattan, Kansas 66506.

Farm Resource Center ⎯⎯⎯⎯⎯
Model. Services state of Illinois. For individuals and families in the farming industry. Provides information and referrals to social work, clergy and other sources who help members deal with various problems, including financial and marital difficulties, alcoholism, drug abuse and suicide. Call: (800) 851-4719. Write: 206 West 5th Street, Metropolis, Illinois 62960.

FETAL ALCOHOL SYNDROME

Fetal Alcohol Network ⎯⎯⎯⎯⎯
International. For parents of persons with fetal alcohol syndrome, a pattern of birth defects affecting the offspring of chronic alcoholics, including growth deficiency, physical defects and mental retardation; also for family members and friends. Promotes public awareness of the dangers of drinking alcohol during pregnancy. Helps members to access appropriate community services, such as alcoholism treatment. Assists in establishing new chapters. Publishes newsletter. Established 1990. Call: (215) 384-1133. Write: 158 Rosemont Avenue, Coatesville, Pennsylvania 19320.

FIRE/EMERGENCY WORKERS: SPOUSES

ASSIST ⎯⎯⎯⎯⎯
National. For spouses of fire fighters and other emergency-related occupations, such as emergency medicine. Aims to help members deal with a spouse's job stress as it affects the entire family. Discussion groups, telephone networking, conferences, other opportunities to exchange support, information. Publishes newsletter, group development guidelines. 35 groups. Established 1983. Call: (717) 741-5704. Write: 2200 South George Street, York, Pennsylvania 17403.

5P- SYNDROME

5P- Society ⎯⎯⎯⎯⎯
For families in which a child has 5P- syndrome, also known as "Cri du chat" syn-

drome, an inherited condition marked by a mewing cry, mental retardation, physical anomalies and the absence of part of a chromosome; also for their families and friends and interested professionals. Discussion groups and other networking opportunities for exchange of support, information. Maintains list of families in U.S. and Canada with children with 5P- syndrome. Publishes newsletter. Organizes annual convention. Call: (913) 469-8900. Write: 11609 Oakmont, Overland Park, Kansas 66210.

GAMBLING

Gam-Anon Family Groups _____
International. For families and friends of compulsive gamblers who find their lives adversely affected by that gambling. Publishes newsletter, group development guidelines. Sponsors "Gam-a-Teen" groups for teenage members. Nearly 400 groups. Established 1960. Call: (718) 352-1671 Tuesday and Thursday, 9–11 A.M. EST. Write: P.O. Box 157, Whitestone, New York 11357.

GAUCHER'S DISEASE

National
Gaucher Foundation _____
For people with Gaucher's disease, the most common genetic disease among Jews. It is characterized by the enlargement of the spleen or liver, abdominal distension, anemia, easy bruising and bleeding, bone pain and fractures. Telephone networking, other opportunities to exchange peer support. Seeks to increase public awareness about the disease. Publishes bimonthly newsletter. Established

1984. Call: (800) 925-8885. Write: 19241 Montgomery Village Avenue, Suite E-21, Gaithersburg, Maryland 20879.

GAY AND LESBIAN

Dignity _____
National. For gay and lesbian Roman Catholics and their families and friends. Activities include celebration of the Roman Catholic Eucharist, various educational and advocacy efforts, social activities, AIDS ministry. Publishes quarterly newsletter. 100 chapters. Established 1969. Call: (202) 861-0017. Write: 1500 Massachusetts Avenue, N.W., #11, Washington, D.C. 20005.

Evangelicals Concerned _____
National. For gay men and lesbians and their families and friends who are Evangelical Christians and who wish to integrate their faith with their homosexuality. Publishes quarterly newsletter, *Record*. Discussion groups, including Bible study groups, for support and exchange of information. Summer and winter conferences. Approximately 25 chapters. Established 1976. Call: (212) 517-3171. Write: Ralph Blair, 311 East 72nd Street, New York, New York 10021.

Homosexuals Anonymous _____
National. Christian men and women who wish not to perform homosexual acts and who seek to change homosexual orientation. Discussion groups for support, exchange of information. Publishes newsletter, group development guidelines and self-help materials. 55 chapters. Established 1980. Call: (215) 376-1146. Write: P.O. Box 7881, Reading, Pennsylvania 19603.

Kaleidescope

Model, active in the Pioneer Valley region of Massachusetts. For older lesbians, gay men, bisexuals and their friends. Monthly meetings for exchange of support, information and various social activities. Publishes newsletter. Established 1988. Call: Corrie, (413) 525-2188 or Warren, (413) 586-4277. Write: P.O. Box 1004, Williamsburg, Massachusetts 01096.

Midwest Men's Center/Chicago

Model. Primarily for gay and bisexual men, though open to all. Various activities to allow members to exchange support, information in connection with their lifestyles, for example, "Men Nurturing Men" support and rap group. Occasional newsletter, *Men Nurturing News*. Call: (312) 878-6003. Write: P.O. Box 2547, Chicago, Illinois 60690.

National Gay & Lesbian Task Force

Advocacy and lobbying for rights of lesbians and gays. Facilitates activities of local and regional lesbian and gay groups through referrals, information, technical assistance. Seeks to educate public at large. Publishes newsletter. Established 1973. Call: (202) 332-6483; TTD (202) 332-6219; fax: (202) 332-0207. Write: 1734 14th Street, N.W., Washington, D.C. 20009.

Parents and Friends of Lesbians and Gays (PFLAG)

National. For parents and friends of lesbians and gays. Discussion groups, telephone networking, other opportunities to exchange support, information in an effort to help membership understand and support their gay and lesbian children and friends. Provides special support services in connection with the AIDS crisis. Publishes various pamphlets, in-

cluding "Why Is My Child Gay? Eleven Scientists Respond." Established 1973. Over 300 chapters; also active in Canada, overseas. Call: (800) 4-FAMILY. Write: P.O. Box 27605, Washington, D.C. 20038.

Presbyterians for Lesbian/Gay Concerns

National. "For all Presbyterians who care about the full participation of lesbians, gays, and bisexuals in the Presbyterian Church and the ministry and outreach of the church with lesbians, gays and bisexuals inside and outside the church." Sponsors regional and national conferences. Publishes monthly newsletter, educational brochures, pamphlets and videos. 20 chapters. Established 1974. Call: (908) 249-1016 days. Write: James D. Anderson, Elder, P.O. Box 38, New Brunswick, New Jersey 08903.

Review

Model. For bisexual and gay married men. Discussion groups, other opportunities to exchange support, information, discuss problem of coming to terms with sexual identity with minimal disruption to family life, and "to end isolation and have fun!" Established 1980. Call: Jerry Walters, (708) 620-6946. Write: P.O. Box 7463, Westchester, Illinois 60154.

SAGE (Senior Action in a Gay Environment)

Model. For elderly gays and lesbians. Activities include support groups (often organized by particular age groups or sex); social activities, such as dances. Publishes newsletter; information kit available. SAGE is interested in fostering the formation of similar groups outside of New York. Established 1978. Call: (212) 721-2247. Write: Arlene Kochman, 208 West 13th Street, New York, New York, 10011.

GLUTEN INTOLERANCE

Celiac Sprue Association/United States of America, Inc.

National. For people with gluten intolerance, the inability to eat gluten, one of the components of wheat flour; also for their families and friends and for interested professionals. 20 chapters. Established 1978. Call: (402) 558-0600. Write: P.O. Box 31700, Omaha, Nebraska 68131.

GLYCOGEN STORAGE DISEASE

Association for Glycogen Storage Disease

National. For families of children with any of the various glycogen storage diseases, which are characterized by the absence or deficiency of the enzymes important to the making or breaking down of glycogen, the principal carbohydrate storage material in humans and animals; also for interested professionals. Telephone networking, conferences, other opportunities to exchange support, information. Seeks to educate public about disease, promote research into its cause and treatments. Publishes newsletter. Established 1979. Call: (319) 785-6038. Write: P.O. Box 896, Durant, Iowa 52747.

GRAVES' DISEASE

National Graves' Disease Foundation

For people with Graves' disease, which is characterized by hyperthyroidism (excessive activity of the thyroid gland, causing increased metabolic rate, rapid heart rate, enlarged thyroid and high blood pressure) and protrusion of the eyeballs; also for families and friends of Graves' disease patients and interested professionals. Discussion groups, telephone networking, pen-pal program, other opportunities to exchange support, information. Provides referrals, funds research, seeks to educate general public about Graves' disease, provides assistance in developing new chapters, organizes conferences, publishes newsletter. Established 1990. Call: (904) 724-0770. Write: 320 Arlington Road, Jacksonville, Florida 32211.

GUILLAIN-BARRE SYNDROME

Guillain-Barre Syndrome Foundation International

For people who suffer from Guillain-Barre syndrome (also called acute idiopathic polyneuritis or Landry's ascending paralysis), a neurological paralytic disorder of unknown cause, characterized by an inflammation of the peripheral nerves (those outside the brain and spinal cord) and by rapid onset of weakness and often paralysis of the legs, arms, breathing muscles and face. Provides hospital and home visitation by recovered patients; other opportunities to exchange support, information. Publishes newsletter. Physician referrals. Over 120 chapters. Established 1983. Call: (215) 667-0131. Write: P.O. Box 262, Wyndewood, Pennsylvania 19096.

HAZARDOUS WASTES

See "Environmental Issues."

HEAD INJURY

National Head Injury Foundation

Members include survivors of head injuries, their families and interested professionals. Provides information and referrals through an 800 telephone help line that also links callers with the "Family Resource Network" for exchange of support, mutual aid. Involved in public education and advocacy efforts. Publishes *National Directory of Head Injury Rehabilitation Services*. 45 chapters; over 400 support groups. Established 1980. Call: (202) 296-6443; fax: (202) 296-8850; (800) 444-6443 (for people with head injury only). Write: 1776 Massachusetts Avenue, N.W., Suite 100, Washington, D.C. 20036.

HEART DISEASE

(See also "High Blood Pressure.")

Coronary Club, Inc.

National. For people with heart disease, including those who have undergone or are facing surgery. Educates members and their families and friends on cardiac health and rehabilitation after surgery. Facilitates networking among members, referrals to parties outside the group. Approximately 20 chapters. Established 1968. Call: (216) 444-3690. Write: 9500 Euclid Avenue, Cleveland, Ohio 44106.

Mended Hearts

National. Members provide encouragement to heart disease patients and their families and friends. Publishes quarterly newsletter; chapter development kit available. Over 200 chapters. Established 1951. Call: (214) 706-1442. Write: 7320 Greenville Avenue, Dallas, Texas 75231.

HEMOPHILIA

See "Blood Disease."

HEPATITIS

(See also "Liver Disease.")

American Hepatitis Foundation

National. For people with hepatitis, a family of diseases marked by inflammation of the liver, and for their families and friends. Discussion groups, other opportunities for exchange of support and information. Provides referrals, sponsors education programs aimed at professionals and general public, promotes research. Services include speakers' bureau. Publishes newsletter. 5 affiliated groups. Established 1982. Call: (212) 891-4066. Write: 30 East 40th Street, New York, New York 10016.

HERPES

Herpes Resource Center

National. Provides self-help, mutual-aid support for people with herpes, any of several inflammatory virus diseases of the skin characterized by clusters of blisters; the most common is herpes simplex. Operates national hotline, which offers support, information and referrals. Also, for families and friends of herpes sufferers. Publishes quarterly newsletter, *The*

Helper. Helps develop local self-help support groups. 90 chapters. Established 1979. Call: (919) 361-2120; hotline: (800) 361-8488 (9 A.M.–7 P.M. Eastern time); fax: (919) 361-8425. Write: P.O. Box 3827, Research Triangle, North Carolina 27709.

HIGH BLOOD PRESSURE

(See also "Heart Disease.")

National Heart, Lung and Blood Institute Information Center _____

A national clearinghouse that provides information on high blood pressure control and assists in locating other sources of education materials and audiovisual aids. Also distributes a variety of publications to physicians and the public. Publishes newsletter. Established 1988. Call: (301) 951-3260. Write: P.O. Box 30105, Bethesda, Maryland 20824.

HIRSCHSPRUNG'S DISEASE

Hirschsprung's Disease _____

International. For parents of children with Hirschsprung's disease, also called congenital intestinal aganglionosis (CIA), which is characterized by a lack of nerve (ganglion) cells in a segment of the bowel; this interferes with the squeezing action called peristalsis that normally moves stool through the colon. Discussion groups, telephone networking, other opportunities for exchange of peer support, information. Maintains database of Hirschsprung families; lending library of videotaped educational meetings. Sponsors conferences.

Publishes newsletter. Established 1984. Call: (802) 257-0603. Write: 22½ Spruce Street, Brattleboro, Vermont 05301.

HISTIOCYTOSIS

Histiocytosis Association of America _____

National. For people who suffer from histiocytosis. Now called Langerhans cell histiocytosis (LCH), this sometimes fatal disease affects about 1,000 children and adults in the U.S. each year and causes histiocytes, a form of white blood cell, to multiply wildly and attack various parts of the body, including the spleen, liver, lungs, skin and lymph nodes. Facilitates networking between histiocytosis families. Promotes research. Publishes newsletter. Provides telephone information and referrals, and holds regional meetings. Established 1985. Call: (800) 548-2758. Write: 609 New York Road, Glassboro, New Jersey 08028.

HOMELESSNESS

Coalition for the Homeless _____

New York area. For people who are homeless, that is, whose primary residence is a shelter or other public space, or who live doubled-up with relatives or friends, moving frequently from place to place. Emphasis on advocacy efforts on behalf of membership, plus service activities, including soup kitchens, rental assistance program, AIDS project, summer camp for homeless children. Also facilitates creation of networks between homeless people for exchange of support, information. Established 1980. Call: (212) 695-8700; fax: (212) 693-8331. Write: 500 Eighth Avenue, 9th Floor, New York, New York 10018.

HOMICIDE VICTIMS

See "Bereavement, Child (Homicide)," "Bereavement: Homicide Victims."

HUMAN PAPILLOMAVIRUS (HPV)

HPV Support Program ————————
National. For people infected with the human papillomavirus (HPV), a group of more than 600 different viruses, which can cause warts on the hands, feet or genitals. Disseminates information and educational materials. Publishes quarterly journal, *HPV News*. The HPV Support Program offers assistance to local self-help/mutual aid support groups. Established 1991. Call: (919) 361-8400; fax: (919) 361-8425. Write: P.O. Box 13827, Research Triangle Park, North Carolina 27709.

HUNTINGTON'S DISEASE

Huntington's Disease Society of America ————————
National. For people with Huntington's disease, also known as Huntington's chorea, a hereditary chorea (a nervous disorder featuring involuntary uncontrollable purposeless movements of the body and face and lack of coordination of the limbs) that develops during adulthood and ends in dementia. Also for families and friends of people with the disease. Discussion groups, other opportunities for exchange of peer support, information. Supports research. Provides educational materials to professionals and the general public. Publishes newsletter three times annually, group development guidelines. 31 chapters. Established 1967. Call: (212) 242-1968 or (800) 345-HDSA. Write: 140 West 22nd Street, 6th Floor, New York, New York 10011.

HYDROCEPHALUS

National Hydrocephalus Foundation ————————
For people with hydrocephalus, an abnormal increase in the quantity of fluid in the cranial cavity, causing disability or death if not treated by a shunt, which drains the fluid. Also for their families, friends and interested professionals. Discussion groups, telephone networking, other opportunities to exchange peer support, information. Conducts symposiums. Maintains reference library; rents video recordings of annual symposia. Publishes quarterly newsletter, brochures and videos for parents, including *Reaching Potential: A Parent's Guide to Hydrocephalus*. 3 affiliated groups. Established 1979. Call: (815) 467-6548; fax: (312) 427-9311. Write: Jim Mazzetti, 400 North Michigan Avenue, Suite 1102, Chicago, Illinois 60611.

HYPOGLYCEMIA

National Hypoglycemia Association ————————
For people with hypoglycemia, a condition characterized by an abnormal decrease in the level of sugar in the blood; also for their families and friends. Discussion groups, telephone networking, home visitation, other op-

portunities to exchange support, information. Provides physician referrals for consultation and evaluation. Publishes newsletter. Established 1984. Call: Lenore Cohen, (201) 670-1189. Write: P.O. Box 120, Ridgewood, New Jersey 07451.

HYSTERECTOMY

HERS (Hysterectomy Educational Resources & Services) Foundation _____
Model. Provides information about alternatives to—and consequences of—hysterectomy. Facilitates formation of networks for exchange of information, support. Publishes quarterly newsletter. Maintains library of audio- and videotapes, other materials. Sponsors conferences. Established 1982. Call: (215) 667-7757. Write: 422 Bryn Mawr Avenue, Bala Cynwyd, Pennsylvania 19004.

ICHTHYOSIS

FIRST (Foundation for Ichthyosis & Related Skin Types) _____
National. For persons with ichthyosis, a group of genetic skin disorders that are characterized by dry, thickened, scaling skin. Maintains a Regional Support Network that connects patients and families to provide emotional support, information. Sponsors local support groups. Holds annual national conference. Advocacy efforts on behalf of membership. Sponsors various educational efforts. Publishes brochures, quarterly newsletter. Established 1981. Call: (800) 545-3266. Write: P.O. Box 20291, Raleigh, North Carolina 27619.

IMMUNODEFICIENCY (PRIMARY)

Immune Deficiency Foundation _____
National. For people with primary immune-deficiency diseases, those that are primarily genetic in origin, unlike AIDS (which results from infection with HIV), or immunodeficiency resulting from chemotherapy or drug therapies designed to block rejection of organ and other implants. Support groups. Publishes newsletter, handbook, group development guidelines. Provides educational materials for patients, families and health professionals. Administers scholarship, fellowship programs. 18 chapters. Established 1980. Call: (800) 296-4IDF. Write: Toni Volk, P.O. Box 586, Columbia, Maryland 21045.

IMPOTENCE

I-Anon _____
National. For partners of men who suffer from impotence. Modified 12-step program. Discussion groups to exchange support, information. See entry for "Impotents Anonymous." Established 1983. Call: (615) 983-6064. Write: P.O. Box 5299, Maryville, Tennessee 37802.

Impotents Anonymous _____
International. For men who suffer from impotence. Modified 12-step program. For referrals, maintains directory of physicians. Discussion groups to exchange support, information. Supplies videotapes and audiocassettes. Publishes quarterly newsletter, chapter development guidelines. Include self-ad-

dressed stamped envelope with all mail queries. Over 125 chapters in the U.S. and abroad. Established 1983. Call: (615) 983-6064. Write: P.O. Box 5299, Maryville, Tennessee 37802.

INCEST

(See also "Child Abuse: Sexual Molestation.")

Incest Survivors Anonymous _____
International. 12-step program. For men, women and teens who were victims of incest as children. Publishes brochures, other literature. Discussion groups, telephone networking, other opportunities to exchange support. Assists in developing new groups. Established 1980. Call: (310) 428-5599. Write: P.O. Box 5613, Long Beach, California 90805.

Incest Survivors Resource Network International (ISRNI) _____
International. A Quaker-affiliated educational resource founded and operated by incest survivors from a variety of professions. Functions mainly by participation in committees and conferences of national and international organizations for human betterment. Established 1983. Call: (505) 521-4260. Write: Anne-Marie or Erik Eriksson, P.O. Box 7375, Las Cruces, New Mexico 88006.

Parents United International, Inc. _____
International (U.S., Canada, Australia and Europe). For families where child sexual abuse has occurred. Serves as an umbrella group for a variety of component organizations, including Daughters and Sons United (for sexually molested children and their siblings) and Adults Molested as Children (adults seeking to recover from molestation they experienced as children). Self-help, especially through discussion group meetings. Seeks to educate public at large about the problem of child sexual abuse. Established 1971. Call: (408) 453-7611, extension 124. Write: 232 Gish Road, San Jose, California 95112.

Survivors of Incest Anonymous _____
International. For men and women 18 years of age and older who were sexually abused as children. 12-step program. Discussion groups, telephone networking, other opportunities to exchange support, information. Information and referral phone lines staffed by volunteers. Maintains speakers bureau. Publishes newsletter and nearly 40 different pamphlets and other informational items. Provides assistance in starting new chapters. 800 chapters worldwide. Established 1982. Call: (410) 433-2365. Write: P.O. Box 21817, Baltimore, Maryland 21222.

VOICES (Victims of Incest Can Emerge Survivors) _____
National. For adults who were victims of childhood incest and sexual abuse. Pen-pal program, other opportunities to exchange support, information. Sponsors conferences around the U.S. Publishes newsletter, group development guidelines, other items as well as audiotapes. Established 1980. Call: (312) 327-1500. Write: P.O. Box 148309, Chicago, Illinois 60614.

INCONTINENCE

Simon Foundation for Incontinence

National. For people who suffer from incontinence. Discussion groups, telephone networking, pen-pal program, other opportunities to exchange peer support and information. Publishes quarterly newsletter and group development guidelines. Established 1983. Call: (708) 864-3913 or (800) 23-SIMON. Write: P.O. Box 815, Wilmette, Illinois 60091.

INFERTILITY

Resolve

National. Support and medical referrals for couples with infertility problems. Services include peer counseling and education for members and the public. Publishes quarterly newsletter, various fact sheets, other printed materials. 52 chapters. Established 1973. Call: (617) 623-0744. Write: 1310 Broadway, Somerville, Massachusetts 02144.

INFLAMMATORY BOWEL DISEASE

Crohn's & Colitis Foundation of America, Inc.

National. For people who suffer from inflammatory bowel disease (IBD): ileitis (Crohn's disease) and ulcerative colitis, which are serious, inflammatory, chronic diseases of the small and large intestines. Also for families and friends of people with IBDs. Promotes formation of support groups. Fund-raises for research. Publishes a quarterly newsletter and chapter development guidelines. Conducts educational seminars. 90 chapters. Established 1967. Call: (212) 685-3440. Write: 444 Park Avenue South, 11th Floor, New York, New York 10016.

INTERRACIAL

Interacc

Model. Established 1983. Support for and advocacy on behalf of interracial couples, their children, biracial adults and interracial adoptive families. Helps deal with concerns and problems such as raising interracial children, rejection from other family members and housing discrimination. Activities include phone and mail networks, discussion group meetings and social events. Publishes a newsletter. Sponsors meetings in New York and New Jersey. Established 1983. Call: Holly and Floyd Sheeger, (718) 657-2271 (evenings). Write: P.O. Box 582, Forest Hills, New York 11375.

INTERSTITIAL CYSTITIS

Interstitial Cystitis Association

National. For people with interstitial cystitis (IC), a chronic inflammation of the bladder wall; also for their families and friends and interested professionals. Discussion groups, telephone networking to exchange support information. Advocacy and fund-raising efforts. Promotes research. Runs conferences and public education programs. Publishes newsletter, group development guidelines, brochures. Over 100 affiliated groups. Established 1984. Call: (212) 979-6057. Write: P.O. Box 1553 Madison Square Station, New York, New York 10159.

INTRAVENTRICULAR HEMORRHAGE

IVH Parents (Intraventricular Hemorrhage)

National. For parents of children with intra- ventricular hemorrhage (IVH), a type of brain hemorrhage. Discussion groups, telephone and computer networking, pen-pal program, other opportunities to exchange peer support, in- formation. Publishes quarterly newsletter. Es- tablished 1984. Call: (305) 232-0381; fax: (305) 232-9890. Write: P.O. Box 56-1111, Miami, Florida 33256.

JEWS

(See also "Alcoholism, Substance Abuse," "Dysautonomia," "Gaucher's Disease," "Marriage," "Tay-Sachs Disease.")

J.A.C.S. (Jewish Alcoholics, Chemically Dependent Persons & Significant Others)

National. For recovering Jewish alcoholics and drug abusers as well as for their families and friends. Employs some 12-step principles. Publishes a newsletter and various other lit- erature. Activities include retreats. Operates speakers bureau. 13 affiliated chapters. Estab- lished 1980. Call: (212) 397-4197. Write: 426 West 58th Street, Suite 555, New York, New York 10019.

JOSEPH DISEASE

International Joseph Disease Foundation (IJDF)

For people with Joseph disease, which is a fatal genetic disorder of the nervous system characterized by weakness in the arms and legs, and a general loss of motor control, resulting in paralysis but no impairment of mental faculties; affects primarily people of Portuguese ancestry. Also for families and friends and interested professionals. Refers patients to medical and other services. Pro- vides clinical examinations and information to general public. Promotes medical research. Established 1977. Call: (510) 443-4600. Write: Rose Marie Silva, P.O. Box 2550, Livermore, California 94550.

KIDNEY DISEASE

American Association of Kidney Patients (AAKP)

National. For people with kidney disease and their families and friends. Discussion groups, telephone networking, other means for ex- changing support, information. Mounts ad- vocacy efforts on behalf of membership. Publishes and distributes various materials, including semiannual magazine, quarterly newspaper, chapter development guidelines, other informational brochures. 20 chapters. Established 1969. Call: (800) 749-2257 or (813) 251-0725. Write: 111 South Parker Street, Suite 405, Tampa, Florida 33606.

Positive Renal Outreach Program (P.R.O.P.)

Model. For people with kidney disease, in- cluding people with kidney transplants, on or preparing to go on dialysis; also for their families and friends. Discussion groups, telephone networking, other activities for exchange of support and information. Provides referrals. Operates speakers' bureau. Publishes newsletter, group development guidelines. Established 1984. Call: (914) 739-6436. Write: P.O. Box 32, Maryknoll, New York 10545.

KLIPPEL-TRENAUNAY SYNDROME

Klippel-Trenaunay Support Group

National. For people with Klippel-Trenaunay syndrome, a rare congenital syndrome of unknown origin characterized by a triad of symptoms: cutaneous capillary malformations ("birthmarks" or port-wine stains), congenital varicose veins and limb hypertrophy (overgrowth). Also for their families. Telephone networking, biennial meeting, other opportunities to exchange peer support, information. Publishes newsletter three or four times annually. Established 1986. Call: (612) 925-2596. Write: 4610 Wooddale Avenue, Edina, Minnesota 55424.

LARYNGECTOMY

International Association of Laryngectomees

For people who are going to have or who have had a laryngectomy (surgical removal of all or part of the larynx, usually due to cancer). Support groups to help patients prepare for and recover from surgery, including learning esophageal speech, a speech technique, useful after a total laryngectomy, that requires swallowing and regurgitating air to produce audible vibrations in the throat. Publishes newsletter, group development guidelines. Approximately 300 chapters. Established 1952. Call: (404) 320-3333. Write: 1599 Clifton Road, N.E., Atlanta, Georgia 30329.

LAW ENFORCEMENT PROFESSIONALS

International Law Enforcement Stress Association

For members of police departments, criminal justice agencies and related organizations and individuals. Discussion groups, telephone networking, other opportunities to exchange support, information. Seeks to help individuals cope with stress associated with their law-enforcement career. Sponsors public education efforts, various community outreach efforts, including home visits. Established 1977. Call: (813) 697-8863. Write: 5485 David Boulevard, Charlotte, Florida 33981.

LEAD POISONING

Parents Against Lead

Model. Established 1986. For parents of children with lead-paint poisoning. Discussion groups, telephone networking, other opportunities to exchange peer support, information. Provides referrals. Advocates legislative action to control uses of lead that lead to poisoning. Provides medical, legal referrals. Established 1986. Call: (410) 727-4226. Write: Lori Shroyer, 28 East Ostend Street, Baltimore, Maryland 21231.

LEARNING DISABILITIES

(See also "Attention-Deficit Disorders.")

Feingold Associations of the United States

National. A nonprofit volunteer organization whose purpose is support of other members in their efforts to improve their children's behavior (including hyperactivity, learning disability, attention deficit disorder) or their own health by implementing a special diet that eliminates foods with synthetic food colors, flavors and certain antioxidant preservatives, thought to cause behavioral problems. Also helps salicylate (aspirin)-sensitive individuals. Publishes newsletter, *Pure Facts*. Sponsors various public education efforts. 12 chapters. Established 1976. Call: (703) 768-FAUS. Write: Box 6550, Alexandria, Virginia 22306.

Learning Disability Association of America

National. For families in which a child has a learning disability (also called "learning disorder"), which is a defect in the ability to learn basic school subjects, such as arithmetic or reading. Provides information, referrals and advocacy. Publishes bimonthly newsletter, chapter development guidelines. Over 800 chapters. Established 1963. Call: (412) 341-1515. Write: Jean Peterson, 4156 Library Road, Pittsburgh, Pennsylvania 15234.

National Network of Learning-Disabled Adults

For adults with learning disabilities (defects in the ability to learn basic school subjects). Consumer rights-style organization of learning disabled adults who want improved educational and employment opportunities. Advocates on behalf of membership at various governmental levels. Promotes improved image of learning-disabled adults. Assists members in improving communication skills. Discussion groups, telephone networking, other opportunities to exchange support, information. Approximately 40 affiliated groups. Established 1980. Write: P.O. Box 32611, Phoenix, Arizona 85064.

Orton Dyslexia Society

National. For people with dyslexia, a disturbance of reading ability. Peer support through meetings, networking, other activities. 77 chapters nationwide. Established 1950. Call: (800) 222-3123. Write: 8600 La Salle Road, Suite 382, Baltimore, Maryland 21204.

LEUKEMIA

Leukemia Family Support Group Program

National. For people with leukemias, lymphomas, multiple myelomas and Hodgkin's disease. Also for families and friends of patients. Organizes groups for exchange of support, information. Groups are facilitated by health and mental health professionals and are held once or twice a month. Provides patient financial aid program. Educational literature available. 45 groups nationwide. Established 1984. Call: (800) 284-4271 extension 126. Write: 600 Third Avenue, New York, New York 10016.

LEUKODYSTROPHY

United Leukodystrophy Foundation, Inc.

National. For people with leukodystrophy, which is any of several genetically determined diseases characterized by degeneration of the white matter of the brain; also for their families and friends. Telephone networking, national conference, other opportunities for exchange of peer support, information. Promotes research. Sponsors public education efforts. Publishes quarterly newsletter. Established 1982. Call: (815) 895-3211 or (800) 728-5483. Write: 2304 Highland Drive, Sycamore, Illinois 60178.

LIFE-THREATENING ILLNESS

Center for Attitudinal Healing, The _____

Model. For people with life-threatening diseases and their families and friends. The center is home to a variety of activities that aid people in dealing with life-threatening illnesses, either their own or of families and friends. The center also offers various nonresidential (off-site) activities, including discussion groups and networking for exchange of support and information. Publishes a wide variety of materials. Established 1975. Call: (415) 435-5022. Write: 19 Main Street, Tiburon, California 94920.

Exceptional Patient Groups _____

Model. For people confronting a life-threatening disease. "To affirm the ability of each human being to meet the challenges, failures, and victories of a life-threatening disease, and to provide emotional, spiritual and social support for living life in a positive and meaningful manner." Discussion groups, telephone networking, other opportunities to exchange support, information. Established 1989. Call: (815) 664-1132. Write: Carol Stevenson, RN, MS, 600 East First Street, Spring Valley, Illinois 61362.

LIVER DISEASE

(See also "Hepatitis.")

American Liver Foundation _____

National. For patients with liver diseases, their families and friends, interested professionals and others. Support groups for and advocacy on behalf of liver-disease patients. Fund-raising for research into causes and cures for liver diseases. Chapters organized by nonprofessional volunteers. Publishes two quarterly newsletters—one for a lay audience, the other for the medical community—and chapter development guidelines. 23 chapters. Established 1976. Call: (800) 223-0179 or (201) 857-2626. Write: 1425 Pompton Avenue, Cedar Grove, New Jersey 07009.

LOU GEHRIG'S DISEASE

See "ALS (Amyotrophic Lateral Sclerosis.)"

LOWE'S SYNDROME

Lowe's Syndrome Association _____

International. For families of patients with Lowe's syndrome, also called oculocerebrorenal syndrome, an inherited disorder with a variety of characteristics, including glaucoma, cataracts, mental retardation and kidney problems. Telephone networking, conferences, other opportunities to exchange support, information. Promotes research. Provides medical and educational information and materials. Publishes informational booklet, newsletter. Established 1983. Call: (317) 743-3634. Write: 222 Lincoln Street, West Lafayette, Indiana 47906.

LUNG DISEASE

(See also "Brown Lung," "Emphysema.")

American Lung Association _____
National. For people who suffer from lung diseases, including chronic bronchitis, emphysema and asthma, and for their families and friends. Various programs, including "Better Breather" support groups, as well as educational outreach programs on asthma and smoking cessation. Speakers bureaus, fundraising activities, professional seminars, video library. Published materials include a newsletter and various educational materials, including posters. 288 affiliated groups nationwide. Established 1904. Call: (413) 737-3506. Write: Phyllis Bertera, 393 Maple Street, Springfield, Massachusetts 01105.

LUPUS

American Lupus Society _____
National. For people with lupus, a chronic disorder of the immune system that causes inflammation of various parts of the body, especially the skin, joints, blood and kidneys, and their families and friends. Seeks to increase public's awareness of lupus; fund-raises for lupus research. Promotes contact between people with lupus through telephone networking, other means. Publishes various printed items, available free of charge, including a quarterly newsletter. 25 chapters. Established 1974. Call: (310) 542-8891 or (800) 331-1802. Write: 3914 Del Amo Boulevard, Suite 922, Torrance, California 90503.

Lupus Foundation of America, Inc., The _____
International. For people with lupus, a chronic disorder of the immune system that causes inflammation of various parts of the body, especially the skin, joints, blood and kidneys. Assists local chapters in their efforts to provide support service. Seeks to educate the public about lupus, which affects approximately one in every 500 people. Supports research into the causes, treatment and cure of lupus. Publishes various booklets and pamphlets. 98 local chapters and over 60 international associated groups in 30 countries. Established 1977. Call: English: (800) 558-0121; Spanish: (800) 558-0231; office: (301) 670-9292. Write: 4 Research Place, Suite 180, Rockville, Maryland 20850.

MALIGNANT HYPERTHERMIA

Malignant Hyperthermia Association of the U.S. (MHAUS) _____
National. For people susceptible to malignant hyperthermia, a rare genetic condition characterized by a chain reaction of symptoms triggered by commonly used general anesthetics and, possibly, other drugs. Symptoms include increased body metabolism, muscle rigidity and fever to 110° F, which can cause death from cardiac arrest, brain damage, internal hemorrhaging or failure of other body systems. Also for their families and friends and interested professionals. Established 1981. Call: (203) 655-3007. Write: Josephine Nichols, P.O. Box 191, Westport, Connecticut 06881.

MALPRACTICE

Litigation Stress Support Group _____
Model. For doctors, dentists, other healthcare workers who are defendants in malprac-

tice suits and for their families and friends. Discussion groups, telephone networking, other opportunities to exchange support, information. Established 1986. Call: (609) 896-1766. Write: 2 Princess Road, Lawrenceville, New Jersey 08648.

MARFAN SYNDROME

National Marfan Foundation _____

For people with Marfan syndrome, which is an inherited disorder characterized by elongation of the long bones and often by ocular and circulatory defects. Also for families and friends of patients and interested professionals. Discussion groups, telephone networking, other opportunities to exchange peer support, information. Promotes research. Provides general information. Publishes quarterly newsletter, group development guidelines, other materials. 9 chapters. Established 1981. Call: (516) 883-8712 or (800) 8MARFAN. Write: 382 Main Street, Port Washington, New York 11050.

MARRIAGE

(See also "Adultery," "Separation, Divorce, Custody.")

W.O.O.M. (Wives of Older Men) _____

National. For women who have married men at least eight years their senior or who are about to do so. Seeks to help its members feel comfortable with their situation. Discussion groups focus on problems that include stepchildren, who may be as old or older than the stepparent, and the generation gap separating the marriage partners. Publishes newsletter

and chapter development guidelines. Established 1988. Call: (809) 747-5586. Write: 1029 Sycamore Avenue, Tinton Falls, New Jersey 07724.

MEN

Men's Support Groups _____

Model. For men interested in personal growth as men. Discussion groups for sharing of support, discussion of experiences of mutual interest and significance to members in their ongoing development as men. Small, informal, peer-led discussion groups meet in members' homes. Various groups in New Jersey since 1978. Call: (609) 683-0968. Write: Tom Landsberg, 21G Andover Circle, Princeton, New Jersey 08540.

MENTAL HEALTH

(See also "Anxiety, Panic, Phobia," "Obsessive-Compulsive Disorder.")

Depressives Anonymous _____

National. For people who suffer from depression and who wish to change patterns of—and attitudes about—living caused by their depression. Discussion groups, other opportunities to exchange support, information. Professionals involved in group activities. Publishes newsletter, provides assistance in starting new chapters. Established 1977. Call: (212) 689-2600 (answering service). Write: 329 East 62nd Street, New York, New York 10021.

Emotional Health Anonymous _____

National. For people with emotional problems, that is, for "any individual whose emotions interfere with their daily living in any way whatsoever, or to any degree, as recognized by themselves." 12-step program includes regular group meetings. Over 40 chapters. Established 1970. Call: (818) 240-3215. Write: P.O. Box 429, Glendale, California 91209.

Emotions Anonymous

International. A 12-step program for people seeking "emotional health." Weekly support groups for emotional problems such as anger, depression, anxiety, phobias, grief. Publishes *Emotions Anonymous,* a daily meditation book, monthly magazine, assorted other literature. Over 1,350 chapters. Established 1971. Call: (612) 647-9712. Write: P.O. Box 4245, St. Paul, Minnesota 55104.

FAIR (Family and Individual Reliance)

Model. Serves Texas. Umbrella organization for groups dealing with mental or emotional illness problems. Separate discussion groups for patients and for their families and friends. Publishes group development guidelines and training manual for group facilitators. Established 1980. Call: (512) 454-3706. Write: Mary Deese, 8401 Shoal Creek Boulevard, Austin, Texas 78758.

H.E.A.L. (Help, Education and Advocacy League)

Active in Connecticut. For families of children (under 18) with emotional or behavior disorders or mental illness. Helps create networks among members for exchange of support, information. Publishes newsletter. Established 1990. Call: (800) 842-1501 or (203) 529-1970. Write: Randy McGovern, 20–30 Beaver Road, Wethersfield, Connecticut 06109.

Helping Hands

Model. Self-help group "formed to provide an alternate approach in servicing people who are suffering from mental disorders in an unstructured environment." Weekly meetings for exchange of information, advice and support, but members also network by phone during the week. Professionals occasionally address open forums where members "can question, challenge and suggest ways of better servicing the community." "Most members are on medication and see their psychiatrist on a regular basis and the group is merely an extension, providing an atmosphere of friendship, through caring, listening and doing for one another when called upon." Established 1984. Call: (617) 475-3388. Write: Rita Martone, 86 Poor Street, Andover, Massachusetts 01810.

International Association for Clear Thinking (I'ACT)

For people who are in need of help with "managing difficult life situations, understanding and controlling anxiety, depression, anger, etc." Members use technique of rational behavior training originated by Maxie C. Maultsby, Jr., M.D. Activities include discussion groups, networking for exchange of support, information. Maintains library of video- and audiotapes. Stages conferences. Published materials include newsletter, group development guidelines, brochures. 72 affiliated groups. Established 1971. Call: (414) 739-8311, (414) 731-5028. Write: P.O. Box 1011, Appleton, Wisconsin 54912.

Mood Disorders Support Group, Inc.

Model. For people with depression or manic depression and for their families and friends. Discussion groups, telephone networking, other opportunities to exchange support, informa-

.A.D. (National Organization
asonal
ive Disorder) _____

ople who suffer from S.A.D. (seasonal
ve disorder), which is a type of mental
er caused by a change of season and
cterized by disturbances in mood—such
oression during fall and winter months;
for their families and friends and for
sted professionals. Helps disseminate in-
ation about S.A.D. among members and
neral public and professionals; promotes
rch into the disorder. Publishes newslet-
for members. Established 1988. Write:
Box 40133, Washington, D.C. 20016.

Our Own of
ntgomery County _____

del. For mental health consumers and ex-
ntal patients. Activities include discussion
ups, social activities, referral service for
community services. Outreach program, including a speakers' bureau, to educate public
about problems confronting ex-mental patients. Maintains a drop-in center. Publishes
quarterly newsletters. Established 1983. Call:
(301) 251-3734. Write: Brian Disher, 213
Monroe Street, Rockville, Maryland 20850.

Reclamation, Inc.

National. For former mental patients working
against stigmatization created by their illness.
Information, referrals regarding social, employment and housing problems. Staffed and
funded primarily by ex-patients. Publishes
newsletter. Call: (512) 833-4946. Write: Don
H. Culwell, Director 2502 Waterford, San
Antonio, Texas 78217.

Recovery, Inc.

International. Community mental health organization founded in 1937 by Dr. Abraham

For people who suffer from depression,
manic depression and for their families and
friends. Seeks to inform general public that
depressive illnesses may result from physical—
not purely mental—factors, such as biochemical imbalances. Administers annual conferences. Publishes chapter development
guidelines. Over 200 affiliated chapters. Established 1986. Call: (800) 82-NDMDA or
(312) 642-0049. Write: 730 North Franklin
#501, Chicago, Illinois 60610.

National Mental Health Consumer Self-Help Clearinghouse

Clearinghouse for information about con-
sumer-run self-help projects focusing on mental health topics. Publishes various materials,
including how-to pamphlets for people interested in starting their own self-help groups.
Established 1985. Call: (215) 735-6367. Write:
311 South Juniper Street, Suite 902, Philadelphia, Pennsylvania 19107.

A. Low, M.D., a neuropsychiatrist. Over 800 groups now meet on a weekly basis in the U.S., Canada and overseas. Offers adults "systematic training in a self-help method for controlling temperamental behavior and handling anxiety, depression and fears." Weekly group meetings are open to the public at no charge. The principal text used to learn the Recovery method is *Mental Health Through Will Training*. Publishes *Recovery Reporter* six times a year for members; and a newsletter, *Recovery, Inc., Reports,* and *Directory of Group Meeting Places* for mental health professionals. Call: (312) 337-5661. Write: 802 N. Dearborn, Chicago, Illinois 60610.

Schizophrenics Anonymous _____

National. For people with schizophrenia or schizophrenia-related disorders. Organized and run by members with the assistance of the Mental Health Association in Michigan. Provides mutual support and opportunities for networking, exchange of information between members. Uses six-step program and reinforces the value of professional help and pharmacotherapy. Group activities vary: weekly meetings, guest speakers, social outings. Encourages development of phone networks. Publishes information brochures, group development guidelines, biennial newsletter and bimonthly leaders' circular. 18 groups in Michigan and a similar number operating throughout the U.S., Canada. Established 1985. Call: (313) 577-6771; fax: (313) 557-5995. Write: 15920 West Twelve Mile Road, Southfield, Michigan 48076.

Stop Abuse by Counselors (Stop ABC) _____

A "national client-advocate organization." Assists victims; works to prevent abuse by mental health care practitioners, such as sexual victimization of client, practicing while chemically dependent, failure to refer when appropriate or to maintain confidentiality, encouragement of client dependency. Seeks to educate general public. Cooperates with research projects. Works to improve professional standards and to further development and passage of remedial legislation. Speakers' bureau. Various published materials, including *What To Do When Psychotherapy Goes Wrong*. Group development packet available. Maintains computerized literature list and list of attorneys specializing in representing clients seeking redress from abuse by counselors. Established 1980. Call: (206) 243-2723. Write: Shirley J. Siegel, P.O. Box 68292, Seattle, Washington 98168.

MENTALLY ILL: FAMILIES AND FRIENDS

NAMI (National Alliance for the Mentally Ill) _____

Membership includes parents, siblings and adult children of mentally ill people and mental health consumers. Umbrella organization for self-help, mutual-aid groups for relatives of mentally ill. Provides various types of support; helps establish networks between members. Advocacy at all levels on behalf of membership. Seeks to educate public about the problems of the mentally ill. Functions as a "stigma clearinghouse" that combats inappropriate representations of the mentally ill in the media. Performs a forensic function by acting as interface between mentally ill and the courts when the former encounter legal problems. Publishes quarterly newsletter and guidelines for developing new affiliate groups. More than 1,000 affiliates. Established 1979. Call: Family Help Hotline, (800) 950-NAMI; other business: (703) 524-7600. Write: 2101 Wilson Boulevard #302, Arlington, Virginia 22201.

Parents Involved Network of Pennsylvania

Active in Pennsylvania. For parents with children, including adolescent children, with serious emotional problems. Self-help groups, telephone networking, other opportunities to exchange support, information. Maintains resources center. Provides information and referrals by phone. Advocates on behalf of specific cases. Lobbies to implement goals of membership at state and local levels. Publishes newsletter. Established 1984. Call: (215) 735-2465; in Pennsylvania: (800) 688-4226; fax: (215) 735-0275. Write: 311 South Juniper Street, Room 902, Philadelphia, Pennsylvania 19107.

Siblings and Adult Children's Network (S.A.C.) of the National Association of the Mentally Ill

For siblings and children of people with mental illness. Discussion groups, other opportunities to exchange support, information. Publishes quarterly newsletter, group development guidelines. Sponsors conferences. Over 100 affiliated groups. Established 1982. Call: (703) 524-7600. Write: 2101 Wilson Boulevard, Suite #302, Arlington, Virginia 22201.

MENTAL RETARDATION

(See also "Cornelia de Lange Syndrome," "Down Syndrome.")

Association for Retarded Citizens (The ARC)

National. For mentally retarded people and their families and friends. Through various activities, provides support and information for and advocacy on behalf of membership. Publishes bimonthly newsletter, group development guidelines. Over 1,200 chapters. Established 1950. Call: (817) 261-6003. Write: 500 East Border Street, #300, Arlington, Texas 76010.

Siblings of the Mentally Retarded

Model. For siblings of the mentally retarded. Discussion groups, telephone networking, other opportunities to exchange support, information. Call: Marjorie Kruckeberg, (806) 358-1681. Write: Marjorie Kruckeberg, P.O. Box 3070, Amarillo, Texas 79116.

Support Group for Mentally Retarded Married Couples

Model. For married mentally retarded couples. Discussion groups, telephone networking, other opportunities to exchange support, information. Groups are facilitated by a professional. Call: Marjorie Kruckeberg, (806) 358-1681. Write: Marjorie Kruckeberg, Box 3070, Amarillo, Texas 79116.

MISSING CHILDREN

Child Find of America, Inc.

International. For parents searching for missing children. Prevents child abduction and locates missing children through investigation, photo distribution. Also assists in mediation (in parental custodial disputes) and public information (programs include educational video for children grades 5–8). Established 1980. Call: (800) I-AM-LOST or (800) A-WAY-OUT or (914) 255-1848. Write: Carolyn

Zogg, P.O. Box 277, New Paltz, New York 12561.

MUCOLIPIDOSIS IV

**Mucolipidosis IV
Foundation, The** _____
National. For children with mucolipidosis IV, one of four different but related rare genetic diseases causing motoric and eye problems; also for their families, friends and interested professionals. Facilitates networking among membership for exchange of support, information. Mounts fund-raising and public education efforts. Established 1984. Call: (914) 425-0639. Write: Lynn Goldblatt, 6 Concord Drive, Monsey, New York 10952.

MUCOPOLYSACCHARIDOSES

**National MPS
(Mucopolysaccharidoses)
Society** _____
For families and friends of people afflicted with mucopolysaccharidoses (MPS's) and mucolipidoses (ML's), rare genetically determined disorders caused by the body's inability to produce certain enzymes. This results in abnormal deposits of complex sugars in tissues and cells, causing progressive damage ranging in severity from bone and joint problems to massive complications involving all organ systems. Discussion groups, telephone networking, other means for exchange of support, information. Seeks to increase professional and public awareness of MPS's and ML's. Raises funds for research. Established 1974. Call: (516) 931-6338. Write: 17 Kraemer Street, Hicksville, New York 11801.

MULTIETHNICITY

(See also "Interracial.")

**Association for
Multi-Ethnic Americans** _____
National. For the multiethnic, interracial community in the U.S. Discussion groups for exchange of support, information. Advocacy efforts on behalf of membership. Seeks to educate general public about multiethnicity, interraciality. Quarterly newsletter, brochure. Encourages and assists in formation of local affiliates. Approximately 17 affiliates. Established 1988. Call: (510) 523-2632. Write: P.O. Box 191726, San Francisco, California 94119.

MULTIPLE BIRTH (TWINS, ETC.)

**National Organization of Mothers of
Twins Clubs** _____
For mothers of twins and other multiple births. Members meet and discuss issues of common concern and exchange information and advice on raising children from multiple births. Over 300 clubs. Established 1960. Call: (505) 275-0955. Write: P.O. Box 23188, Albuquerque, New Mexico 87192.

**Twinless Twins Support
Group International** _____
More than 350 members in each of the 50 states and Europe and Africa. For twins of all ages who have experienced the death or loss through adoption of their twin sibling. Members network via telephone, mail. Special care to remember birth and death dates of deceased twins of members. Counsels members through bereavement following the death of a twin,

and for the rest of their lives. Helps reunite twins separated through adoption. Publishes bimonthly newsletter, *Twins Letter*. Established 1985. Call: (219) 627-5414. Write: Dr. Raymond W. Brandt, 11220 St. Joe Road, Fort Wayne, Indiana 46835.

MULTIPLE SCLEROSIS

Multiple Sclerosis Service Organization, Inc.

Model. For people with multiple sclerosis, a chronic neurological condition, most often affecting young adults, characterized by hardened (sclerotic) tissue in the brain or spinal cord, associated with speech disturbances, incoordination, visual problems, bladder dysfunction, and muscle weakness; also for their families and friends. Chapters provide peer support and counseling; information and referrals; social and exercise programs and events. Sponsors conferences and workshops. Publishes quarterly newsletter. 4 chapters. Established 1949. Call: (201) 429-9890. Write: 146 Park Avenue, Randolph, New Jersey 07869.

National Multiple Sclerosis Society

For people with multiple sclerosis, a chronic neurological condition, most often affecting young adults, characterized by hardened (sclerotic) tissue in the brain or spinal cord, associated with speech disturbances, incoordination, visual problems, bladder dysfunction, and muscle weakness; also for families and friends of patients. Discussion groups, other opportunities for exchange of support, information. Provides referrals, education. Publishes newsletter. 140 chapters and branches have over 1,000 affiliated groups. Established

1946. Call: (800) LEARN-MS (800/532-7667). Write: 733 Third Avenue, New York, New York 10017.

MYALGIC ENCEPHALOMYELITIS

Myalgic Encephalomyelitis Association

International. For people with myalgic encephalomyelitis, an acute concurrent inflammation of the brain and spinal cord, causing severe muscular pain; also for families and friends of patients and interested professionals. Discussion groups, pen-pal program, conferences, other opportunities to exchange peer support, information. Advises medical professionals, health care services, general public on the disease. Offers assistance in developing new chapters. 480 affiliated groups. Established 1976. Call: Myalgic Encephalomyelitis Association, 011-44-375-642466. Write: 0375 642466 Stanhope House, High Street, Stanford-le-Hope, Essex SS17 OHA England.

MYASTHENIA GRAVIS

Myasthenia Gravis Foundation

National. For people with myasthenia gravis, a disease characterized by muscular weakness, especially in the muscles of the face, tongue and neck; also, for families and friends of patients. Discussion groups, telephone networking, conferences, other opportunities to exchange peer support, information. Provides referrals, other support services. Publishes newsletter. Maintains patient registry. Sponsors annual and scientific meetings, medical symposia. Administers research fellowships. 43 chapters. Established 1952. Call: (312) 427-6252. Write: 53 West Jackson Boulevard, Suite 660, Chicago, Illinois 60604.

NARCOLEPSY

American Narcolepsy Association

National. For persons with narcolepsy, a condition characterized by a frequent and uncontrollable need for sleep. Discussion groups, telephone networking, other opportunities to exchange peer support, information. Publishes quarterly newsletter. Approximately 40 affiliated chapters. Established 1977. Call: (415) 788-4793. Write: P.O. Box 26230, San Francisco, California 94126.

NEUROMETABOLIC DISORDERS

Association for Neuro Metabolic Disorders

National. For families with children who have one of the many different metabolic disorders that affect the brain, including phenylketonuria (PKU), maple syrup urine disease, galactosemia and biotinidase deficiency. Seeks to interconnect member families for exchange of support, information, including through informal discussion groups. Advocates research into causes, cures of neurometabolic disorders. Publishes newsletter, membership roster. Activities include yearly parent conference and picnic. Established 1981. Call: (419) 885-1497. Write: Cheryl Volk, 5223 Brookfield Lane, Sylvania, Ohio 43560.

OBSESSIVE-COMPULSIVE DISORDER

Obsessive-Compulsive Anonymous

National. For people who suffer from obsessive-compulsive disorders, an anxiety disorder characterized by recurrent, persistent ideas, thoughts, images or impulses that intrude into consciousness and are experienced, at least initially, as intrusive and senseless. Individuals engage in repetitive, purposeful, intentional behaviors performed in response to an obsession and designed to neutralize the obsession. A 12-step program. Offers guidance in starting new groups. 50 affiliated groups. Established 1988. Call: (516) 741-4901. Write: P.O. Box 215, New Hyde Park, New York 11040.

Obsessive-Compulsive Disorder Association of the National Capitol Area, Inc.

Regional. For people with obsessive-compulsive disorders (disorders characterized by recurrent, persistent ideas, thoughts, images or impulses that intrude into consciousness and are experienced, at least initially, as intrusive and senseless) and trichotillomania, a compulsion to pull one's own hair. Provides information, referrals and mutual support. Publishes newsletter and group development guidelines. Six affiliated groups. Established 1988. Call: (703) 379-8510. Write: Robert Hess, P. O. Box 11837, Alexandria, Virginia 22312.

Obsessive Compulsive Foundation (OCF)

National. For people with obsessive-compulsive disorders (disorders characterized by recurrent, persistent ideas, thoughts, images or impulses that intrude into consciousness and are experienced, at least initially, as intrusive and senseless); also for families and friends of sufferers and for interested professionals. Chapters provide support and information to member. Provides referrals to medical doctors and psychologists. Maintains updated listings of self-help and professional-led groups. Publishes a bimonthly newsletter. 4 chapters. Established 1987. Call: (203) 772-0565. Write: P.O. Box 9573, New Haven, Connecticut 06535.

ORGAN TRANSPLANT

Transplant Recipients International Organization (TRIO) _____

For transplant recipients, families, friends and medical professionals. Discussion groups, other opportunities for exchange of peer-group support, information. Seeks to educate public about organ donation. Publishes newsletter, group development guidelines. Sponsors annual national conference. 43 chapters. Established 1983. Call: (412) 687-2210; fax: (412) 687-7190. Write: Veronica K. Meury, 244 North Bellefield Avenue, Pittsburgh, Pennsylvania 15213.

OSTEOGENESIS IMPERFECTA

Osteogenesis Imperfecta Foundation _____

National. For families where a member suffers from osteogenesis imperfecta, a hereditary disease characterized by brittleness of the body's long bones. Telephone networking, other opportunities to exchange peer support, information. Promotes research. Publishes quarterly newsletter. Established 1970. Call: (813) 282-

1161. Write: 5005 West Laurel Street, #210, Tampa, Florida 33607.

OSTEOPOROSIS

National Osteoporosis Foundation _____

For people with osteoporosis, a disease in which the bones become porous and therefore fragile; also for their families and friends and interested professionals. Seeks to educate professionals and the general public. Provides direct support for research. Advocates increased federal research efforts. Provides referrals. Publishes newsletter, other materials useful to support groups. Encourages development of new chapters. Established 1984. Call: (202) 223-2226. Write: 2100 M Street, N.W., Suite 602, Washington, D.C. 20037.

OSTOMY

United Ostomy Association _____

National. For persons with ostomies, which are artificial passages surgically created in the body for the elimination of wastes, such as a colostomy or an ileostomy. Helps members return to normal life. Active in educational and advocacy efforts on a national level on behalf of its members. Provides support, including educational material and chapter development guidelines, to its affiliated groups. Maintains library of audiovisual materials. Holds conferences. Publishes various materials. Runs youth camp. Over 700 chapters. Established 1962. Call: (800) 826-0826; (714) 660-8624; fax: (714) 660-9262. Write: 36 Executive Park, #120, Irvine, California 92714.

OVERWEIGHT, OVEREATING

(See also "Eating Disorders.")

Gastroplasty Support Group

Model. For patients and professionals who wish to volunteer their time to organize discussion groups for people who have had or will have gastroplasty, an operation whose goal is to help people lose weight through vertical banded gastroplasty, a surgical procedure to the stomach. Established 1985. Call: (201) 374-1717. Write: Dr. Lubomyr Kuzmak, 340 East Northfield Road, Suite 1-D, Livingston, New Jersey 07039.

National Association to Advance Fat Acceptance (N.A.A.F.A.)

Seeks to improve the quality of life for fat people in ways other than dieting. Seeks to end size discrimination and give fat people the tools for self-empowerment through public education, advocacy, research and member support. Publishes newsletter eight times annually. Pen-pal and dating services. Annual convention. 60 chapters. Established 1969. Call: (916) 443-0303. Write: P.O. Box 188620, Sacramento, California 95818.

National Association to Aid Fat Americans (N.A.A.F.A.)

For overweight people, whether or not they wish to lose weight. Discussion groups, telephone networking, other opportunities for members to support each other in their effort to improve their low self-esteem associated with obesity. Seeks to educate the public at large about obesity. Over 50 chapters. Established 1969. Call: (916) 443-0303. Write: P.O. Box 188620, Sacramento, California 95818.

O-Anon

International. 12-step recovery program for codependents of overeaters—for people who wish to disengage themselves from the food-related problems of friends and family members and learn to lead happy, independent lives. Publishes newsletter. 50 affiliated groups. Established 1975. Write: P.O. Box 4305, San Pedro, California 90731.

Overeaters Anonymous

International. For all individuals who have a desire to stop eating compulsively. 12-step program. Special meetings for young people and newcomers. Publishes monthly magazine *Lifeline* and a bimonthly newsletter, plus books pamphlets, recordings, group guidelines. 9,719 groups in 42 countries. Established 1960. Call: (310) 618-8835; for meetings only: (800) 743-8703. Write: P.O. Box 92870, Los Angeles, California 90009.

TOPS (Take off Pounds Sensibly)

International. For overweight people who wish to reduce their weight to a certain level and maintain it. Weekly meetings for exchange of support; members provide each other with positive reinforcement and motivation. Publishes newsletter, nutritional guide. Over 11,600 chapters. Established 1948. Call: Information about local groups: (800) 932-8677; national headquarters: (414) 482-4620. Write: P.O. Box 07360, Milwaukee, Wisconsin 53207.

OXALOSIS AND HYPEROXALURIA

Oxalosis and Hyperoxaluria Foundation

National. For people with hyperoxaluria, a rare, genetic metabolic disease that causes a type of kidney stones and kidney failure; also for their families and friends. Telephone networking, pen-pal programs, newsletter. Fundraising activities. Supports research. Sponsors annual conference. Seeks to educate patients, families, medical professionals and general public. Materials available include brochure, "Understanding Oxalosis and Hyperoxaluria," low-oxalate diet guidelines, newsletter (back issues available), reprints of medical journal articles. Established 1987. Call: (206) 631-0386; fax: call to arrange. Write: Anne M. Dayton, P.O. Box 1632, Kent, Washington 98035.

PAIN, CHRONIC

American Chronic Pain Association, Inc. _____

International. For people who suffer from chronic pain. Groups for mutual support, exchange of information, tips on dealing with chronic pain. Publishes quarterly newsletter, group development guidelines, workbook. Sponsors outreach program to clinics; administers phone network. Over 600 groups in the U.S. and five foreign countries. Established 1980. Call: (916) 632-0922. Write: P.O. Box 850, Rocklin, California 95677.

National Chronic Pain Outreach Association, Inc. _____

A clearinghouse for information about chronic pain and its management. Sponsors public information and educational efforts aimed at the general public, chronic-pain sufferers, and health care professionals. Publishes quarterly newsletter, *Lifeline*, support-group starter kit, over 50 pamphlets, audio cassettes, membership directory. Makes referrals to support groups (maintains a computerized "Support Group Registry" of chronic pain support groups

in the U.S. and Canada) and to pain clinics and pain specialists. Established 1980. Call: (301) 652-4948; fax: (301) 907-0745. Write: 7979 Old Georgetown Road, Suite 100, Bethesda, Maryland 20814.

PARENTING, GENERAL

(See also "Child Custody," "Missing Children," "Problem Children.")

F.E.M.A.L.E. ("Formerly Employed Mothers at the Leading Edge") _____

National. Formerly, F.E.M.A.L.E. was an acronym for "Formerly Employed Mothers at Loose Ends." For women who have left the paid workforce to raise their children at home, dealing with transitions between paid employment and at-home motherhood; does not oppose mothers who work outside the home full time. Local chapters hold regular meetings for exchange of support, information. Meetings are organized around a topic or book discussions or guest speaker. Sponsors playgroups, babysitting co-ops, various social activities. Publishes membership directory, *Female Forum*, a monthly newsletter. Advocates on behalf of membership on issues such as improved and expanded child care options, mandated family-leave policies, child care and tax legislation that does not discriminate against parents who choose to forgo paid employment in order to care for their children. Established 1987. Call: (708) 941-3553. Write: P.O. Box 31, Elmhurst, Illinois 60126.

National Committee for Citizens in Education _____

For parents and other citizens interested in taking a more active part in the school system. Facilitates creation of networks of local parents groups, the better to work actively on improving schools. Group development guidelines, various published materials available. Over 500 groups. Established 1973. Call: (202) 408-0447. Write: 900 Second Street, N.E., Suite 8, Washington, D.C. 20002.

No Kidding!

International. For married or single people who have decided not to have children, are postponing having them, are undecided or are unable to have them. Activities include social events. 39 chapters. Established 1984. Call: (604) 538-7736. Write: Box 76982, Station S, Vancouver, British Columbia V5R 5S7.

Post-Partum Education for Parents (P.E.P.)

Model. For parents of newborn children in need of support, assistance during initial period after childbirth. Discussion groups, telephone networking, other opportunities for members to provide mutual support, information on basic infant care and adjustment to new parental role. Publishes *Guide for Establishing a Parent Support Program in Your Community.* Established 1977. Call: (805) 564-3888. Write: P.O. Box 6154, Santa Barbara, California 93110.

Stepfamily Association of America, Inc.

National. For stepfamilies, that is, families where there is a stepfather or stepmother. Discussion groups run by local chapters for exchange of support, information. Provides educational resources to interested parties, chapter development information. Administers annual conference. Publishes quarterly newsletter. Approximately 70 chapters. Established 1979. Call: (402) 477-7837. Write: 215

Centennial Mall South #212, Lincoln, Nebraska 68508.

PARENTING: SINGLE PARENTS

International Youth Council

For teenage children of single-parent homes. Discussion groups, telephone networking, social events, other opportunities for members to share experiences and solutions to common problems, socialize with one another. Sponsored by local chapters of Parents Without Partners (see entry). 40 chapters. Established 1972. Call: (800) 637-7974 or (301) 588-9354; fax: (301) 588-9216. Write: 8807 Colesville Road, Silver Spring, Maryland 20910.

Parents Without Partners

National. For single parents (most divorced, but some widowed). Discussion groups, other opportunities to exchange support, information. Publishes group development guidelines, newsletter, other materials. 735 chapters. Established 1957. Call: (301) 588-9354; (800) 637-7974; fax: (301) 588-9216. Write: 8807 Colesville Road, Silver Spring, Maryland 20910.

Single Mothers by Choice

National. "To provide support and information to single women who have chosen or who are considering single motherhood." Telephone networking, other opportunities for exchange of support, information. Connects members anonymously with social scientists, journalists, other people researching phenomenon of single motherhood. Not an advocacy group. Publishes quarterly newsletter and other literature. Exact number of affiliated groups not known, but active in all 50 states and Canada. Established 1981. Call: Jane Mattes, (212) 988-0993. Write: Jane Mattes, P.O. Box 1642, Gracie Square Station, New York, New York 10028.

Single Parent Resource Center

International. Umbrella organization for single-parent self-help/mutual aid groups. Provides information and referrals. Maintains resource library. Holds seminars. Provides consultation. Publishes newsletter, group development guidelines. Interested in developing programs for single parents and mothers coming out of prison. Established 1975. Call: (212) 947-0221. Write: 141 West 28th Street, New York, New York 10010.

Unwed Parents Anonymous

Model. For people whose lives are affected by out-of-wedlock pregnancy and parenting. Encourages sexual abstinence outside of marriage. Activities include discussion groups for exchange of support. Publishes newsletter, group development guidelines. 4 affiliated groups. Established 1979. Call: (602) 952-1463. Write: P.O. Box 44556, Phoenix, Arizona 85064.

Women on Their Own, Inc. (W.O.T.O.)

National. For single, divorced or widowed women raising children on their own. Discussion groups, telephone networking, other opportunities to exchange support, advice on topics including childcare, employment. Administers speakers' bureau, loan programs. Advocates on behalf of membership. Makes referrals. Publishes quarterly newsletter, mem-

bership telephone directory to aid in networking. Administers conferences. Founded 1982. Call: Joyce Knox, Director, (609) 871-1499. Write: P.O. Box 1026, Willingboro, New Jersey 08046.

PARKINSON'S DISEASE

American Parkinson's Disease Association

National. For people with Parkinson's disease, a neurological disorder, and their families and friends. Network of over 350 support groups. Promotes research. Maintains 45 information and referral centers nationwide. Publishes chapter development guidelines and quarterly newsletter. 85 chapters. Established 1961. Call: In New York State, (718) 981-8001; elsewhere, (800) 223-APDA. Write: Frank Williams, 60 Bay Street, Suite 401, Staten Island, New York 10301.

Parkinson's Educational Program

National. For people with Parkinson's disease, a neurological disorder, and their families and friends. Activities include support groups, educational outreaches to medical professionals and regional conferences. Refers patients to local groups and physicians. Publishes a monthly newsletter and group development guidelines. Over 500 groups. Established 1981. Call: (800) 344-7872. Write: 3900 Birch Street, #105, Newport Beach, California 92660.

Parkinson's Support Groups of America

National. For people with Parkinson's disease, a neurological disorder, and for their families and friends. Goal is to help adjust their lives to cope with this chronic illness. Activities include support groups; annual convention and other opportunities to network and exchange ideas and information; speakers bureau. Publishes a newsletter and chapter development guidelines. Over 150 affiliated groups. Established 1980. Call: (301) 937-1545. Write: 11376 Cherry Hill Road, #204, Beltsville, Maryland 20705.

PEDIATRIC PSEUDO-OBSTRUCTION

North American Pediatric Pseudo-obstruction Society, Inc. _____
International. For families where a child has been diagnosed with intestinal pseudo-obstruction or other gastrointestinal motility disorders, conditions in which the normal process of food digestion is disrupted, causing symptoms including nausea, bloating, vomiting, leading to death in some cases. Discussion groups, telephone networking, conferences, other opportunities to exchange support, information. Seeks to educate general public about these disorders. Promotes research. Established 1988. Call: (617) 395-4255. Write: P.O. Box 772, Medford, Massachusetts 02155.

P.I.D. (PELVIC INFLAMMATORY DISEASE)

Canadian P.I.D. Society _____
National. For women with pelvic inflammatory disease (PID), an infection or inflammation of a woman's reproductive organs that can affect the uterus (womb), Fallopian tubes, ovaries and tissue surrounding these organs. Also for their families, health care professionals, community groups and the general public. Distributes information, provides support and promotes public education and prevention. Provides free telephone information, counseling and resource and referral services. Facilitates self-help telephone support networks for women with PID. Develops and distributes public education materials, including a PID brochure, PID booklet, and a true/false public education questionnaire. Maintains a resource library with over 1,500 medical research articles on PID and related topics. Conducts public education and prevention program. Also provides services to many individuals and organizations in the United States. Established 1986. Call: (604) 684-5704. Write: P.O. Box 33804, Station D, Vancouver, B.C., Canada V6J 4L6.

POLIO

International Polio Network _____
For polio survivors, and for their families and friends, and for interested health care professionals. Polio is a disease caused by a viral infection; its characteristics are fever, paralysis and atrophy of skeletal muscles. Although new polio infections are relatively rare now, there are still numerous survivors from polio epidemics antedating the Salk polio vaccine (1953). Sponsors international conferences (tapes and transcripts available). Discussion groups, workshops, other opportunities for exchange of peer support, information. Publishes quarterly newsletter, annual directory of clinics, health professionals and support groups, including an international section. Established 1958. Call: (314) 534-0475. Write:

Joan Headley, 5100 Oakland Avenue, #206, St. Louis, Missouri 63110.

POLLUTION

See "Environmental Issues."

PORPHYRIA

**American
Porphyria Foundation** _____
National. For persons with porphyria, which is any of several metabolic abnormalities, usually hereditary, characterized by extreme sensitivity to light. Also for families and friends of patients and interested professionals. Discussion groups, telephone networking, pen-pal programs, other opportunities to exchange peer support, information. Promotes research, provides education to health care professionals and general public. Publishes quarterly newsletter. 40 groups. Established 1982. Call: (713) 266-9617. Write: Desiree Lyon, P.O. Box 22712, Houston, Texas 77063.

PRADER-WILLI
SYNDROME

**Prader-Willi
Syndrome Association** _____
National. For parents of children with Prader-Willi syndrome, a congenital disorder whose characteristics include short stature, mental retardation, abnormally small hands and feet and uncontrolled appetite leading to extreme obesity. Telephone networking, pen-pal program, other opportunities to exchange peer support and information. Publishes bimonthly

newsletter, handbook and chapter development guidelines. 26 chapters. Established 1975. Call: (800) 926-4797; fax: (612) 928-9133. Write: 6490 Excelsior Boulevard, E-102, St. Louis Park, Minnesota 55426.

PREMATURE, HIGH-RISK,
SICK INFANTS

(See also "Sick, Disabled Children")

Intensive Caring Unlimited _____
Model. For parents who share a variety of birth-related experiences, including premature or sick-at-birth baby, high-risk pregnancy, child with developmental issues, death of a baby. Telephone networking to exchange support. Provides peer counseling, education, referrals. Publishes newsletter. Serves greater Philadelphia and southern New Jersey. Established 1978. Call: Lenette, (215) 233-6994. Write: 910 Bent Lane, Philadelphia, Pennsylvania 19118.

Parent Care _____
National. For families, professionals, others concerned with problem of infants who require special care at birth, such as premature babies. Provides information, referrals and support to parents, who organize in groups to exchange support. Maintains resource directory, sponsors annual international conference and occasional seminars. Publishes quarterly newsletter, group development guidelines. Over 130 groups. Established 1982. Call: (317) 872-9913. Write: 9401 Colgate Street, Indianapolis, Indiana 46268.

PROBLEM CHILDREN

(See also "Parenting, General.")

Because I Love You

Model. For parents whose children have problems such as substance abuse, truancy, juvenile delinquency. Goal of support groups is to help parents regain self-esteem, control of their homes. 8 affiliated groups. Established 1981. Call: (213) 659-5289. Write: P.O. Box 35175, Los Angeles, California 90035.

Tough Love

International. For families disrupted by problematic behavior of one or more children. Discussion groups for parents. Publishes quarterly newsletter and chapter development guidelines. Over 2,000 affiliated groups. Established 1980. Call: (800) 333-1069, Monday–Friday, 9 A.M.–5 P.M., EST: leave messages at other hours. Write: Box 1069, Doylestown, Pennsylvania 18901.

PROSTITUTION

See "Sex Industry."

PRUNE-BELLY SYNDROME

**Prune Belly
Syndrome Network**

National. For people who suffer from prune-belly syndrome (abdominal muscle deficiency syndrome), a congenital absence (partial or complete) of abdominal muscles, in which the outline of the intestines is visible through the protruding abdominal wall. Telephone networking, pen-pal program, other opportunities to exchange peer support, information. Established 1984. Call: (602) 730-6364. Write: Barbara Hopkins, 1005 East Carver Road, Tempe, Arizona 85284.

PSORIASIS

**National
Psoriasis Foundation**

For people with psoriasis, a chronic skin disease characterized by red patches covered with white scales. Discussion groups, telephone networking, pen-pal program, other opportunities for exchange of support, information. Fund-raises for research into causes, treatments, cure. Publishes bimonthly newsletter. Established 1968. Call: (503) 297-1545; fax: (503) 292-9341. Write: 6443 S.W. Beaverton Highway, Suite 210, Portland, Oregon 97221.

PUBLIC SPEAKING, FEAR OF

Toastmasters International

For people who suffer from fear of speaking before an audience. Various activities where members can exchange support and information as well as opportunities to practice and improve public speaking skills. Over 7,000 chapters. Established 1924. Call: (714) 858-8255. Write: P.O. Box 9052, Mission Viejo, California 92690.

RAPE

See "Crime Victims."

RARE DISORDERS

**National Organization for
Rare Disorders**

Clearinghouse for information concerning rare disorders. Facilitates networking among families where there are members with same or similar disorders to promote exchange of mutual aid, support and information. Also serves as clearinghouse for information about so-called orphan drugs and orphan devices and about their availability to patients, physicians, other health care workers. Call: (203) 746-6518. Write: P.O. Box 8923, New Fairfield, Connecticut 06812.

RESPIRATORY DISEASE

White Lung Association _____

National. For victims of asbestosis, also known as White Lung Disease, a disease of the lungs caused by the habitual inhalation of asbestos; also for people with asbestos-related cancers and for families and friends of patients. Activities include mutual aid meetings for members and advocacy on their behalf. Promotes public awareness of the dangers of asbestos, with particular attention to workers who are at risk of exposure. Publishes quarterly newsletter and chapter development guidelines. Films and videotapes available for educational purposes. Over 200 chapters. Established 1979. Call: (410) 243-5864. Write: P.O. Box 1483, Baltimore, Maryland 21203.

REYE'S SYNDROME

National Reye's Syndrome Foundation _____

For families where an individual has—or has had—Reye's syndrome, an often fatal brain disease, especially of childhood, characterized by fever, vomiting, fatty infiltration of the liver and swelling of the brain. Local chapter meetings for exchange of peer support, information. Provides information and referrals.

Encourages research. Publishes newsletter. Approximately 140 affiliates. Established 1974. Call: (800) 233-7393. Write: 426 North Lewis Street, Bryan, Ohio 43506.

RUBINSTEIN-TAYBI SYNDROME

Rubinstein-Taybi Parents Group _____

National. For parents of children with Rubinstein-Taybi syndrome, a constellation of congenital anomalies, including mental retardation, facial deformities, broad thumbs, big toes and possible heart, lung or kidney defects. Telephone networking, other opportunities for exchange of peer support, information. Established 1984. Call: (913) 282-6237. Write: Garry and Lorrie Baxter, 414 East Kansas, Smith Center, Kansas 66967.

RUSSELL-SILVER SYNDROME

Association for Children with Russell-Silver Syndrome _____

International. For families where a child has been diagnosed with Russell-Silver syndrome, characterized by short stature, limb asymmetry, low birthweight, triangular-shape face, hypoglycemia, in-curved fifth fingers, café au lait spots. Discussion groups, telephone networking, other opportunities for exchange of peer support, information. Encourages research, seeks to heighten public's awareness of syndrome. Publishes quarterly newsletter, brochures. Established 1989. Call: (201) 377-4531. Write: 22 Hoyt Street, Madison, New Jersey 07940.

SCLERODERMA

Scleroderma Federation _____

International. For people with scleroderma, a disease that is usually slowly progressive, characterized by the deposition of fibrous connective tissue in the skin and often in internal organs; also for their families and friends. Support groups, telephone networking, other opportunities for exchanging support, information. Provides referrals, advice and education. Fund-raises for research. Videotapes available. Publishes quarterly newsletter. 17 groups. Established 1983. Call: (508) 535-6600. Write: 1 Newbury Street, Peabody, Massachusetts 01960.

SEPARATION, DIVORCE, CUSTODY

Association of Children for Enforcement of Support (A.C.E.S.) _____

National. For parents with custody of children, but who have difficulty collecting child support payments. Information and referrals to local child support services. Publishes newsletter. 265 affiliated groups. Established 1984. Call: (419) 476-2511 or (800) 537-7072. Write: 723 Phillips Avenue, Suite 216, Toledo, Ohio 42612.

Children's Rights Council _____

National. For parents interested in reform of child custody laws. Provides information and referrals. Activities include advocacy efforts, conferences. 23 affiliated groups. Established 1985. Call: (202) 547-NCCR. Write: David L. Levy, President, 220 Eye Street, N.E., Washington, D.C. 20002.

Committee for Mother & Child Rights, Inc. _____

National. For mothers with custody problems due to divorce, contested custody. Telephone networking for exchange of information, support. Call: (703) 722-3652. Write: 210 Ole Orchard Drive, Clearbrook, Virginia 22624.

Divorce Anonymous _____

Model. For people undergoing separation or divorce. 12-step program. Discussion groups, telephone networking for exchange of support and information. Six affiliated groups active in southern California. Established 1987. Call: (213) 651-2930. Write: Christine Archambault, 543 North Fairfax Avenue, Los Angeles, California 90036.

E.X.P.O.S.E. (Ex-Partners of Servicemen for Equality) _____

National. Nonprofit, volunteer organization "dedicated to achieving equity for the ex-wives of service men. Our special concern is the older woman whose primary career in her long-term marriage was that of military wife and homemaker. Our members have been married an average of 25 years." Lobbies on behalf of membership. Provides information about legal rights and referrals to legal assistance. Publishes handbook, *Guide for Military Separation and Divorce.* 35 chapters, more than 4,000 members. Established 1981. Call: (703) 941-5844 or (703) 255-2917 (24-hour hotline). Write: P.O. Box 11191, Alexandria, Virginia 22312.

Grandparents'-Children's Rights, Inc. _____

National. Not a self-help group per se, but a clearinghouse for information on other groups involved in the issue of grandparents' rights vis-à-vis their grandchildren. May serve as a source of information about local support groups for grandparent problems, such as those who have gained and then lost custody of abused grandchildren; and information about advocacy on behalf of grandparents at the local, state and national level. Established 1982. Call: (517) 339-8663. Write: Lee and Lucille Sumpter, 5728 Bayonne Avenue, Haslett, Michigan 48840.

Joint Custody Association

International. For parents with children in the process of divorce who want joint custody. Provides information about family law including recent research and decisions. Lobbies at the state level for changes in law favorable to equitable joint custody. Publishes and distributes informational material. 250 affiliated groups. Established 1979. Call: (310) 475-5352. Write: James A. Cook, President, 10606 Wilkins Avenue, Los Angeles, California 90024.

Mothers Without Custody

National. For women who have lost custody of their children through separation or divorce. Discussion groups, telephone networking, other opportunities for exchange of support, information. Other activities include public education efforts. Publishes bimonthly newsletter, group development kit. 25 chapters. Established 1981. Call: (713) 840-1622. Write: P.O. Box 27418, Houston, Texas 77227.

National Child Support Advocacy Coalition (N.C.S.A.C.)

Umbrella organization for numerous independent groups nationwide that help families deal with the problem of enforcing and collecting child support. Advocates on behalf of membership at all levels of government. Helps membership network; assists the development of new local and regional groups. Publishes quarterly newsletter. Sponsors annual confer-

ence. Founded 1984. Write: P.O. Box 420, Mendersonville, Tennessee 37077.

National Congress for Men and Children

For men who feel that their rights are being denied, especially regarding divorce decisions, such as child custody. Provides information and referrals. Publishes newsletter. 54 affiliated groups. Established 1980. Call: (215) 576-0177. Write: Ken Lewis, P.O. Box 202, Glenside, Pennsylvania 19038.

National Organization for Men

Primarily an advocacy organization seeking equal rights for men in such matters—mostly relating to divorce—as child custody and division of property, or where it perceives that men are being discriminated against. The organization does not address issues relating to gay men, or to abortion as it involves men. Sponsors support groups where men with similar experiences and problems in these areas can exchange support, information. Conducts educational seminars. Publishes newsletter, *The Quest*. Approximately 13,000 members and 40 affiliated chapters; others in formation. Established 1983. Call: (212) 686-MALE. Write: 11 Park Place, New York, New York 10007.

New Beginnings, Inc.

Model. For separated and divorced men and women in the Washington, D.C. area; one chapter in Greensboro, North Carolina. Discussion groups, guest-speaker events, social events, workshops, other networking opportunities for exchange of support, information. Publishes newsletter, materials to assist in developing new groups. Established 1979. Call: (301) 384-0111. Write: 13129 Clifton Road, Silver Spring, Maryland 20904.

**North American Conference of
Separated and
Divorced Catholics** _____

National. For families of all faiths where there
has been divorce or separation. Discussion
groups, conferences, other opportunities for
support, exchange of information about the
religious, educational and psychological impact of separation, divorce and remarriage.
Publishes newsletter, group development
guidelines. Over 3,000 affiliated groups. Established 1975. Call: (401) 943-7903. Write:
Dorothy J. Levesque, 83 St. Mary's Drive,
Cranston, Rhode Island 02920.

SEX INDUSTRY

Prostitutes Anonymous _____

National. For men and women involved in
any aspect of the sex industry (prostitution,
phone sex, sex shows including nude dancing,
modeling and acting for film and print por-
nography) who wish to end their involvement
permanently. 12-step program. Discussion
groups, telephone networking, other opportunities to exchange support, information.
Special program for studying the 12 steps by
mail for people in areas where there are no
meetings. Established 1987. Call: (818) 905-
2188. Write: 11225 Magnolia Boulevard,
#181, North Hollywood, California 91601.

SEXUAL ADDICTION

**C.O.S.A. (Codependents of
Sex Addicts)** _____

National. 12-step program for spouses, lovers,
families and friends of sex addicts. Publishes
two volumes of *C.O.S.A. Stories,* various brochures, group development guidelines. Ap-

proximately 100 groups. Established 1980.
Call: (612) 637-6904. Write: P.O. Box 14537,
Minneapolis, Minnesota 55414.

S-Anon _____

International. 12-step group for spouses, lovers, families and friends of "sexaholics" (sex-
addicted persons). Assists in formation of new
groups. Publishes quarterly newsletter. New-
comer's packet and other literature also available. Sponsors semiannual international
conferences. Cooperates with Sexaholics
Anonymous (see entry). Numerous affiliated
groups and contacts in U.S., Canada and Europe. Established 1984. Call: (818) 990-6910.
Write: P.O. Box 5117, Sherman Oaks, California 91413.

Sex Addicts Anonymous _____

National. 12-step program for people seeking
to recover from addiction to compulsive sexual behavior. Provides guidelines for starting
new groups. Publishes educational booklet.
Approximately 450 groups. Established 1977.
Call: (612) 339-0217. Write: P.O. Box 3038,
Minneapolis, Minnesota 55403.

Sexaholics Anonymous _____

International. 12-step program for people who
seek "sexual sobriety" and release from self-
destructive patterns of compulsive sexual behavior and thinking. Activities include meetings and telephone networking; publishes
newsletter; provides chapter development
guidelines. Over 700 chapters. Established
1979. Call: (818) 704-9854. Write: P.O. Box
300, Simi Valley, California 93062.

**Sex & Love
Addicts Anonymous** _____

International. 12-step fellowship for people
seeking to recover from addiction to sex, ob-
sessive love or emotional relationships. Pub-

lishes book, *Sex and Love Addicts Anonymous,* quarterly newsletter and other literature. Provides group development guidelines. 500 affiliated groups. Established 1976. Write: P.O. Box 119, New Town Branch, Boston, Massachusetts 02258.

SHORT PEOPLE

Human Growth Foundation

National. For parents of short children and for people with growth disorders of any type. Discussion groups, other opportunities for exchange of support, information. Publishes monthly newsletter, group development guidelines. 58 chapters. Established 1965. Call: (703) 883-1773 or (800) 451-6434. Write: P.O. Box 3090, Falls Church, Virginia 22043.

Little People of America

National. For people four feet ten inches or less. Discussion groups, other opportunities for exchange of support, information. Special program for teenagers. Publishes newsletter. 45 chapters active in 13 national districts. Established 1957. Call: (301) 589-0730. Write: P.O. Box 9897, Washington, D. C. 20016.

SICK, DISABLED CHILDREN

(See also "Caregivers," "Premature, High-Risk, Sick Infants.")

Association of Birth Defect Children

National. For families of children with birth defects due to mother's or father's exposure to pesticides, chemicals, drugs, radiation, other substances in the environment. Helps create networks between parents for exchange of support, information. Publishes quarterly newsletter, maintains national birth-defect registry. Established 1982. Call: (407) 629-1466. Write: 5400 Diplomat Circle, Suite 270, Orlando, Florida 32810.

Keshet

Model. For disabled Jewish children and their families and friends. To help membership "realize their dreams, while participating as fully as possible in the mainstream of Jewish life." Activities include parent and sibling support groups, day and Sunday school, summer day camps, special events, including holiday celebration. Provides information, referrals. Mounts advocacy efforts on behalf of membership, which now exceeds 200. Established 1982. Call: (312) 588-0551. Write: Susan Wolfson, 3525 Peterson T17, Chicago, Illinois 60659.

Parents Helping Parents

Model. For families of children with disabilities. Discussion groups, other opportunities for exchange of resources, information between parents and other family members; social activities for children. Provides peer counseling. Conducts outreach visits to prospective new member families. Maintains resource center of printed and other materials for use by members. Sponsors annual symposium. Publishes newsletter, group development guidelines. 2 chapters. Established 1976. Call: (408) 288-5010. Write: 535 Race Street, Suite 140, San Jose, California 95126.

S.K.I.P. ("Sick Kids Need Involved People"), Inc.

National voluntary organization. For families of children with complex health care needs, including developmental disabilities, inherited disorders, conditions that require mechanical assistance or support and needs associated with conditions resulting from accidents of birth. Assists families in bringing home children from hospital or facilities, helps keep them home. Provides advice, referrals. Each chapter helps create networks among members for exchange of support, information by phone, in person. Various publications, including annual, *Families to Families*. 22 affiliated groups nationwide. Established 1983. Call: (212) 421-9160. Write: Kathy Schwaninger, 990 Second Avenue, New York, New York 10022.

SJÖGREN'S SYNDROME

**Sjögren's
Syndrome Foundation** _____

International. For people with Sjögren's syndrome, a chronic autoimmune disease, characterized by dry eyes, mouth, nose and vagina, with related effects on other parts of the body, including skin, lungs, kidneys, digestive tract; affects women nine times more often than men. The foundation sponsors educational symposia for patients and professionals; publishes monthly newsletter, *The Moisture Seekers,* and *The Sjögren's Syndrome Handbook.* Provides guidelines for local chapters, which offer programs including discussion groups for exchange of support, information. Numerous U.S., Canadian and overseas chapters. Established 1983. Call: (516) 767-2866. Write: Elaine K. Harris, 382 Main Street, Port Washington, New York 11050.

SMOKING

Nicotine Anonymous _____

International. For people who want to recover from a self-diagnosed addiction to nicotine and live without smoking. Formerly called Smokers Anonymous. 12-step program. Discussion groups for exchanging support, information. Publishes newsletter, group development guidelines. Over 250 groups. Established 1985. Call: (415) 922-8575. Write: 2118 Greenwich Street, San Francisco, California 94123.

SOTOS SYNDROME

**Sotos Syndrome
Support Association** _____

National. For families of children with Sotos syndrome (also known as cerebral gigantism), a brain-based condition marked by certain physical characteristics (such as larger-than-normal head) and resulting in childhood developmental delays. Discussion groups, telephone networking, other opportunities for exchange of peer support, information. Provides referrals. Sponsors annual conferences. Publishes newsletter, pamphlet, and booklet on "family feelings." Established 1984. Call: (402) 556-2445. Write: 4686 Vinton, Omaha, Nebraska 68106.

SOUTHEAST ASIANS

Southeast Asia Center _____

Chicago area. For refugees from Southeast Asia. Facilitates networking between members for exchange of support, information. Provides advocacy, cultural orientation, English-as-a-second-language instruction, assistance with homework, counseling, day care, other services on behalf of member clients. Seeks to help Southeast Asian refugees participate effectively in U.S. society, culture, and to "help build bridges of cooperation and understanding between people of Eastern and Western cultural backgrounds." Established 1979. Call: (312) 989-6927. Write: Peter R. Porr, 1124 West Ainslie, Chicago, Illinois 60640.

SPASMODIC DYSPHONIA

National Spasmodic Dysphonia Association

For people with spasmodic dysphonia, a neurological condition affecting the vocal muscles of the larynx, causing abnormal involuntary movements and rendering speech effortful and often strangled; also for families and friends. Stimulates increased access to information and resources; promotes public education; advocates increased research; encourages formation of local support groups. Established 1990. Write: P.O. Box 1574, Birmingham, Michigan 48009.

SPASMODIC TORTICOLLIS

National Spasmodic Torticollis Association

For people with spasmodic torticollis (ST), a painful neurological disorder that affects the muscles of the neck, causing the head to pull, turn or jerk toward the shoulder; also for families and friends of patients. Discussion groups, telephone networking, pen-pal program, other opportunities to exchange peer-group support, information. Publishes newsletter, group development guidelines. Chapters in 40 states. Established 1983. Call: (800) HURTFUL. Write: P.O. Box 476, Elm Grove, Wisconsin 53122.

SPINA BIFIDA

Spina Bifida Association of America

National. For people with spina bifida, a congenital defect of the spine. Facilitates educational and vocational development of membership. Publishes newsletter, chapter development guidelines. 110 chapters. Established 1972. Call: (202) 944-3285; fax: (202) 944-3295. Write: 4590 MacArthur Boulevard, N.W., Suite 250, Washington, D.C. 20007.

SPINAL-CORD INJURY

National Spinal Cord Injury Association

For persons with spinal cord injury, their families and friends and interested professionals. Discussion groups for support, exchange of information. Publishes quarterly magazine, group development guidelines, resource directory. 60-plus chapters and support groups. Established in 1948 by the Paralyzed Veterans Association, (see entry), to improve quality of care available to those with spinal cord injuries. Call: (800) 962-9629 or (617) 935-2722. Write: Rebecca White, 600 West Cummings Park, Suite 2000, Woburn, Massachusetts 01801.

Spinal Cord Society

National. For people with spinal cord injuries, their families and friends and interested professionals. Promotes research for treatments and a cure. Works to heighten public awareness. Sponsors outreach efforts to individuals with the injury. Publishes monthly newsletter. Nearly 200 affiliated chapters. Established

1978. Call: (218) 739-5252. Write: Charles Carson, Wendell Road, Fergus Falls, Minnesota 56537.

SPINAL MUSCULAR ATROPHY

Families of Spinal Muscular Atrophy (S.M.A.)

National. For families of patients with various types of spinal-muscle atrophy (SMA), including Werdnig-Hoffman disease, benign congenital hypotonia, juvenile progressive spinal muscular atrophy and adult progressive spinal muscular atrophy. Telephone networking, pen-pal program, other opportunities for exchange of peer support, information. Publishes bimonthly newsletter. Informational videotapes available. 4 chapters. Established 1984. Call: (708) 432-5551. Write: P.O. Box 1465, Highland Park, Illinois 60035.

STROKE

Courage Stroke Network

National. For people who have had strokes. Discussion groups, other opportunities for exchange of support, information. Provides referrals, conducts public education efforts, produces annual seminar, trains peer counselors, publishes two newsletters, *Stroke Connection* and *Stroke of Luck, The Stroke Fact Book* and *A Stroke Survivor's Workout* exercise video. Over 800 chapters. Established 1979. Call: (800) 553-6321 or (612) 520-0464; fax: (612) 520-0577. Write: 3915 Golden Valley Road, Golden Valley, Minnesota 55422.

National Stroke Association

For stroke survivors, their families and friends, interested professionals and the general public. Discussion groups, other opportunities for exchange of support, information. Administers an information and referral center. Grants research fellowships. Publishes training manual for long-term caregivers to stroke victims, as well as a professional journal, *Stroke: Clinical Updates*. 8 chapters. Established 1984. Call: (303) 762-9922. Write: 300 East Hampden Avenue, Suite 240, Englewood, Colorado 80110.

Stroke Clubs

National. For persons who have had strokes and their families and friends. Discussion groups, social and recreational events, other opportunities for exchange of support and information. Established 1968. Call: (800) AHA-USA1. Write: 7272 Greenville Avenue, Dallas, Texas 75231.

STURGE-WEBER SYNDROME

Sturge-Weber Foundation, The

International. For families and friends of people with Sturge-Weber syndrome (encephalotrigeminal angiomatosis), a congenital, nonfamilial disorder of unknown incidence and cause; characterized by a congenital facial birthmark (port wine stain) and neurological abnormalities as well as eye and internal organ irregularities. Facilitates creation of networks—including by telephone and pen-pal program—among members for exchange of support, information. Facilitates research, disseminates information to general public. Publishes quarterly newsletter. Established 1987. Call: (303) 360-7290 or (800) 627-5482. Write: P.O. Box 460931, Aurora, Colorado 80046.

STUTTERING

Compulsive Stutterers Anonymous

National. For people who stutter. 12-step program. "Talking gently and not hiding our stuttering is our primary purpose." Discussion groups and telephone networking help group members exchange support and information, and practice speech-modification techniques or tools learned through professional speech therapy. Publishes pamphlets, brochures, groups development guidelines. Established 1989. Call: (708) 272-3712. Write: P.O. Box 1406, Park Ridge, Illinois 60068.

International Foundation for Stutterers, Inc.

For people who stutter. Combines speech therapy with self-help, mutual aid approach. Seeks to educate professionals and general public about stuttering. Discussion groups, telephone networking, other opportunities for exchange of support and information between members. Administers speakers' bureau. Publishes group development guidelines. Established 1980. Call: (609) 275-3806. Write: P.O. Box 462, Belle Mead, New Jersey 08502.

National Stuttering Project

For people who stutter. Discussion groups where members can exchange support and information and work on their verbal skills. Publishes monthly newsletter, group development guidelines. Over 80 groups. Estab-

lished 1977. Write: 2151 Irving Street #208, San Francisco, California 94122.

Speak Easy International Foundation, Inc.

For adults as well as adolescents who stutter. Discussion groups, telephone networking, other opportunities for exchange of support, information and peer counseling. Publishes quarterly newsletter. Annual symposium. 8 chapters. Established 1981. Call: (201) 262-0895. Write: Bob or Antoinette Gathman, 233 Concord Drive, Paramus, New Jersey 07652.

SUICIDE

(See also "Bereavement: Suicide.")

American Association of Suicidology

National. For people who have survived suicide attempts. Umbrella organization that promotes self-help groups for suicide survivors. Publishes newsletter. Call: (303) 692-0985. Write: 2459 South Ash, Denver, Colorado 80222.

National Hemlock Society

For people—many of whom suffer from terminal illnesses—who believe that terminally ill adults have the right to some control over their own dying. Also for their families and friends. Local affiliates have discussion groups, telephone networking, other opportunities to exchange support, information. Publishes quarterly newsletter and distributes several books on euthanasia for the terminally ill. Over 57,000 members. Chapters in most states. Established 1980. Call: (503) 342-5748. Write: P.O. Box 11380, Eugene, Oregon 97440.

Samaritans, The _____
National. For the suicidal, lonely and distressed. Provides suicide prevention, "befriending" services via 24-hour telephone line. 7 affiliates. Established 1974. Call: (617) 247-0220. Write: 500 Commonwealth Avenue, Boston, Massachusetts 02215.

SYRINGOMYELIA

**American Syringomyelia
Alliance Project** _____
National. For people with syringomyelia, often called SM, a chronic progressive disease primarily of the spinal cord, causing sensory disturbances, muscle atrophy and spasticity. Telephone networking, special children's network, annual convention in June, other opportunities for members to exchange support, information. Publishes various materials. Seeks to promote public awareness of problem, research. Active in 49 states and overseas. Established 1988. Call: (903) 236-7079; fax: (903) 757-7456. Write: Patricia Williams, P.O. Box 1586, Longview, Texas 75606.

TALL PEOPLE

Tall Clubs International _____
Various activities, especially social events, where tall men (6'2" and over) and tall women (5'10" and over) can meet, exchange support, form friendships and relationships. Advocacy for the special needs of the tall community, such as appropriately sized clothing from the apparel industry. Provides information and referrals. Publishes newsletter, group development guidelines. 54 chapters. Established 1938. Call: Leave message at (800) 521-2512.

Write: P.O. Box 4301, Huntington Beach, California 92605.

TAY-SACHS DISEASE

**National Tay-Sachs & Allied
Diseases Association** _____
For families and friends of children with Tay-Sachs and allied diseases (lysosomal storage diseases), which are rare, fatal, hereditary disorders, chiefly affecting infants and children, usually of Eastern European Jewish background. The disease is characterized by a common biochemical defect: the inability of body cells to dispose of certain metabolic waste products, causing a variety of debilitating symptoms; usually fatal early in childhood. Discussion groups for parents to exchange peer-group support, information. Seeks to heighten awareness of professionals and general public. Sponsors genetic screening for carriers of Tay-Sachs and related disorders. Promotes research, quality control of labs working on problem. Offers various services to member families. Established 1957. Call: (617) 277-4463. Write: 2001 Beacon Street, Brookline, Massachusetts 02146.

TEEN PREGNANCY

Parents Too Soon _____
Active in Illinois. For teenagers who need pregnancy and parenting counseling and services in areas that include day care, parent support, home visiting, public aid, job services, education, family planning, prenatal care, WIC (Women and Infant Children Program) and substance abuse. Provides information, referrals and education. Over 60 chapters active. Established 1983. Call: (800) 422-5587

8:30 A.M.–midnight, Monday–Friday, 1:30–9 P.M. Saturday and Sunday. Write: Shelly Lambert, 535 West Jefferson Street, Springfield, Illinois 62761.

THROMBOCYTOPENIA ABSENT RADIUS SYNDROME

T.A.R.S.A. (Thrombocytopenia Absent Radius Syndrome Anonymous) _____

International. For families of children with TAR, a congenital disease whose sufferers are characterized by short arms, low blood platelet count, and, occasionally, knee and ankle problems. Telephone networking, pen-pal program, other opportunities for exchange of peer support, information. Publishes annual newsletter. Established 1981. Call: (609) 927-0418. Write: Ed Purinton, 312 Sherwood Drive, R.D. 1, Linwood, New Jersey 08221.

TOURETTE SYNDROME

Tourette Syndrome Association, Inc. _____

National. For people with Tourette syndrome, a neurological condition characterized by involuntary movements (tics) and vocalizations; also for families and friends of patients and interested professionals. Provides various services to members, including physician referrals. Funds research. Publishes chapter development guidelines, medical information and materials for teachers. Audiovisuals available. 45 chapters. Established 1972. Call: (718) 224-2999 or (800) 237-0717. Write: 42-40 Bell Boulevard, Bayside, New York 11361.

TRANSVESTITES

International Foundation for Gender Education (I.F.G.E.) _____

For male and female cross-dressers (transvestites) as well as for anyone who is conflicted about his or her gender, including transsexuals (people whose desire to become members of the opposite gender is sometimes treated by surgery that transforms genitals and other elements of their physiology); and for the families and friends. Maintains lists of self-help groups of interest to membership. Publishes a journal, *TV/TS Tapestry*. Established 1984. Call: (617) 894-8340 or (617) 899-2212. Write: P.O. Box 367, Wayland, Massachusetts 01778.

Society for the Second Self _____

National. Also known as the Tri-Ess Sorority. For heterosexual male cross-dressers (transvestites). Support and information through a variety of activities, including pen-pal program, annual convention, discussion groups. Various special events "en femme," where members dress as women, use their female name, and so on. Publishes newsletter, group development guidelines. National directory of members. Seeks to protect privacy of members, all activities conducted confidentially. 24 chapters. Established 1976. Call: (209) 688-9246. Write: P.O. Box 194, Tulare, California 93275.

WACS ("Wives Associated with Crossdressers Society") _____

National. For wives and partners of male crossdressers (transvestites). Affiliated with Society for the Second Self (see entry). Publishes occasional newsletter to facilitate communications, networking among members. Established 1991. Call: (512) 438-7604. Write:

Cynthia Phillips, P.O. Box 17, Belverde, Texas 78163.

TRAUMA

Trauma Recovery, Inc. _____
Model. For people recovering from serious injuries and their families and friends. Discussion groups, telephone networking, other opportunities to exchange support, information. Members assist each other with practical help for everyday problems. 2 affiliated groups. Established 1979. Call: (301) 255-3074. Write: Linda Wolfe, 2201 Argonne Drive, Baltimore, Maryland 21218.

TREACHER COLLINS SYNDROME

Treacher Collins Family Foundation _____
National. For individuals with Treacher Collins syndrome, also called mandibulofacial dysostosis or Franceschetti-Klein syndrome, a rare and very complex genetic condition involving underdevelopment of the structures of the head and face as well as certain other occasional problems, including hearing loss, eating difficulties and breathing problems. (Otherwise, TC patients have normal development and intelligence.) Also for families and friends of TC patients. Telephone networking, pen-pal program, other opportunities for exchange of peer-group support, information. Makes referrals. Maintains U.S. and Canadian resource list, library of materials relating to TC syndrome. Publishes newsletter, list of members to facilitate networking, various other materials. Established 1988. Call:

(802) 649-3020. Write: P.O. Box 683, Norwich, Vermont 05055.

TRISOMY

S.O.F.T. (Support Organization for Trisomy) _____
National. For families of children—living or deceased—with trisomy 13, trisomy 18 and other genetic disorders. Discussion groups, regional and annual international meetings, pen-pal program, telephone networking, other opportunities to exchange peer-group support, information. Manages speakers' bureau. Seeks to educate professionals. Publishes quarterly newsletter, various books, including *T18—A Book for Families; T13—A Guidebook; Common Problems of Children With T18 or T13.* 54 chapters. Established 1979. Call: (716) 594-4621; fax: same as telephone number, but call first. Write: Barbara Van Herreweghe, 2982 South Union Street, Rochester, New York 14624.

TUBE FEEDING

(See also "Caregiving.")

Oley Foundation, Inc. _____
National. For people requiring long-term specialized nutritional therapy, including tube feeding. Network of clinicians and patients through the U.S. and several other countries. Activities include annual research registry of patients in the U.S. and Canada; monthly publication, *Lifelineletter;* outreach system to provide support, information for patients; annual conference. Established 1983. Call: (518) 445-5079 or (800) 776-OLEY. Write: Joan

Bishop Albany Medical Center A-23, Albany, New York 12208.

Tuberous Sclerosis

National Tuberous Sclerosis Association

For families and friends of people with tuberous sclerosis, also called Bourneville's disease or epiloia, a genetic disorder marked by seizures, mental retardation and multiple tumors of the skin, brain and eyes. Discussion groups, telephone networking, pen-pal program, other opportunities for exchanging peer-group support, information. Promotes research. Publishes quarterly newsletter, group development guidelines. Affiliates or contacts in 35 states. Established 1975. Call: (301) 459-9888 or (800) 225-NTSA. Write: 8000 Corporate Drive, Suite 120, Landover, Maryland 20785.

Tumor

Acoustic Neuroma Association

National. Support and information for patients who have suffered from acoustic neuromas (also known by a variety of other terms, including acoustic neurilemoma or schwannoma, cerebellopontine angle tumor, or eighth nerve tumor), which are benign growths of the cranial nerves. Services include chapter development guidelines and newsletter. Over 30 chapters. Established 1981. Call: (404) 237-8023. Write: P.O. Box 12402, Atlanta, Georgia 30355.

American Brain Tumor Association

National. For people who have or who have had brain tumors; also for families and friends of patients and interested professionals. Maintains lists of brain-tumor support groups. Makes referrals. Distributes information about treatment facilities. Publishes patient education materials and triannual newsletter, *Message Line*. Established 1973. Call: (312) 286-5571; fax: (312) 549-5561; patient services: (800) 886-2282. Write: 3725 North Talman Avenue, Chicago, Illinois 60618.

Turner's Syndrome

Turner's Syndrome Society of Canada

National in Canada. For girls and women with Turner's syndrome, a genetically determined condition characterized by infertility and short stature; also for families of Turner's syndrome patients. Pen-pal program, annual conferences, other opportunities to exchange peer-group support, information. Provides referrals, education to members. Publishes newsletter, tapes, chapter development guidelines. Numerous chapters throughout the provinces. Established 1981. Call: (416) 660-7766. Write: 7777 Keele Street, Second Floor, Concord, Ontario, Canada L4K 1Y7.

Turner's Syndrome Society of the U.S.

National. For girls and women with Turner's syndrome, a genetically determined condition characterized by infertility and short stature, and for their families. Discussion groups, annual conferences, other opportunities for exchange of peer-group support, information. Seeks to increase public awareness of syndrome. Publishes bimonthly newsletter, group development guidelines. 9 chapters. Established 1988. Call: (612) 475-9944. Write: 768-214 Twelve Oaks, 15500 Wayzata, Wayzata, Minnesota 55391.

USHER'S SYNDROME

(See also "Blindness, Visual Impairment," "Deafness Hearing Impairment.")

Usher's Syndrome Self-Help Network

National. Maintains a database of people who suffer from Usher's syndrome, a congenital disorder that causes deafness and retinitis pigmentosa; also lists families and friends of Usher's syndrome sufferers. People listed in database are available for networking by phone or correspondence. Established 1983. Call: (800) 683-5555 or (410) 225-9400; TDD (410) 225-9409. Write: 1401 Mount Royal Avenue, 4th Floor, Baltimore, Maryland 21217.

VENTILATOR USERS

Care for Life, Inc.

National. For people whose breathing depends on use of a ventilator (also known as a respirator), a mechanical device that "breathes" for people when they are no longer able to do so themselves. Also for families and friends of users. Helps create networks between members for informal exchange of support, information by phone. Established 1980. Call: (312) 883-1018. Write: 1018 West Diversey Parkway, Chicago, Illinois 60614.

International Ventilator Users Network

For people whose breathing is assisted by ventilators—mechanical devices that "breathe" for people when they are no longer able to do so themselves; also for families and friends and interested professionals. Members communicate via newsletter, *IVUN News*. Spon-

sors conferences. Founded 1958. Call: (314) 534-0475. Write: 5100 Oakland Avenue, #206, St. Louis, Missouri 63110.

VESTIBULAR (BALANCE) DISORDERS

Vestibular Disorders Association

National. For people who suffer from dizziness and balance disorders due to inner-ear (vestibular) problems. Discussion groups, telephone networking, other opportunities for exchange of support, information. Other activities include public education, resource library. Publishes quarterly newsletter, booklets, videotapes, group development guidelines. 70 affiliated groups. Established 1983. Call: (503) 229-7705; fax: (503) 229-8064. Write: Jerry Underwood, P.O. Box 4467, Portland, Oregon 97208.

VETERANS

(See also "Blindness, Visual Impairment.")

Concerned Americans for Military Improvements (C.A.M.I.)

National. For military personnel (active or veteran) who are or believe they are victims of military malpractice, such as preventable accidents, or other injustices. Also for their families and friends. Discussion groups, telephone networking, conferences, other opportunities for exchange of information and support. Publishes newsletter. Assists in formation of new chapters. Over 30 chapters. Established 1982. Call: (401) 943-5165. Write:

Mary Day, 293 Webster Avenue, Cranston, Rhode Island 02909.

Disabled American Veterans _____
National. For disabled veterans and their families. Provides professional benefit counseling and claim-filing assistance to veterans and their families free of charge. Local chapters provide opportunities for exchange of support, information. Members assist fellow veterans in several ways, including extensive volunteer programs at Veterans Administration medical facilities. Advocates legislation that benefits disabled veterans. Publishes monthly magazine, group development guidelines. Over 2,760 chapters. Established 1920. Call: (606) 441-7300. Write: P.O. Box 14301, Cincinnati, Ohio 45250.

Paralyzed Veterans of America _____
National. For military veterans with spinal cord injury or disease. Various activities provide members with a network for exchange of support, information. Lobbies on behalf of membership. Administers sports and recreation program. Mounts public education efforts. Over 40 chapters nationwide. Established 1947. Call: (202) USA-1300; fax: (202) 785-4452. Write: 801 Eighteenth Street, N.W., Washington, D.C. 20006.

Vietnam Veterans of America _____
National. For Vietnam War era veterans and their families and friends. Advocacy on behalf of membership on pertinent issues, such as Agent Orange-related medical disorders, post-traumatic stress. Publishes monthly newsletter, group development guidelines. Nearly 600 chapters. Founded 1978. Call: (202) 628-2700. Write: 1224 M Street, N.W., Washington, D.C. 20005.

VITILIGO

National Vitiligo Foundation _____
For persons with vitiligo, a skin disease manifested by smooth white spots on various parts of the body. Discussion groups, telephone networking to exchange support, information. Fund-raises for research. Publishes semiannual newsletter, chapter development guidelines. 10 chapters. Established 1985. Call: (903) 534-2925; fax: (903) 534-8075. Write: Amy Jones, P.O. Box 6337, Tyler, Texas 75711.

WERDNIG-HOFFMAN DISEASE

Werdnig-Hoffman Parents Group _____
Model. For parents of children with Werdnig-Hoffman disease, also known as infantile muscular atrophy, Hoffman's muscular atrophy, familial spinal muscular atrophy, infantile progressive spinal muscular atrophy—a hereditary disease marked by progressive muscular wasting due to degeneration of the spinal cord, beginning in an infant's first year and causing 80% mortality by the fourth. Telephone networking, recreational activities, other opportunities to exchange peer-group support, information. Publishes quarterly newsletter. Call: (415) 570-6166. Write: c/o M.D.A., 561 Pilgrim Drive, #C, Foster City, California 94404.

WIDOWS/WIDOWERS

See "Bereavement: Spouse."

WILLIAMS SYNDROME

Williams Syndrome Association

National. For families and friends of people with Williams syndrome, a congenital disorder marked by mental deficiency, mild growth deficiency as well as a variety of heart and other problems; also for interested professionals. Telephone networking, other opportunities to exchange peer-group support, information. Seeks to inform professionals and general public about syndrome. Publishes quarterly newsletter. Maintains library of videotapes, off-prints. 10 regional chapters active throughout U.S. Established 1983. Call: (314) 227-4411. Write: P.O. Box 3297, Ballwin, Missouri 63022.

WILSON'S DISEASE

Wilson's Disease Association

National. For people with Wilson's disease, a rare but treatable genetic disorder characterized by excess storage of copper in the body tissues, particularly in the liver, kidneys, brain and corneas of the eyes, leading to liver disease, kidney malfunction, neurologic malfunction and a distinctive rusty-brown discoloration of the cornea. Also for their families and friends and interested professionals. Helps members network for exchange of support, information. Seeks to educate general public about disease. Disburses funds to foster research and provides direct financial aid to members. Cooperates with other, related organizations. Established 1979. Call: (703) 636-3014 or (703) 636-3003. Write: Carol Terry, President, P.O. Box 75324, Washington, D.C. 20013.

WOMEN

(See also "Aging," "Alcoholism, Substance Abuse," "Endometriosis," "Hysterectomy," "Osteoporosis," and "P.I.D. [Pelvic Inflammatory Disease"])

Midlife Women's Support Group

Model. For women over 40. Encourages enjoyable, meaningful lives in middle age and beyond. Discussion groups, workshops, other opportunities to exchange support, information. Specific topics addressed include: life after raising a family, after divorce or death of spouse; dealing with feelings resulting from childlessness; medical problems associated with midlife. One-page information flyer available. Workshops on specific subjects, such as optimism and hypnosis. Established 1979. Call: (718) 875-1420. Write: Rose Langfelder, 30 Third Avenue, Brooklyn, New York 11217.

National Organization for Women

Members include women and men. Advocates equality for both genders. Activities include advocacy efforts, education meetings and national newsletter. Provides chapter development guidelines. Over 800 chapters. Established 1966. Call: (202) 331-0066. Write: 1000 16th Street, N.W., Suite 700, Washington, D.C. 20036.

WORKAHOLISM

Workaholics Anonymous

International. For people who overwork compulsively; also for their families and friends. 12-step program. Meetings, other opportunities to exchange support, information. Assistance and guidelines for developing new chapters. Literature available. Provides information, materials for related program, Work-Anon, "a program of recovery for those in a relationship with a workaholic." Founded 1983. Call: (310) 859-5804. Write: P.O. Box 61501, Los Angeles, California 90066.

Clearinghouses

U.S.: NATIONAL

American Self-Help Clearinghouse. Contact: St. Clares-Riverside Medical Center, Denville, New Jersey 07834. Call: (201) 625-7101, Fax: (201) 625-8848; TDD: (201) 625-9053.

National Self-Help Clearinghouse. Contact: Frank Riessman, Director, City University of New York Graduate Center, Room 620, 25 West 43rd Street, Room 620, New York, New York 10036. Call: (212) 642-2944.

CALIFORNIA

Culver City

Southern Tri-County Regional Self-Help Center. Contact: Al Jenkins, Coordinator, 5839 Green Valley Circle, Suite 100, Culver City, California 90230. Call: (310) 645-9890.

Davis

Northern Self-Help Clearinghouse, Western Division. Contact: Elaine Talley, Coordinator, Mental Health Association of Yolo County, P.O. Box 447, Davis, California 95617. Call: (916) 756-8181.

Los Angeles

California Self-Help Center. Contact: Fran Jammott Dory, Executive Director, U.C.L.A. Psychology Department, 405 Hildegard Avenue, Los Angeles, California 90024. Call: In California: (800) 222-LINK, Outside California: (310) 825-1799.

Merced

Central Region Self-Help Center. (For Central California) Contact: Mary Jo Burns, Coordinator, Merced County Department of Mental Health, 650 West 19th Street, Merced, California 95340. Call: (209) 725-3752.

Riverside

Self-Help Information & Networking Exchange (S.H.I.N.E.). Contact: Karen Banker, Coordinator, Riverside Mental Health Association, 3763 Arlinton Avenue, Suite 103, Riverside, California 92508. Call: (714) 684-6051.

Sacramento

Northern Region Self-Help Center, Eastern Division. (For Northern California) Contact: Pat Camper, Coordinator, Mental Health Association of Sacramento, 8912 Volunteer Lane, Room 210, Sacramento, California 95819. Call: (916) 368-3100.

San Diego

Southern Self-Help Center. (For Southern California) Contact: Joe Horton, Coordinator, Mental Health Association, 3958 Third Avenue, San Diego, California 92103. Call: (619) 298-3152.

San Francisco

Bay Area Self-Help Center. (For the Bay area) Contact: Duff Axsom, Coordinator. Mental Health Association, 2398 Pine Street, San Francisco, California 94115. Call: (415) 921-4401, Fax: (415) 921-1911.

CONNECTICUT

Connecticut Self-Help/Mutual-Support Network. Contact: Carol Shaff, Director, 389 Whitney Avenue, New Haven, Connecticut 06511. Call: (203) 789-7645.

ILLINOIS

Champaign

Self-Help Center. (For Northern Illinois) Contact: Mellen Kennedy, Coordinator, Family Service of Champaign County, 405 South State Street, Champaign, Illinois 61820. Call: (217) 352-0099, Fax: (217) 352-9512.

Decatur

Macon County Support Group Network. Contact: Macon County Health Department, 1221 East Condit, Decatur, Illinois 62521. Call: (217) 429-HELP.

Evanston

Illinois Self-Help Center. (Statewide) Contact: Daryl Isenberg, Executive Director, 1600 Dodge Avenue, Suite S-122, Evanston, Illinois 60201. Call: Inquiries and referrals: (312) 328-0470, Administration: (312) 328-0471; fax: (312) 328-0754.

IOWA

Iowa Self-Help Clearinghouse. Contact: Carla Reed, Director, Iowa Pilot Parents, Inc., 33 North 12th Street, Fort Dodge, Iowa 50501. Call: Iowa: (800) 383-4777 or (515) 576-5870; outside Iowa: (515) 576-5870.

KANSAS

Kansas Self-Help Network. Contact: Gregory J. Meissen, Director, Wichita State University, Campus Box 34, Wichita, Kansas 67208. Call: In Kansas: (800) 445-0116; Outside Kansas: (316) 689-3843.

MASSACHUSETTS

Massachusetts Clearinghouse of Mutual-Help Groups. Contact: Warren Schumacher, Director, University of Massachusetts Cooperative Extension, 113 Skinner Hall, Amherst, Massachusetts 01003. Call: (413) 545-2313.

MICHIGAN

Benton Harbor

Center for Self-Help. (Southern Michigan) Contact: Pat Friend, Director, Riverwood

Center, P.O. Box 547, Benton Harbor, Michigan 49022. Call: (800) 336-0341; in Michigan only, (616) 925-0594.

Michigan Self-Help Clearinghouse. Contact: Toni Young, Coordinator, Michigan Protection & Advocacy Service, 106 West Allegan, Suite 210, Lansing, Michigan 48933. Call: In Michigan: (800) 336-0341; outside Michigan: (517) 484-7373.

MINNESOTA

Minnesota First Call for Help. Contact: Diane Faulds, Coordinator, 116 East 4th Street, Suite 310, St. Paul, Minnesota 55101. Call: Information and referrals: (612) 224-1133; administration: (612) 291-8427.

MISSOURI

Kansas City

The Support Group Clearinghouse. Contact: Julie Broyle, Coordinator, Kansas City Association for Mental Health, 1009 Baltimore Avenue, Suite 5-FL, Kansas City, Missouri 64105. Call: (816) 472-HELP.

St. Louis

St. Louis Self-Help Clearinghouse. Contact: Peggy Corski, Coordinator, Greater St. Louis Mental Health Association, 1905 South Grand Boulevard, St. Louis, Missouri 63104. Call: (314) 773-1399.

NEBRASKA

Nebraska Self-Help Information Services. Contact: Barbara Fox, Director, 1601 Euclid

Avenue, Lincoln, Nebraska 68502. Call: (402) 476-9668.

NEW JERSEY

New Jersey Self-Help Clearinghouse. Contact: Edward J. Madara, Director, St. Clares-Riverside Medical Center, 25 Pocono Road, Denville, New Jersey 07834. Call: In New Jersey: (800) 367-6274; outside New Jersey: (201) 625-9565; TDD: (201) 625-9053.

NEW YORK

Brooklyn

Brooklyn Self-Help Clearinghouse. Contact: Rose Langfelder, Director, Height Hills Mental Health Center, 20 Third Avenue, Brooklyn, New York 11217. Call: (718) 875-1420.

White Plains

Westchester Self-Help Clearinghouse. Contact: Leslie Borck Jameson, Director, 456 North Street, White Plains, New York 10605. Call: (914) 949-6301.

NORTH CAROLINA

Mecklenberg County

Supportworks. Contact: Joal Fischer, Director, 1012 Kings Drive, Suite 923, Charlotte, North Carolina 28283. Call: (704) 331-9500.

OHIO

Dayton

Greater Dayton Self-Help Clearinghouse. Contact: Shari Peace, Coordinator, Family

Services Association, 184 Salem Avenue, Dayton, Ohio 45406. Call: (513) 225-3004.

OREGON

Portland

Northwest Regional Self-Help Clearinghouse. (Northwest). Contact: Judy Hadley, Coordinator, 718 West Burnside Avenue, Portland, Oregon 97209. Call: Information and referrals: (503) 222-5555; administration: (503) 226-9360.

PENNSYLVANIA

Pittsburgh

Self-Help Group Network of the Pittsburgh Area. Contact: Betty Hepner, Coordinator, 1323 Forbes Avenue Suite 200, Pittsburgh, Pennsylvania 15219. Call: (412) 261-5363; fax: (412) 471-2722.

Scranton

Self-Help Information & Networking Exchange (S.H.I.N.E.). (Northeast). Contact: Gail Bauer, Director, Voluntary Action Center of Northeast Pennsylvania, 225 West Washington, Park Plaza, Lower Level, Scranton, Pennsylvania 18503. Call: (717) 961-1234.

SOUTH CAROLINA

West Columbia

Midland Area Support Group Network. Contact: Nancy Farrar, Director, Lexington Medical Center, 2720 Sunset Boulevard, West Columbia, South Carolina 29169. Call: Infor-

mation and referrals: (803) 791-9227, Administration: (803) 791-2049.

TENNESSEE

Knoxville

Support Group Clearinghouse of Knox County. Contact: Judy Balloff, Coordinator, Mental Health Association of Knox County, 6712 Kingston Pike, Suite 203, Knoxville, Tennessee 37919. Call: (615) 584-3736.

Memphis

Self-Help Clearinghouse. (Memphis and Shelby counties) Contact: Carol Barnett, Coordinator, Mental Health Association, 2400 Poplar Avenue, Memphis, Tennessee 38112. Call: (901) 323-8485; fax: (901) 323-0858.

TEXAS

Austin

Texas Self-Help Clearinghouse. (statewide) Contact: Christine Devall, Coordinator, Mental Health Association in Texas, 8401 Shoal Creek Boulevard, Austin, Texas 78758. Call: (512) 454-3706.

Dallas

Dallas Self-Help Clearinghouse. Contact: Carol Madison, Director, Mental Health Association, 2929 Carlisle, Suite 350, Dallas, Texas 75204. Call: (214) 871-2420.

Fort Worth

Tarrant County Self-Help Clearinghouse. (For central Texas) Contact: Roxanne Rudy, Coordinator, Mental Health Association of

Tarrant County, 3136 West 4th Street, Fort Worth, Texas 76107. Call: (817) 335-5405.

Houston

Houston Area Self-Help Clearinghouse. (For southeast Texas) Contact: Dianne Long, Co-ordinator, Mental Health Association in Houston and Harris Counties, 2211 Norfolk Street, Suite 810, Houston, Texas 77098. Call: (713) 523-8963.

San Antonio

Greater San Antonio Self-Help Clearinghouse. Contact: Mental Health in Greater San Antonio, 901 Northeast Loop 410, Suite 500, San Antonio, Texas 78209. Call: (512) 826-2288.

VIRGINIA

Annandale Church

Self-Help Clearinghouse of Greater Washington. (Washington, D.C. area) Contact: Lisa Saisselin, Coordinator, Mental Health Association of Virginia, 7630 Little River Turnpike, Suite 206, Annandale Church, Virginia 22003. Call: (703) 941-5465.

Falls Church

Self-Help Clearinghouse of Greater Washington. Contact: Mental Health Association of Northern Virginia, 100 North Washington Street, Suite 232, Falls Church, Virginia 22046. Call: (703) 536-4100.

Canada

ALBERTA

Family Life Education Council. Contact; Sonia Eisler, Executive Director, 33 Twelfth Avenue, S.W., Calgary, Alberta, Canada T2R 0G9. Call: (403) 262-1117.

BRITISH COLUMBIA

Self-Help Collaboration Project. Contact: Rae Folster, Coordinator, United Way of the Lower Mainland, 1625 West Eighth Avenue, Vancouver, British Columbia, Canada V6J 1T6. Call: (604) 731-7781.

NOVA SCOTIA

The Self-Help Connection. Contact: Margot Clarke, Coordinator, Mental Health Association, 63 King Street, Halifax, Nova Scotia, Canada B3J 2R7. Call: (902) 466-2011.

ONTARIO

Canadian Council on Social Development/ Conseil Canadien de Développement Social. (Nationwide) P.O. Box 3505, Station C, Ottawa, Ontario, Canada K1Y 4G1. Call: (613) 728-1865; Fax: (613) 728-9387.

Self-Help Clearinghouse of Metropolitan Toronto. Contact: Janet McCloud, Director, 40 Orchard View Boulevard, Suite 215, Toronto, Ontario, Canada M4R 1B9. Call: (416) 487-4355.

WINNIPEG

Winnipeg Self-Help Resource Clearinghouse. Contact: Bernice Marmel, Director, NorWest Coop & Health Center, 103-61 Tyndall Avenue, Winnipeg, Manitoba, Canada R2X 2T4. Call: (204) 589-5500, (204) 633-5955.

3

How to Start a Self-Help Group

If after consulting your local self-help clearinghouse and national organizations listed in Chapter 2, you discover there are no groups for your particular problem in your area, you may wish to start one yourself. The clearinghouse staff will prove invaluable in coaching you through the process and alerting you to resources in your community. But the following information on starting your own self-help group will be a useful outline of what the process will entail and a point of reference for beginning that process.

FINDING OTHERS

Since self-help is all about people helping each other in groups, the first step is to find other people with your problem to form the group. If the problem is health related (say, breast cancer), network among your health care providers, including doctors and nurses, and other staff at institutions, including hospitals and counseling centers. Also, place fliers on bulletin boards at the institutions. Advertising in community papers, especially weeklies—which often run "community bulletin board" pages where ads are free or inexpensive—may also be an effective route for locating others with a wide range of problems that are not just health related.

Finding other potential members for the group may be difficult at first. But once you have found a few, the task of finding more—like all other tasks relating to the group—can be shared, and progress will be made quickly. Once the group is established and its activities have achieved a certain momentum, news of

its existence will get around through word-of-mouth, further advertising, perhaps some publicity (more on this below) and referrals from sympathetic professionals. Soon new members will begin to appear spontaneously. In fact, eventually you may encounter one of self-help's perennial problems: too *many* members in your group.

DEFINING YOUR GROUP AND ITS GOALS

Although its value may become apparent only later when your group is up and running, it is important to formulate a statement of purpose as soon as possible after the group's formation. Above all, this statement should define who are going to be members of the group. As an example of problem areas where such a statement of purpose is crucial, take alcoholism and substance abuse. Today, many—perhaps even most—recovering alcoholics have also had problems with drugs, including prescription, self-prescribed over-the-counter and illicit. Yet others, often older alcoholics, have not. And often the latter do not feel comfortable at discussions of drug abuse. For an alcoholism self-help group to be effective—and for all potential members to feel comfortable participating—it needs to decide whether its purpose is to help people who are "cross-addicted" (alcoholic and drug addicted) or just alcoholic.

Any additional restrictions on membership and attendance should also be clarified in the statement of purpose. For example, it is common for family members and friends of people with a particular problem to attend the group's meetings. And yet some people only feel comfortable discussing their problem—for example, overeating—exclusively in the presence of others who share that problem. So it should be decided whether all or at least some of the group's meetings will be "closed"—restricted to those people who suffer directly from the problem being addressed. Another, similar problem may occur in groups for serious illnesses. For example, in breast cancer support groups, it should be decided up front whether people who are terminally ill will attend the same meeting as people who are recovering from the illness.

In this statement of purpose, the group should also define its goals and methods for achieving them. Such a statement may be important for people when they contemplate joining the group. While some self-help groups meet primarily to exchange mutual support, others pursue activities—ranging from lobbying to civil disobedience including arrest—in an effort to improve the membership's situation in society at large. These activities and their consequences may be more than some people had bargained for when they joined. A good example are groups for people concerned about HIV, the virus that causes AIDS. They range from, at one end of the spectrum, support groups organized by Body Positive of New York, where people meet weekly for eight to ten weeks to discuss adjusting to the news that they've tested positive for HIV; to ACT-UP ("AIDS Coalition to Unleash Power"), which mounts highly publicized demonstrations including acts of civil disobedience that often result in arrests. Needless to say, people should be told in advance whether the activities of a self-help group they're considering joining include being photographed by the media and arrested by the police. In fact, in the case of HIV, where prejudice and financial, insurance-related problems still plague

victims, people may want assurance that all aspects of their participation in the group are in strict confidence.

THE FIRST MEETING

Before the initial meeting can take place, you must decide upon a time and—what is more difficult—a space. Many self-help groups have started out in the homes of members. This has the advantage of reinforcing the familial atmosphere typical of much of self-help, but the disadvantage that makes it unsuitable in the long run—it places pressure on the host. Nor is rotating the meeting between homes of various members any better in the long run, because when a meeting place is a moving target, locating the meeting place easily is difficult for new members. Many people who arrive at their first meeting are shy or even frightened and apprehensive; many finally walk through the door of a self-help meeting only after having gotten to the location many times before, only to turn around and return home. Imagine the disappointment of someone finally mustering the courage to attend a meeting and then discovering that he or she has come to the wrong venue.

The best solution to the location problem is to find space—for which you may have to pay rent—at a local facility, such as a church, temple or library, and to hold the meeting at a regular time, say, weekly. Self-help groups—like individuals and families—have a certain pride of place. A clean, quiet, well-lighted meeting room is more important than you'd think in creating self-help meetings from which members reap ongoing benefits and enjoy attending. It will be worth the extra effort to locate such a venue. If the group addresses a medical problem, try to avoid holding the meeting in a health care facility, which may have negative, counterproductive associations for group members. Neutral ground, such as a YMCA or the meeting room of a local business, is a good bet.

For the first meeting, the founding members should take responsibility for a variety of duties, including: conducting the meeting; determining its content, for example, a speaker; greeting people at the door and providing hospitality (coffee and tea); acting as phone and mail contact; and performing secretarial duties, including collecting money to defray costs (more on this below). Ultimately, these duties may be distributed—and redistributed every so often according to some plan, say, semiannual elections—among whatever sort of leadership structure (probably minimal) that will emerge as the most effective to achieve the group's goals.

The focus of the first meeting—of any self-help group meeting, really—should be an open discussion where participants share and discuss their experiences with and feelings about the common problem that has brought them together in the first place. That's what self-help is all about. But in addition, at the first few meetings of a new self-help group, topics of discussion could include the group's statement of purpose and also what organization the group needs to achieve those goals. Most self-helpers would agree that a group should have only as much organization as it needs, and no more. If the group's activities are confined to discussion groups where members exchange support and information concerning, say, gambling, a group chairperson or leader, elected for terms of office of six months, will probably be sufficient; his or her duties may be limited to choosing a topic for—or a speaker to lead—the discussion; opening and closing the meeting; and performing secretarial duties, including "passing the basket," if that is done. On the other hand, if the group is a national organization with hundreds of affiliated groups and involved in lobbying and fund-raising efforts on the national, regional and local levels, a far more complicated structure such as a board of directors will be necessary.

UP AND RUNNING

Once your group has achieved a critical mass and its program of activities is launched, a variety of problems, issues and considerations will probably emerge. Here are some notes describing them, with suggestions for their solution.

Group Size: Six to ten is best. If there are fewer, there may not be enough different experiences and feelings to share; if there are more, reclusive members may get lost in the shuffle. If membership goes beyond 20, try breaking the meeting into two or more discussion groups for at least part of the meeting. Always try to seat participants in a circle, whether around a table or not: that way, everyone has a front-row seat, encouraging participation, and no one can hide out in the back.

Confidentiality: To a certain extent, people will share openly about their experiences with and feelings about their problem based on the level of confidentiality accorded their participation in the group. In many groups, members know each other on a first-name basis only, but as they get to know each other and form friendships, even relationships, outside the group—one of the greatest benefits of participation in self-help—this is dropped. But strict confidentiality is not uncommon, and an announcement to that effect may be made at some point in the meeting. In Alcoholics Anonymous—the model for so many other self-help groups—there's a well-known formula, often printed on a little placard hung on the meeting room walls along with other slogans: "Who you see here, what you hear here, let it stay here."

Supportive Atmosphere: Since self-help groups are made up of human beings, they are subject to all the usual human foibles. Certain members will despise each other the minute they meet; others will have love affairs, break up, and remain aloof and embittered (one may even leave the group to avoid awkwardness); still others will seek to use the group as an opportunity to act out their need to control or dominate others. Certain people may form cliques that leave nonmembers feeling left out. Such behavior, fortunately, is hardly typical. Inasmuch as it is a problem, it can be minimized by taking a few concrete steps that will foster an atmosphere of congeniality, friendship, even love, that occurs spontaneously in self-help rooms where people gather together to help each other cope with a common problem. Very little, perhaps nothing, need be said explicitly: certain actions will speak louder and more effectively than any words.

- *Greet New Members:* Have someone at the door greeting new members as they arrive; also, ask them to introduce themselves at the beginning of the meeting.
- *Introductions:* At large meetings, ask everyone to introduce themselves to the people sitting to their left and right; many people hate wearing name tags, but they do serve their purpose.
- *Buddy System:* Encourage a buddy or sponsor system, where each new member is taken under the wing of an older one, who explains the operations of the group, introduces him or her to other, established members and deals with certain problems—often by phone or in person, not at the meeting—on a one-on-one basis.

- *No Cross Talk:* Consider a policy of no "cross talk." Cross talk is a form of discussion whereby a few group members— two or three—discuss a topic in rapid fire among themselves. It effectively closes the rest of the group out of the discussion and makes it possible for those members to have a heated disagreement over an issue. Instead, encourage people to speak at an appropriate length, commenting on and responding to the topic, and then yield the floor to someone else.
- *Facilitator:* The facilitator or chairperson should seek to move the discussion along. He or she does this by encouraging—but not pressuring—quieter members to speak by at least offering the opportunity; and by reminding (very subtly and only when absolutely necessary) talkative members that there are others who remain to speak in the limited amount of time available. Facilitators are often members of the group, occasionally with some training at a facilitator's workshop. Occasionally, a professional may facilitate the meeting.

NEWSLETTERS AND OTHER PUBLISHED MATERIALS

Newsletters and other printed materials can be crucial to the success and growth of your group. But they needn't be elaborate; a single-sided photo-copied page is perfectly sufficient. Today's desktop-publishing software and laser printers are bringing professional-looking printed pieces well within the grasp of many PC users. But if there are any graphic artists in the group, encourage them to donate their talents, if not their equipment. It will increase their sense of belonging to the group. In this as in all cases, when group members give, they receive back even more in return. There's an old AA saying, "In order to keep it, you've got to give it away."

As far as its contents are concerned, the newsletter should above all include a calendar of events for the period in which it is current, listing meetings and extracurricular activities, such as social events. It should also include the telephone and mailing address for group members who've volunteered to serve as contacts. Every issue could include the group's statement of purpose in an abbreviated, mottolike form.

For the group's members, a newsletter is a concrete expression of the group's existence and goals; it helps create the perceptions that, in participating in the group's activities, they are part of a significant, tangible phenomenon. For newcomers, the newsletter will serve as an important "leave-behind" piece that will shape their perception of the group and of the desirability of belonging to it. Finally, the newsletter can be mailed as a backup item to publicity, fund-raising and lobbying campaigns, and in response to inquiries about your group through the mail.

EXPANDING THE SCOPE OF YOUR GROUP'S ACTIVITIES

Many groups are content to focus their energies on discussion meetings that facilitate the exchange of support and practical information. For Alcoholics Anonymous and the other orthodox 12-step groups, any widening beyond such ambitions—for example, outreach efforts, such as publicity and advertising, fund-raising and lobbying—is a violation of several of the "Twelve Traditions" that guide these groups. In today's self-help community, even among non-12-steppers, there are purists who

believe that when a group expands its activities beyond the confines of mutual aid and support, it is no longer truly self-help.

But not all groups are alike. For many, an important part of their activities is outreach to the world beyond the meeting. These outreach efforts include communications about the group and its activities and goals, fundraising to meet operating costs and systematic attempts to incorporate its viewpoints into the media and to achieve its goals by lobbying at various levels of government for legislation it favors.

The following suggestions will serve as a starting point for your group, should it decide to expand its activities in these directions.

Advertising and Public Relations: At the beginning of the group's existence, a limited amount of communications work may have been necessary to assemble a critical mass of participants and get the group off the ground, up and running. But later, communications may be a systematic and ongoing activity designed to keep new members coming into the fold.

Self-helpers who want to spread the word about their groups should investigate two aspects of communications: *advertising,* where you pay for space in print media, such as newspapers, or pay for time in television and radio broadcasts; and *publicity* or *public relations,* where you seek to interest—without payment, of course—editors and writers to provide coverage of stories relating to your group and, as much as possible, incorporate your point of view in any discussion of issues related to your group's interests.

Since most self-help groups have limited financial means, public relations is always more attractive than advertising. The theory of public relations is this: Print and broadcast editors are always overworked and in search of new stories. So, if you can (1) convince an editor that your group and its activities are news-worthy, and (2) *pre*report its story by submitting a letter describing the story, or a news release that contains at least enough information to give a reporter a head start, chances are you will get coverage. Sometimes editors are even willing to accept a complete news feature; if there's a by-line, it might go to a member of the group with a professional or other distinction, or a relatively high profile in the community. And there's a bonus that makes public relations superior to advertising: Since the coverage is by a disinterested third party, the press, public relations is, by definition, a more credible way of shaping public perception.

Some of the most important tools for achieving your public relations ends are conceiving events in terms of news stories and creating releases that describe those events concisely. A press release should always describe an event—an announcement, an award, a demonstration—and should list the proverbial "five w's": "who, what, when, why, where." For example, "Breast Cancer Support Group Celebrates 10th Anniversary with Teach-In at Holy Name Hospital Next Saturday." At the top of the release should be the name and phone number of a person who can be contacted for further information. A release such as this would probably generate a so-called news story, a type of journalism that focuses on the purely factual aspects of the story—in this case, a tenth-anniversary celebration.

Another way to bring the story of your group to the media's attention is to write a "query letter," not necessarily pegged to any particular news event, that describes the group and its members in general terms. For that same breast cancer support group, such a letter could describe how the illness has affected a member of your group and illustrate how the activity of your group has helped her cope with this change in her life. Such a query letter would probably generate a "news feature" that, in contrast to a news story, contains interpretive, subjective and personal material, often profiling the experiences of one or more individuals.

Though it costs money, advertising should not be out of the question, since some ad space in print media and ad time in radio and occasionally even television *are* free. For example, many daily and weekly papers and some radio and TV programs run "community news bulletin boards" where a brief ad may be run free of charge. Even if you do have to pay, media space in weekly papers is often quite cheap. And with desktop publishing software and laser printers, it is possible for you to submit to the publisher so-called camera-ready art for a fraction of what it used to cost for the same work to be done by a professional. Network among the members of your group—and have them, in turn, network among their families and friends—to find a professional graphic artist willing to do this job for little or no money, or someone with the correct PC, software and laser printer. (Incidentally, this camera-ready art can—with little or no alteration—be photoreproduced and used for fliers, posters and so forth.)

Since you are paying for the media coverage, you have complete or near complete control over the contents. The ad copy for the breast cancer support group, for example, would probably announce its existence, tell where and when it meets, who is invited (for example, just patients or their families too), and give a contact name and number. If there is some stigma attached to participation in a self-help group—for example, Parents Anonymous, for people grappling with child abuse issues—you may wish to give only a phone number that people can call to learn the time and location of the meeting. Otherwise, group participants may worry, with some justification, that in a small community their attendance at the meeting may become general knowledge.

Fund-Raising: The greatest resource at your group's disposal is the people in it. Nevertheless, it takes cash to cover expenses, however minimal. At the low end, perhaps most groups need money to cover rent and hospitality at meetings, and little else; at the high end—at large, national or international groups that serve as umbrella organizations—costs include salary and benefits for staff and various other operating costs.

Different groups have different ways of meeting these expenses. Twelve-step organizations based on Alcoholics Anonymous are "fully self-supporting, declining outside contributions" (AA Tradition Number Seven). Even the General Services Office of Alcoholics Anonymous in New York City, a large and complex apparatus that services thousands of AA groups internationally, is supported through funds from AA's constituent groups. Donations of more than $200 are not accepted.

But AA is not the only model for creating new self-help groups. Your group may want to explore fund-raising as a means for generating income by reaching out beyond the group. Here are a few suggestions on how it's done.

Determine Your Needs, and Fund-Raise Only If Necessary: Determine what your group's goals are and then how much you need to meet expenses incurred by a program of activities designed to meet those goals. Embark on fund-raising only if there's a deficit. Otherwise, generate income by "passing the hat" at each meeting. Do it halfway through the meeting: You might miss latecomers, if you do it earlier, and risk the perception of an inappropriate emphasis on money; and if you do it later, you may miss people who have to leave early. At AA meetings, there's an unspoken tradition of putting one dollar in the basket. But don't hesitate to suggest a specific amount for the donation if, for example, you pay a high rent for your meeting space.

Dues: If additional funds are still needed, you may want to consider annual membership dues. If so, the amount is usually nominal, say, $10 to $25 annually. Certain self-help purists feel this is another procedure that violates the voluntary and informal nature of self-help. But once again, there are many models for self-help—and a good deal of leeway in its definition.

Various Fund-Raising Activities: Finally, there are a variety of special events you can mount to generate cash. They include raffles, dances, white-elephant sales and so forth. Such events have an added advantage: They draw the group's members—and their families and friends and interested professionals—together at an event that can promote group solidarity and a familial atmosphere, and help create or firm up networks. Later these networks can be used for exchange of support and information.

Ask for Specific Amounts: Whether you ask for contributions at each meeting or an annual membership fee—or both—remember one rule that holds for all levels of fund-raising: Quote specific amounts when you ask for donations. The basic figure could be related to the actual cost of operating the group for each member; another, higher figure would allow for an additional contribution; and a lower figure could be quoted for those with a limited income due to disability or unemployment. If you have reason to believe that a potential donor might give a large sum of money, ask for it.

Personalize Fund-Raising: People are more willing to give when asked in person. Do so. Also, send a thank-you note when the fund-raising is over.

Keep accurate records of who gave what when. Your best potential donors are people who have given before. Be sure to send them thank-you notes. Accurate records of who gave what previously will be invaluable.

Social Action: Most self-help groups aim to help their members cope with the problems life has dealt them; others set out to attack the problem itself through social action. Some self-help purists feel that such action-oriented activities push at the conceptual boundaries of self-help. But such action—performed in solidarity with other members of the group—is a constructive channel for the anger members feel when confronted with their particular problem. And who can deny that people feel the same self-help benefits—a sense of belonging, of empowerment—when they gather together to take direct action to solve the problem?

Some of the most famous self-help groups fall into this category, including M.A.D.D. (Mothers Against Drunk Driving) and ACT-UP (AIDS Coalition to Unleash Power). On the more conventional end of the activist spectrum is M.A.D.D., whose members include mothers and other family members of people killed by drunken drivers. M.A.D.D. has been instrumental in publicizing the problem of insufficient punishment of drunken drivers and lobbying for more stringent laws and sentencing for those convicted of breaking them. At the unconventional end is ACT-UP, which opened a whole new era in action-oriented self-help through its aggressive demonstrations and other activities designed to catch the attention of media and politicians and increase AIDS awareness. Interestingly, in recent years, the ACT-UP style has been adopted with success by other self-help organizations for people with health problems, particularly breast cancer.

Disadvantages to activism include the more elaborate structure it requires and the negative perceptions from society at large that it might create for your group. Extreme activism could result in potential members' reluctance to join; this is particularly true of ACT-UP, whose notorious "Church Demo," staged December 10, 1989 at New York City's St. Patrick's Cathedral, did little to endear itself to many sectors of local and national society, though it did garner the media attention it sought.

Should your group decide to adopt activist means to achieve its goals—no matter where its style of activism lies on the spectrum that runs from M.A.D.D. to ACT-UP—there are a number of basic activities you'll want to explore:

Form Coalitions with Other Groups That Have Similar Goals: Since social activism can be expensive and, to a certain extent, effective in proportion to the number of people involved in it (for example, the larger a public demonstration, the larger its impact), seek to form alliances with other groups that have goals similar to yours. It'll cost less and make more noise. While your cancer self-help group needn't merge with others in your area for purposes of holding support-group meetings—to the contrary in fact, since the smaller the discussion group, the better—it will probably want to join forces if you decide, for example, to march on Washington, D.C. to demand increased funding for research.

Monitor the Media, Get the Coverage You Want: In as systematic a way as is possible—which might include hiring a clipping service—monitor the coverage your problem area is receiving in the media. If you note general or specific errors and problems in the news clips you assemble, write to the appropriate editors, state your criticisms and, if possible, seek to set up a brief meeting to discuss them.

This media-related form of activism is similar to public relations, but less intent on generating specific clips and more intent on effecting the contours, if not the content, of media reporting.

Monitor Government, Get the Legislation You Want: While hiring professional lobbyists is beyond the means of most self-help organizations, it is possible to influence your representatives in the state and federal legislatures. Once you have a set of specific demands supported by research and documentation that can, if possible, be left with your legislator, make an appointment to see him or her, or the proper representatives. Be sure to identify yourselves as registered voters in his or her district. One member should be designated to represent the group in the discussion, which should be concise, amicable and marked by a fruitful exchange of ideas in both directions. Foster any relationships that the meeting might produce and—whether or not you get what you want—follow up in the future with similar or related demands that would benefit your group.

Further Reading

Alcoholics Anonymous World Services, Inc. *Alcoholics Anonymous,* 2d ed. New York: Alcoholics Anonymous World Services, 1955.

Dory, Frances J. *Building Self-help Groups Among Older Persons: A Training Curriculum to Prepare Organizers.* New York: New Careers Training Laboratory, City University of New York, 1979.

Evans, Glen. *The Family Circle Guide to Self-help.* New York: Ballantine Books, 1979.

Gartner, A., and Riessman, F. *HELP: A Working Guide to Self-help Groups.* New York: New Viewpoints/Vision Books, 1980.

Hill, Karen. *Helping You Helps Me.* Ottawa, Ontario: Canadian Council on Social Development, 1983.

Humm, Andy. *How to Organize a Self-help Group.* New York: National Self-help Clearinghouse, 1979.

Mallory, Lucretia. *Leading Self-help Groups.* New York: Family Service Association of America, 1984.

A Note About Professionals and Self-Help

Today, despite its growing credibility among health and human services professionals, self-help is at best still only a marginal element in the training curricula for social workers, psychotherapists, clinical psychologists, physicians and others. Professionals interested in correcting the effects of this curricular imbalance in their own training can begin by an examination of the growing professional literature on the topic. To do so, see "Relationships with Professionals," pp. 16–18 in David Spiegel, "The Recent Literature: Self-Help and Mutual Support Groups" (1980). For further, more up-to-date bibliographic references as well as theoretical and empirical discussions, including a case study, see, for example, "The Mental Health Professionals and Mutual Help Programs," in Alan Gartner and Frank Riessman's *The Self-Help Revolution* (1984). A useful one-volume handbook for professionals is *Mutual Help Groups: A Guide For Mental Health Workers* (Rockville, Maryland: U.S. Department of Health, Education, and Welfare, 1978), by Phyllis R. Silverman, a leader in the development of human service programs that are amalgams of professional and nonprofessional elements.

Meanwhile, the following text will serve as an introduction to the topic of the relationship between self-help and the helping professions, especially for nonprofessionals interested in the historical and social scientific context of their self-help activities.

While self-helpers and professionals have often historically been—and still are—at odds with one another both conceptually and practically, professionals were crucial to the founding and running of several of the oldest and best-known self-help organizations; contrary to popular belief, not all self-help organizations are purely grassroots phenomena. For example, Dr. William Duncan Silkworth, M.D., a neurologist who in the early 1930s treated Bill Wilson, the cofounder (with Dr. Bob Smith) of Alcoholics Anonymous, contributed significantly to the AA program in a number of ways: He provided key elements to its theoretical base, especially the disease concept of alcoholism; and he gave the program perhaps its earliest professional stamp of approval, his essay, "A Doctor's Opinion," which opens *The Big Book* of Alcoholics Anonymous.

But in a turn of events that would set a pattern for the relationship between professionals and self-helpers of the 12-step variety, the rapport between AA and professional health care was cut short. The Towns Hospital in New York City—where Dr. Silkworth treated Wilson and numerous other alcoholics during the Prohibition Era—became so impressed with the success of the fledgling AA program that it offered Wilson the post of an in-house peer counselor to alcoholics. The AA community soon agreed, however, that financial remuneration for 12-step work—activities that reach out and carry the AA message of recovery to suffering alcoholics—would compromise the nature and success of the outreach itself. This determinedly antiprofessional stance was later articulated in "Tradition Eight" of the AA program; see *Twelve Steps and Twelve Traditions* (Alcoholics Anonymous, 1953). In actual practice, however, alcoholics recovering in AA often accept remunerative work as alcoholism counselors, sometimes after professional training—for example, in the "Credentialed Alcoholism Counselor" programs that operate in most states. Acquiring these credentials and working in the capacity of paid counselor is not, however, construed as a violation of the Eighth Tradition, since such counselors do not claim to represent AA and therefore do not break their anonymity, the program's "spiritual foundation."

In other, non-12-step sectors of the self-help world, lay participants have been incorporated into the structure of professional organizations. But significant friction often occurs over credentialism, an issue that clearly divides professionals, whose expertise in dealing with human problems is academic and formal, and nonprofessionals, for whom it is experiential and informal. This friction is aggravated at institutions such as residential drug rehabilitation programs that are supported by tax dollars or third-party insurance payments, because these institutions must therefore receive a stamp of approval by independent organizations, such as the Joint Commission on Hospital Accreditation (JCHA). Conforming to the hospital model inherent in standards of the JCHA has often blunted the effectiveness of the self-help elements that these institutions had successfully incorporated, much to the frustration of the personnel.

On the flip side from professional institutes that employ self-helpers are self-help organizations that incorporate professionals in their activities. Since pure self-help organizations—which are nonprofessional, peer-oriented, informal, and not-for-profit—do not have to answer to the exigencies of accreditation, the rapport between professionals and nonprofessionals may be beneficial under the best circumstances. Examples include Recovery, Inc., for ex-mental patients, founded by Dr. Abraham Low, M.D. in 1937, and Parents Anonymous, a support group for parents prone to child abuse. Recovery, Inc. groups use materials developed by Dr. Low, including sound recordings. Parents Anonymous groups include a professional "sponsor," often with social work or other professional training, who facilitates the activities of the group by guiding its chairperson.

Parents Anonymous, in fact, may serve as a paradigm for the successful collaboration between professionals and self-help, where the former, to use a popular self-help slogan, is kept "on tap, not on top." Once again con-trary to popular belief, self-helpers are not necessarily antiprofessional; often they welcome the involvement of professionals in the activities of their group. But friction occurs when the professional violates the informal, experiential, peer-oriented spirit of self-help; in the words of Parents Anonymous, the professional must "leave his/her professional aura at home, enabling all involved to interact on an equal level." (Willen, Mildred L. "Parents Anonymous: The Professional's Role as Sponsor." In A. Gartner and F. Reissman, eds. *The Self-Help Revolution*. New York: Human Services Press, 1984, pp. 109–119.) For a case study of how professionals successfully interacted with a self-help group for people with life-threatening illnesses, see Wollert, Richard, Knight, Bob, and Levy, Leon. "Make Today Count: A Collaborative Model for Professional and Self-Help Groups." In A. Gartner and F. Reissman, eds. *The Self-Help Revolution*. New York: Human Services Press, 1984, pp. 129–137. This study contains some particularly useful clues about rapport-building techniques and the decorum professionals should employ and observe in interacting with self-helpers. In brief, professionals should learn as much as possible about the group through observation of meetings and friendly interaction with group members; avoid flashing credentials or engaging in obviously social-scientific behavior (such as taking notes at meetings); offer friendly advice, not paternalistic directions, and do so sparingly and when asked.

Whatever the potential pitfalls of the professional-nonprofessional interface, many self-help groups are interested in the participation by professionals, whether as guest speakers—for example, medical specialists giving presentations about recent advances in the treatment of a disease—or as consultants who can critique the activities of the group in order to increase its efficiency.

For their part, professionals convinced of the efficacy of self-help—and they are relatively few—greatly value the availability of self-help as a resource for their clients and patients. Based on the experience of the few decades that make up "the self-help revolution," the most successful combination seems to occur when the two tracks are mostly parallel, only occasionally intersecting, but certainly not overlapping. Notable unhappiness has occurred when paternalistic professionals have sought to co-opt the activities of a group, thereby alienating its members, or have exploited groups as "feeder channels" for their own professional services.

There is potential for friction in the interface between professionals and self-help. And for many members of the professional community, self-help continues to hold relatively low credibility; for others, it may even be a threat. Nevertheless, it seems likely—given the crisis that looms over the health and human services sector of our society, and the attractiveness of self-help for the consumer—that the resources of self-help, which will never suffer professional burnout, will be a key ingredient in the health and human services of the future.

The Twelve Steps and Twelve Traditions of Alcoholics Anonymous

Recently there has been an unfortunate tendency to confuse all "self-help" with the so-called 12-step fellowships or recovery groups that derive their form and (explicitly spiritual) content from the Twelve Steps and Twelve Traditions of Alcoholics Anonymous. In fact, 12-step fellowships and recovery-oriented self-help groups are probably a minority; the majority consist of groups for people with various medical problems. Nevertheless, 12-step programs are numerous and important.

In addition, some self-help authorities have suggested that even groups that do not espouse 12-step-style spirituality can nevertheless profit from the largely organizational, practical suggestions of AA's Twelve Traditions.

So, with the permission of Alcoholics Anonymous World Services, the public relations apparatus of the AA community, the "Twelve and Twelve" are reprinted here. It should be noted, however, that the significance of the Twelve Traditions for non-12-step groups will be more apparent from the "long form" of the traditions, contained in *Twelve Steps and Twelve Traditions*.[1]

---

[1] Alcoholics Anonymous, *Twelve Steps and Twelve Traditions* (New York: Alcoholics Anonymous, 1952).

THE TWELVE SUGGESTED STEPS

1. We admitted that we were powerless over alcohol—that our lives had become unmanageable.
2. Came to believe that a Power greater than ourselves could restore us to sanity.
3. Made a decision to turn our will and our lives over to the care of God, *as we understood Him.*
4. Made a searching and fearless moral inventory of ourselves.
5. Admitted to God, to ourselves and to another human being the exact nature of our wrongs.
6. Were entirely ready to have God remove all these defects of character.
7. Humbly asked Him to remove our shortcomings.
8. Made a list of all persons we had harmed, and became willing to make amends to them all.
9. Made direct amends to such people wherever possible, except when to do so would injure them or others.
10. Continued to take personal inventory, and when we were wrong promptly admitted it.
11. Sought through prayer and meditation to improve our conscious contact with God *as we understood him*, praying only for knowledge of His will for us and the power to carry that out.
12. Having had a spiritual awakening as the result of these steps, we tried to carry this message to alcoholics, and to practice these principles in all our affairs.

THE TWELVE TRADITIONS

1. Our common welfare should come first; personal recovery depends upon A.A. unity.

2. For our group purpose there is but one ultimate authority—a loving God as He may express Himself in our group conscience. Our leaders are but trusted servants—they do not govern.

3. The only requirement for A.A. membership is a desire to stop drinking.

4. Each group should be autonomous except in matters affecting other groups or A.A. as a whole.

5. Each group has but one primary purpose—to carry its message to the alcoholic who still suffers.

6. An A.A. group ought never endorse, finance or lend the A.A. name to any related facility or outside enterprise, lest problems of money, property and prestige divert us from our primary purpose.

7. Every A. A. group ought to be fully self-supporting, declining outside contributions.

8. Alcoholics Anonymous should remain forever nonprofessional, but our service centers may employ special workers.

9. A.A., as such, ought never be organized; but we may create service boards or committees directly responsible to those they serve.

10. Alcoholics Anonymous has no opinion on outside issues; hence the A.A. name ought never be drawn into public controversy.

11. Our public relations policy is based on attraction rather than promotion; we need always maintain personal anonymity at the level of press, radio and films.

12. Anonymity is the spiritual foundation of all our Traditions, ever reminding us to place principles before personalities.

Computers and Self-Help

The key to self-help is interaction among people who share a common problem. But what if it's impossible to gather in a group? Ironically, this possibility is especially great for certain people who need self-help most, for example, those housebound by agoraphobia or serious disabilities, or those separated from one another by geographical isolation, for example, alcoholics living in sparsely populated rural areas; or people with extremely rare diseases, where there may be only a handful of patients in the entire country.[1]

Luckily, high technology and the do-it-yourself imagination that animates all of self-help have teamed up to create a fascinating, inexpensive solution for this problem: computerized self-help meetings via telecommunications (telephone) hookups. Instead of gathering at a specific time and place, members of electronic self-help groups "meet" at a specific time and digital location in a computer information service, such as CompuServ, Genie, Prodigy or America OnLine.

Details may vary as a function of the computer hardware and software and computer information service, but here is, in general terms, how an electronic self-help meeting takes place:

Each member must have the following:

- a *personal computer;*
- a *modem:* this is an inexpensive hardware device that translates digital pulses from the computer into analog signals transmittable by telephone—and vice-versa—so that computers can "talk" to each other over the phone;
- a *telecommunications software program,* such as Crosstalk (for IBM-PC-compatible computers) or Microphone (for Macintosh computers) that runs on the personal computer and organizes the entire event *at the user's end;*
- a *standard telephone line,* such as the one a common telephone is hooked up to;
- a *membership in an information service,* such as CompuServ. Computers at the information service's headquarters organize the incoming signals from subscribers' computers and structure the various events—including the "conference facility" service used by the self-help meeting.

At the appointed time for the meeting, the user turns on his or her PC, activates the telecommunications software program, which produces a series of menus that the user works through. For example, at a certain point, a menu will ask the user for the telephone number of the information service, which the telecommunications program then dials.

Then the software program at the information service takes over and displays on the user's PC another series of menus. Working through these menus, the user is able to choose an option to go to the "conference facility" where the group is going to meet. Upon "arriving" at the meeting, the user—along with all the other participating members of the computer self-help group—is looking at a blank computer screen. The meeting is ready to begin. Instead of talking to each other in a room, the self-help group members, one at a time, type what they have to say to each other; their words appear instantaneously on the computer screens of all participants.

---

[1] The problem of spreading the benefits of self-help to people unable to meet with fellow sufferers is not new. In the early days of AA, when there were few meetings anywhere, the stories at the back of the *Big Book* of Alcoholics Anonymous were intended for the many people who were unable to come to meetings to hear other alcoholics "share their experience, strength and hope."

Because only one person can type at a time, a certain etiquette is observed. For example, each person may type a signal such as "GA" when he or she is finished to signal that someone else can "go ahead." To increase the orderliness of the meeting, often a group leader calls on people one at a time.

So far, self-help meetings are known to have occurred by computer via telephone lines for people with a variety of problems: alcoholics recovering through Alcoholics Anonymous; agoraphobics, under the auspices of the Phobia Society of America; and people who suffer from Ehlers-Danlos syndrome, a group of inherited diseases of the connective tissues. There's a big difference between meeting physically in a room and hearing people share their experiences and support through speech and "meetings" where people's words are flashed on a computer screen in real time as they are typed at several distant locations. But, according to participants in such meetings, the important result is the same: People no longer feel so alone, so powerless in the face of their problem.

Another telecommunications-based modality for exchange self-help is the bulletin board system (BBS). A BBS is a service, usually free, that permits the user to post information—especially queries for information—and pick up replies. Like information networks, a BBS requires a personal computer, telecommunications software and a telephone line. Originally, BBSs were developed by computer enthusiasts who wanted to communicate with each other on computer-related matters of mutual concern. But today BBSs are increasingly the locus for many different types of activity, including the self-help exchange on

health, mental health and "recovery" problems. For example, there is an AIDS BBS in the San Francisco area—accessible by long-distance phone from anywhere in the world, of course—through which AIDS patients and their families, friends and interested professionals may place and pick up messages on AIDS-related matters. For a listing of over 300 such health-related bulletin board services, send $5.00 and a legal-size self-addressed stamped envelope to: Ed Del Gross, 29 Golfview Drive, Apartment A-2, Neward, Delaware 19702.

Most BBSs are free, though you will usually be required to "register" the first time you call by leaving your name, address and so forth. As is the case with information networks, BBSs will fill your computer screen with a variety of user-friendly menus.

The leading authority on self-help via computers and telecommunications hookup is Edward J. Madara, director of the American Self-Help Clearinghouse, Denville, New Jersey, and a seminal figure in the self-help movement. (See "Further Reading" for a reference to his monograph on computer self-help.) Mr. Madara and his staff answer self-help-related queries posted in the Self-Help/Support section of the GoodHealth Forum of CompuServ (70275, 1003). If you need basic information on setting yourself up to participate in computer self-help, call the Clearinghouse at (201) 625-7101.

The ever-increasing popularity of personal computers combined with the growth of self-help can only mean a future increase of this novel and effective way for people to help themselves by helping each other.

Further Reading

Ferguson, Tom, M.D. "Running a Self-Help Group by Computer." *Medical Self-Care Magazine* (November/December 1987):80.

Madara, Edward J. "Using Your Home Computer for Mutual Help." In Barbara J. White and Edward J. Madara, compilers and edi-tors. *The Self-help Sourcebook; Finding and Forming Mutual Aid Self-help Groups,* 4th ed. Denville, New Jersey: American Self-Help Clearinghouse, St. Clares-Riverside Medical Center, 1992.

Index

Boldface type indicates major subject areas

American Hepatitis Foundation 80
American Juvenile Arthritis Organization 46
American Liver Foundation 89
American Lung Association 90
American Lupus Society 90
American Narcolepsy Association 98
American Parkinson's Disease Association 103
American Porphyria Foundation 105
American Self-Help Clearinghouse 124
American Society for Deaf Children 65
American Society for Psychoprophylaxis in Obstetrics
  (ASPO/Lamaze) 59
American Society of Handicapped Physicians 68
American Syringomyelia Alliance Project 116
American Tinnitus Association 65
amputation 44–45
Amputees in Motion (AIM) 44
amyotrophic lateral sclerosis (ALS) 44
A.N.A.D. (National Association of Anorexia Nervosa
  and Associated Disorders) 72
anemia 54, 63, 75–76
anorexia nervosa 71–72
Anorexia Nervosa and Related Eating Disorders
  (ANRED) 71–72
anxiety disorders 45 See also obsessive-compulsive
  disorder
Anxiety Disorders Association of America 45
aplastic anemia 54, 75
Aplastic Anemia Foundation of America 54
apnea 45–46
ARC (AIDS-related complex) 39
ARC, The (Association for Retarded Citizens) 95
A.R.T. ("Academics Recovering Together") 41
arthritis 45
Arthritis Foundation 46
arthrogryposis 46
artists 45
A.R.T.S. Anonymous (Artists Recovering through the
  Twelve Steps) 46
asbestosis 107
Asian-Americans 112–113
ASPO/Lamaze (American Society for Psychoprophylaxis
  in Obstetrics) 59
ASSIST 76
Association for Children with Russell-Silver Syndrome
  107
Association for Glycogen Storage Disease 79
Association for Macular Diseases, Inc. 52
Association for Multi-Ethnic Americans 96
Association for Neuro Metabolic Disorders 98
Association for Retarded Citizens (The ARC) 95
Association of Birth Defect Children 111
Association of Children for Enforcement of Support
  (A.C.E.S.) 108
Association of Late-Deafened Adults (ALDA) 65–66
asthma 46, 90
ataxia 46–47
atresia 71

attention-deficit disorders 47, 88
Attention Disorders Association of Parents and
  Professionals Together (ADAPPT) 47
autism 47
Autism Society of America 47
automobile accidents 69–70
Avenues: A National Support Group for Arthrogryposis
  46
AVRT (Addictive Voice Recognition Training) 43
A.W.A.K.E. Network (Alert, Well and Keeping
  Energetic) 45–46

B

balance disorders 120
Bald-Headed Men of America 47–48
baldness 47–48
Barker, Robert A. 4
Batterers Anonymous 48
batteres 48
BBS (bulletin board system) 153
BEBASHI (Blacks Educating Blacks about Sexual-Health
  Issues) 39
Because I Love You 106
Beckwith-Wiedemann Support Network 48
Beckwith-Wiedemann syndrome 48
Believe the Children 58
Bender, Eugene I. 5
benign congenital hypotonia 114
benign essential blepharospasm 48
Benign Essential Blepharospasm Research Foundation,
  Inc. 48
Bereaved Parents 49
bereavement 48–51
Bethany Place AIDS Service Organization 39
Big Book, The (Alcoholics Anonymous) 144
biological families 37–38
biotinidase deficiency 98
biracial families 85
birth defects 111
Birth Parent and Relative Group of Canada 37
birth parents 37–38
bisexuals 78
Black Americans 39, 54
Blacks Educating Blacks about Sexual-Health Issues
  (BEBASHI) 39
Blinded Veterans Association 52
blindness 52–53 See also retinitis pigmentosa
blood disease 54 See also AIDS; anemia; hemophilia;
  leukemia
Body Positive of New York 39
Bone Marrow Transplant Family Support Network 54
bone-marrow transplants 54
Borman, Leonard 4
Bourneville's disease (tuberous sclerosis) 119
Bradshaw, John 4, 6
brain tumors 119

breast cancer 55
breast feeding 60
bronchitis 90
Brown Lung Association 55
brown lung disease (byssinosis) 55
bulimia 71–72
bulletin board system (BBS) 153
Burns United Support Group 55
burn victims 55–56
byssinosis 55

C

California clearinghouses 124–125
Calix Society 41
C.A.M.I. (Concerned Americans for Military Improvements) 120–121
CAN (Cult Awareness Network) 64–65
Canada
  clearinghouses 129
  self-help groups 37, 74, 104, 119
Canadian P.I.D. Society 104
cancer 55–56, 62–63
Cancer Support Network 56
Candlelighters Childhood Cancer Foundation 56
CAPS (Children of Aging Parents) 56
car accidents 69–70
Care for Life, Inc. 120
caregivers 44, 56–57
Caregivers of Patients with Memory Loss 56
Carnegie, Dale 4
Catholics See Roman Catholics
Catholics United for Spiritual Action (C.U.S.A.) 68
Celiac Sprue Association/United States of America, Inc. 79
Center for Attitudinal Healing, The 89
Center for Loss in Multiple Birth (C.L.I.M.B.), Inc. 49
cerebellopontine angle tumor (acoustic neuroma) 119
cerebral gigantism (Sotos syndrome) 112
cerebral palsy 6, 57
CFIDS Association, Inc. 61
CFS (chronic-fatigue syndrome) 61
C.H.A.D.D. (Children with Attention-Deficit Disorders) 47
Charcot-Marie-Tooth Association 57–58
Charcot-Marie-Tooth (CMT) disease 57–58
chemical hypersensitivity 58
child abuse 36, 58–59, 84
childbirth 59–60
child care 59–60
Child Find of America, Inc. 95–96
children See also childbirth; child care; infants; specific diseases or conditions of childhood (e.g., cystic fibrosis)
  abuse 36, 58–59, 84
  adoption 35–37
  of alcoholics 41
  arthritis 46

behavior problems 47, 88, 92, 105–106
bereavement for 49–50
cancer 56
custody of 60–61, 108–109
of deaf adults 66
deafness 65
with disabilities 88, 111–112
drug abuse prevention among 42
in foster homes 36
with health care need 111–112
lead poisoning 87
mental illness 92
of mentally ill adults 95
missing 95–96
as murder victims 48–49
support payments for 108–109
Children of Aging Parents (CAPS) 56
Children of Deaf Adults (C.O.D.A.) 66
Children's Rights Council 108
Children with Attention-Deficit Disorders (C.H.A.D.D.) 47
child support 108–109
Christians 43, 77–78 See also Roman Catholics
Chronic Dysmotility Support Group 70
chronic-fatigue syndrome (CFS) 61
chronic illness 57, 61, 68
chronic pain 101
CIA (congenital intestinal aganglionosis) 81
cigarettes See smoking
Citizen's Clearinghouse for Hazardous Wastes 74
civil rights 58
clearinghouses 34, 124–129
cleft palate 61
Cleft Palate Association 61
C.L.I.M.B., Inc. (Center for Loss in Multiple Birth, Inc.) 49
CMT disease (Charcot-Marie-Tooth disease) 57–58
coalition-building 140
Coalition for the Homeless 81
Cocaine Anonymous 41–42
Cochlear Implant Club International 61–62
cochlear implants 61–62
C.O.D.A. (Children of Deaf Adults) 66
codependency 62
Co-Dependents Anonymous 62
Codependents Anonymous for Helping Professionals (CoDAHP) 62
Codependents of Sex Addicts (C.O.S.A.) 110
colitis 85
colleges 41
colorectal cancer 62–63
colostomy 99
Coma Recovery Association 63
comas 63
Committee for Mother and Child Rights, Inc. 108
Committee for Single Adoptive Parents 36
Compassionate Friends 49
compulsive stealing 64
Compulsive Stutterers Anonymous 115
computers 152–154

Epstein-Barr virus 61
esophageal speech 87
ethnic organizations 6
euthanasia 115
Evangelicals Concerned 77
Exceptional Patient Groups 89
E.X.P.O.S.E. (Ex-Partners of Servicemen for Equality) 108
Extra Effort (X.E.) 73

F

Faces 75
facial disfigurement 61, 75
F.A.C.T. (Forgotten and Abused Children and Teens) 36
F.A.C.T.S. (Farmers Assistance, Counseling, and Training Service) 76
FAIR (Family and Individual Reliance) 92
familial spinal muscular atrophy (Werdnig-Hoffman disease) 114, 121
families See also children; parents; siblings; spouses
   with emotional or mental problems 92
   of farmers 76
   of homicide victims 50
   interracial 85
   stepfamilies 102
   of substance abusers 42
Families Anonymous 42
Families of Homicide Victims Support Group 50
Families of Spinal Muscular Atrophy (S.M.A.) 114
Family and Individual Reliance (FAIR) 92
family-centered maternity care (FCMC) 59–60
Fanconi anemia 75–76
Fanconi Anemia Support Group 75–76
Farmers Assistance, Counseling, and Training Service (F.A.C.T.S.) 76
farm families 76
Farm Resource Center 76
Feingold Associations of the United States 88
F.E.M.A.L.E. ("Formerly Employed Mothers at the Leading Edge") 101
fetal abnormality 35
Fetal Alcohol Network 76
fetal alcohol syndrome 76
fire fighters 76
FIRST (Foundation for Ichthyosis and Related Skin Types) 83
5P-Society 76–77
5P-syndrome 76–77
Focus 65
Forensic Committee of N.A.M.I. (National Alliance for the Mentally Ill) 64
Forgotten and Abused Children and Teens (F.A.C.T.) 36
Formerly Employed Mothers at the Leading Edge (F.E.M.A.L.E.) 101
Fortune Society 64
Forty Plus of New York 73
Forty Plus of Philadelphia 73

Forward Face 75
foster children 36
Foundation for Ichthyosis and Related Skin Types (FIRST) 83
Franceschetti-Klein syndrome (Treacher Collins syndrome) 118
Franken, Al 6
F.R.I.A. (Friends and Relatives of Institutionalized Aged, Inc.) 57
Friendly Societies 5–6
Friends and Relatives of Institutionalized Aged, Inc. (F.R.I.A.) 57
fund-raising 139

G

galactosemia 98
Gam-Anon Family Groups 77
gambling 77
Gartner, Alan 7, 144
Gastroplasty Support Group 100
Gaucher's disease 77
gay men 39–40, 77–78
Gay Men's Health Crisis 39–40
Genetic Pregnancy Termination Support Group 35
gluten intolerance 79
glycogen storage disease 79
grandparents 58, 108–109
Grandparents'-Children's Rights, Inc. 108–109
Grandparents Raising Grandchildren 58
Graves' disease 79
grief See bereavement
growth disorders 111, 116
Guillain-barre syndrome 79
Guillain-Barre Syndrome Foundation International 79

H

HANDI (Hemophilia and AIDS/HIV Network for the Dissemination of Information) 40
handicapped 68
hazardous wastes 74, 111
head injury 80
H.E.A.L. (Help, Education and Advocacy League) 92
H.E.A.L. (Human Ecology Action League, Inc.) 74
Health and Human Services, U.S. Department of 7–8
health care professionals 68, 90, 94, 144–146
hearing impairment 65–66
Heartbeat 51
heart disease 80
Help, Education and Advocacy League (H.E.A.L.) 92
"helper-helpee principle" 5
Helping Hands 92
Hemochromatosis Research Foundation, Inc. 54
hemophilia 40, 54

Kaminer, Wendy 6
Kansas clearinghouse 125
Katz, Alfred H. 5
Keshet 111
kidney disease 86–87
Killilea, M. 7
kleptomaniacs 64
Kleptomaniacs/Shoplifters Anonymous 64
Klippel-Trenaunay Support Group 87
Klippel-Trenaunay syndrome 87
Koop, C. Everett 10
Kropotkin, Petr 5

L

La Leche League 60
Lamaze, Fernand 59
Landry's ascending paralysis (Guillain-Barre syndrome) 79
Langerhans cell histiocytosis (LCH) 81
laryngectomy 87
Latin-American Parents Organization 36
Latinos 39
law enforcement officers 50–51, 87
Lawyers Assistance Program of Connecticut, Inc. 42
lead poisoning 87
LEAPS across the Heartland
   ("Lower-Extremity-Amputees Providing Support")
   44–45
learning disabilities 88 See also attention-deficit
   disorders
Learning Disability Association of America 88
lesbians 77–78
leukemia 88
Leukemia Family Support Group Program 88
leukodystrophy 88–89
life-threatening illness 89
Lighthouse National Center for Vision and Aging 53
limb deficiency 44–45
Litigation Stress Support Group 90–91
Little People of America 111
liver disease 80, 89
Lou Gehrig's disease (amyotrophic lateral sclerosis) 44
Love-N-Addiction 62
Low, Abraham A. 6, 93–94, 145
Lower-Extremity-Amputees Providing Support (LEAPS
   across the Heartland) 44–45
Lowe's sydrome 89
Lowe's Syndrome Association 89
low vision 52–53
lung disease 55, 90, 107 See also emphysema
lupus 90
Lupus Foundation of America, Inc., The 90
lymphoma 88
lysosomal storage diseases 116

M

macular degeneration 52
Madara, Edward J. 153
M.A.D.D. (Mothers Against Drunk Driving) 69–70, 140
malignant hyperthermia 90
Malignant Hyperthermia Association of the U.S.
   (MHAUS) 90
malpractice 90–91
mandibulofacial dysostosis (Treacher Collins syndrome)
   118
manic depression 92–93
maple syrup urine disease 98
Marfan syndrome 91
marriage 38, 91, 95 See also divorce; spouses
Massachusetts clearinghouse 125
Maultsby Jr., Maxie C. 92
measles, mumps, rubella (MMR) vaccine 69
MELD (Minnesota Early Learning Design) 60
membership dues 139
memory loss 56
men
   baldness 47–48
   child molesting 58–59
   custody rights 109
   homosexuality 39–40, 77–78
   impotence 83–84
   personal growth 91
   woman battering 48
Mended Hearts 80
Men's Support Groups 91
mental health/mental illness 42, 64, 91–95 See also
   anxiety disorder; obsessive-compulsive disorder
mental retardation 63, 69, 95
Messies Anonymous 69
MHAUS (Malignant Hyperthermia Association of the
   U.S.) 90
Michigan clearinghouses 125–126
Midlife Women's Support Group 122
Midwest Men's Center/Chicago 78
midwifery 60
military widows 51
mill fever (byssinosis) 55
Minnesota clearinghouse 126
Minnesota Early Learning Design (MELD) 60
minorities See specific groups (e.g., Black Americans)
miscarriage 50
missing children 95–96
Missouri clearinghouses 126
MMR (measles, mumps, rubella) vaccine 69
model groups 33
Molesters Anonymous 58–59
mood-altering pills 43
Mood Disorders Support Group, Inc. 92–93
Mothers Against Drunk Driving (M.A.D.D.) 69–70, 140
Mothers Without Custody 60–61, 109
motor vehicle accidents 69–70

Single Mothers by Choice 102–103
Single Parent Resource Center 103
single parents 36, 102–103
Sjögren's syndrome 112
Sjögren's Syndrome Foundation 112
S.K.I.P. ("Sick Kids Need Involved People"), Inc. 111–112
sleep apnea 45–46
sleep disorders 45–46, 98
SM (syringomyelia) 116
SMA (spinal muscular atrophy) 114, 121
S.M.A. (Families of Spinal Muscular Atrophy) 114
smoking 112
social activism 140
Society for the Second Self 117
Society of Military Widows 51
S.O.F.T. (Support Organization for Trisomy) 118
S.O.S. (Survivors of Suicide) 51
S.O.S.A.D. (Save Our Sons and Daughters) 49
Sotos syndrome 112
Sotos Syndrome Support Association 112
Sources of Help in Airing and Resolving Experiences:
    Pregnancy and Infant Loss Support, Inc. (SHARE) 50
South Carolina clearinghouse 127
Southeast Asia Center 112–113
S.O.W.N. (Supportive Older Women's Network, The)
    38
spasmodic dysphonia 113
spasmodic torticollis (ST) 113
spasmodic winking (benign essential blepharospasm) 48
Speak Easy International Foundation, Inc. 115
Speaking for Ourselves 67
Spiegel, David 9, 144
spina bifida 113
Spina Bifida Association of America 113
spinal cord injury 113–114, 121
Spinal Cord Society 113–114
spinal muscular atrophy (SMA) 114, 121
spouses
    age difference between 91
    of chronically ill 57
    death of 50–51
    of emergency workers 76
    of transvestites 117–118
ST (spasmodic torticollis) 113
stepfamilies 102
Stepfamily Association of America, Inc. 102
stillbirth 50
Stone, W. Clement 4
Stop Abuse by Counselors (Stop ABC) 94
stress See post-traumatic stress
stroke 114
Stroke Clubs 114
Students Against Driving Drunk (S.A.D.D.) 70
Sturge-Weber Foundation, Inc. 114–115
Sturge-Weber syndrome 114–115
stuttering 115
substance abuse 41–43, 86
sudden infant death syndrome (SIDS) 49–50

suicide 51, 115–116
Support Group for Mentally Retarded Married Couples 95
Support Group for People Who Love Too Much 62
Supportive Older Women's Network, The (S.O.W.N.)
    38
Support Organization for Trisomy (S.O.F.T.) 118
Surgeon General's Workshop on Self-Help and Public
    Health (Department of Health and Human Services) 8
Survivors of Homicide 50
Survivors of Incest Anonymous 84
Survivors of Suicide (S.O.S.) 51
syringomyelia (SM) 116

T

Take Off Pounds Sensibly (TOPS) 100
Tall Clubs International 116
tall people 116
T.A.R.S.A. (Thrombocytopenia Absent Radius
    Syndrome Anonymous) 117
Tay-Sachs disease 116
TC syndrome (Treacher Collins syndrome) 118
teenagers
    alcoholism 41
    pregnancy 116–117
    in single-parent homes 102
Tennessee clearinghouses 127
terminal illness 115
tetanus vaccine 69
Texas clearinghouses 127–128
thalassemia (Cooley's anemia) 63
THEOS (They Help Each Other Spiritually) 51
Thrombocytopenia Absent Radius syndrome 117
Thrombocytopenia Absent Radius Syndrome
    Anonymous (T.A.R.S.A.) 117
tinnitus 65
Toastmasters International 106
tobacco See smoking
TOPS (Take Off Pounds Sensibly) 100
Tough Love 106
Tourette syndrome 117
Tourette Syndrome Association, Inc. 117
toxic waste 74
trade unions 6
traffic accidents 59–60
Transplant Recipients International Organization
    (TRIO) 99
transvestites 117–118
trauma 64, 118 See also post-traumatic stress
Trauma Recovery, Inc. 118
Treacher Collins Family Foundation 118
Treacher Collins syndrome 118
trichotillomania 98
TRIO (Transplant Recipients International
    Organization) 99
trisomy 118
tube feeding 118–119

tuberous sclerosis 119
tumors 119
Turner's syndrome 119
Turner's Syndrome Society of Canada 119
Turner's Syndrome Society of the U.S. 119
twelve-step program (Alcoholics Anonymous) 6–8, 144, 148–149
Twelve Steps and Twelve Traditions (Alcoholics Anonymous) 6, 144, 148–149
Twinless Twins Support Group International 96–97
twins 49, 96–97

U

ulcerative colitis 85
Uncommon Survivors (US) 61
unemployment 73
Unite, Inc. 50
United Cerebral Palsy Associations, Inc. 57
United Cerebral Palsy Foundation 6
United Leukodystrophy Foundation, Inc. 88–89
United Ostomy Association 99
universities 41
Unwed Parents Anonymous 103
US (Uncommon Survivors) 61
U.S.-Canadian Endometriosis Association 74
Usher's Syndrome Self-Help Network 120

V

vaccine victims 69
ventilator users 120
vestibular disorders 120
Vestibular Disorders Association 120
veterans 52, 120–121
Victims of Child Abuse Laws (VOCAL) 58
Victims of Incest Can Emerge Survivors (VOICES) 84
Vietnam Veterans of America 121
Virgina clearinghouses 128
Vision Foundation, Inc. 53
Vision Northwest 53
visual impairment 52–53
vitiligo 121
VOCAL (Victims of Child Abuse Laws) 58
VOICES (Victims of Incest Can Emerge Survivors) 84

W

WACS ("Wives Associated with Crossdressers Society") 117–118

W.A.T.C.H. (Women and Their Cheating Husbands) 38
Well Spouse Foundation 57
Werdnig-Hoffman disease 114, 121
Werdnig-Hoffman Parents Group 121
We the People Living with AIDS/HIV of the Delaware Valley 40
White Lung Association 107
white lung disease (asbestosis) 107
whooping cough (pertussis) vaccine 69
Widowed Persons Service 51
widows and widowers 50–51
Williams syndrome 122
Williams Syndrome Association 122
Wilson, Bill 6, 144
Wilson's disease 122
Wilson's Disease Association 122
wives *See* spouses
Wives Associated with Crossdressers Society (WACS) 117–118
Wives of Older Men (W.O.O.M.) 91
women 122
  adultery of husbands 38
  aging 38
  alcoholism 43
  breast feeding 60
  as caregivers 57
  child custody 60–61, 108–109
  codependency 62
  divorce 108
  drug side effects 67
  employment 73–74
  health problems 55, 74, 83, 99, 104, 119
  leaving work to raise children 101
  married to older men 91
  married to transvestites 117–118
  single mothers 102–103
  widows 50–51
Women and Their Cheating Husbands (W.A.T.C.H.) 38
Women Employed 74
Women for Sobriety 43
Women on Their Own, Inc. (W.O.T.O.) 103
Women's Alliance for Job Equality (W.A.J.E.) 73–74
Women Who Love Too Much (Robin Norwood) 4, 62
Workaholics Anonymous 122–123
workaholism 73, 122–123

X

X.E. (Extra Effort) 73